THE

Well-Furnished
GARDEN

THE
Well-Furnished
GARDEN

Using paths, pavilions, beds, and borders; statues, pots, ironwork,
stonework, rockwork, and all manner of ornaments and furniture to create
charming, romantic, and fanciful garden effects

Michael Balston

SIMON AND SCHUSTER
NEW YORK

To Meriel

I am most grateful to the many kind people who have given me
their valuable time and discussed various aspects of this book
during its preparation, as well as those who have corresponded with
me by letter. I would also like to thank the many designers,
photographers and owners whose ideas, photographs and gardens
appear in the book.

Many thanks also to Carl Callaghan, Diana Clarkson and Paola
Muscari, who all helped with the research, and to the publishers'
team, Bob Saxton, Denise Brown and Brigitte Arora.

I am indebted too to Rosemary Verey for the use of her library, and
for her encouragement, moral support and good humour.

M. B.

Executive Editor **Bob Saxton**   Executive Art Editor **Denise Brown**
Assistant Designer **Susie Lanni**   Picture Research **Brigitte Arora**
Additional Picture Research **Caroline Smith**   Production **Philip Collyer**

Published by Simon and Schuster
A Division of Simon & Schuster, Inc.
Simon & Schuster Building, Rockefeller Center
1230 Avenue of the Americas
New York, New York 10020

Edited and designed by Mitchell Beazley International Ltd,
Artists House, 14-15 Manette Street, London W1V 5LB

Library of Congress Cataloging in Publication Data

Balston, Michael, 1944-
   The well-furnished garden.
   Bibliography: p.180
   Includes index.
   1. Garden ornaments and furniture.   I. Title.
SB473.5.B35   1987   712'.6   86-17667
ISBN 0-671-63474-7

1 2 3 4 5 6 7 8 9 10

The author and publishers will be grateful for any information
which will assist them in keeping future editions up to date.
Although all reasonable care has been taken in the preparation of
this book, neither the publishers nor the author can accept any
liability for any consequences arising from the use thereof, or from
the information contained herein.

Typeset by *Bookworm Typesetting, Manchester*
Colour reproduction by *Anglia Reproductions Ltd, Witham*
Printed by *Printer Industria Grafica SA, Barcelona*

Introduction *6*

GARDEN TRADITIONS

The Ancient World *12*
Oriental Gardens *14*
The Islamic World *18*
Medieval Europe *22*

Renaissance Italy *24*
Baroque France *28*
After Versailles *32*
The English Landscape *35*

The Nineteenth Century *40*
The Twentieth Century *45*
Creative Conservation *49*

GARDEN STRUCTURE AND ORNAMENT

The Potential Today *54*
Functional Requirements *55*
Space and Scale *59*
Colour and Texture *67*

Ground Form and Surface *77*
Enclosure and Buildings *87*
Water *97*
Sculptural Forms *101*

Structure with Plants *105*
Movables *109*

CATALOGUE OF GARDEN FEATURES

Garden Structure
Edgings *116*
Paths and Paving *117*
Steps and Stairs *119*
Balustrades and Railings *122*
Fences *123*
Gates and Gateways *125*
Trelliswork *129*
Pergolas, Tunnels and
  Colonnades *131*
Walls and Ha-has *132*

Buildings
Arbours and Pavilions *134*
Dovecotes and Aviaries *137*

Conservatories, Greenhouses
  and Orangeries *138*
Follies and Temples *140*

Water
Boat Houses *142*
Bridges *142*
Pools, Canals and Lakes *145*
Cascades and Fountains *148*

Plants and Trees
Avenues *151*
Training *153*
Mazes *154*
Topiary and Hedges *155*
Parterres, Knots, Bedding
  and Borders *158*

Sculptural Form
Obelisks and Columns *160*
Statues and Sculptural Objects *161*
Stone Seats *164*
Sundials *166*
Urns and Vases *167*
Grottoes and Rockwork *170*

Movables
Garden Furniture *171*
Seats *172*
Plant Containers *175*

Glossary *178*   Bibliography *180*   Directory of Ornament *182*   Index *187*   Picture Credits *190*

INTRODUCTION

In a crowded high-pressure world, the quiet satisfactions of the garden become increasingly important. There, to some extent, we can re-establish our links with nature and its cycles. There, we can exercise our creative imagination and individuality, unharassed by the intrusions of a standardized, highly commercialized society. There, we can make and cherish a calm and ordered environment that satisfies both our aesthetic sensibilities and our functional needs.

Today, gardeners tend to pay more attention to horticulture than to architecture or ornament, and this is clearly reflected in the vast literature about gardens and gardening that is currently available. However, this has not always been the pattern, and indeed during the last few years the pendulum has begun to swing back toward a greater interest in non-horticultural features – a trend which this book reflects and encourages.

The principal subject of these pages is the architecture and sculpture of the garden – using both terms in their broadest sense to include, for example, buildings, enclosures, changes of level, pools, lakes, and decorative features such as urns and seats. Plants themselves are discussed mainly in terms of their architectural or sculptural aspects and the contributions they make to colour and texture. As well as dealing with such features in their historical context, the book considers their use as part of the design process, especially from the point of view of concepts such as three-dimensional form, spatial and visual relationships, quality of materials, and harmony and contrast.

At least until the 19th century, gardens throughout the world have displayed a close interdependence between plants and architecture. Even in the sweeping landscapes of 18th-century England or the very different traditions of the Orient, buildings have been the vital foil that reveals the beauty of lakes, hills and trees. In the Western classical tradition, architecture and sculpture supported a central idea – often, an expression of the garden-owner's status through a system of symbolic references. In the Baroque garden all the elements were fully integrated, but then, gradually, the designs became more fragmented. With the tumultuous changes of the 19th century, the laying out or revamping of so many old gardens in a confused medley of styles and the creation of mile upon mile of suburban gardens, architecture and sculpture in the garden began to lose their coherence. In the more ostentatious gardens there was a promiscuity of ornament, designed to impress by quantity rather than by its contribution to a theme. This led to the weakening of the intellectual rationale of the garden – a tendency that perhaps contributed to the development this century of the compartmented garden, which can be coherent without an overbearingly powerful central theme, presenting new ideas in each discrete section.

Today, gardens seldom rely on philosophical ideas or symbolic allusions. The garden is no longer the nourishment for the mind that it was in the Renaissance. Rather more prosaically, we tend to use functional necessity as the basis on which to generate spaces and

Nature contained

The garden is a personal creation, an interplay of human intelligence (here expressed in the ordered yews and path) and natural cycles of growth, decay and rebirth.

Function and delight

This swimming pool in California shows how with creative thought, the functional can become exciting.

Architecture (*opposite*)

The garden is as much architecture as horticulture. This arbour sheltering a statue is the visual climax of its space.

Plants for structure

The interest of plants lies as much in
their form as in their flowers. This
clump of pampas grass has a sculptural
strength that dominates its space. The
effect slowly changes with the year,
pushing up glorious plumes from the
tangled leaves in the late summer.

Contrasts

Here, the radiating spikes of *Furcraea*
are juxtaposed with a bust of Neptune.
Such contrasts of materials, forms and
textures are among the inventions that
make the garden a place of magic.

Tumbling water *(opposite)*

This rocky cascade, crowned by a
simple pavilion, embodies so much that
is romantic in the garden. Sunbeams
slant across the leaning tree trunk to
light the riverbank and make the
cascade sparkle. Sound as well as sight
plays a part in the overall effect.

enclosures – and, to some degree, visual axes, focal points, colours and textures. However,
an analysis of functional requirements alone can only suggest a garden that is convenient. To
produce one that grips the soul, we must search deeply in our innermost feelings and
imagination, as well as in our knowledge of other people's creations, both past and present.
The collective experience of centuries of garden-making has much to teach us.

Aspects of this collective experience form the first section of this book. This does not
attempt to be a comprehensive garden history, but an introduction to architectural and
sculptural themes in garden design over the last two thousand years. The gardens discussed
and illustrated are, of course, only partially representative of their age. They were made for
the privileged few with wealth and power, and can have had little relevance to the plots of
lesser mortals. However, they are of tremendous interest to us today as a source of ideas.

Historic gardens are a product of their age, determined by the social and political
background, by the philosophical and architectural thought of the time, as well as by
available labour and finance. Today, we live and work against a background thoroughly
different from anything in the past. Although substantial houses and gardens are still
widespread, the middle classes of today, in comparison with those of the 19th century, are
sorely limited in space and finance, and the cost of construction or artistic works has risen
disproportionately to our disposable income. Thus, a knowledge of the past must be used
with caution. Indiscriminate copying of historic layouts and details will lead to problems of
finance and maintenance, or of finding skilled artists or craftsmen, quite apart from the
question of appropriateness to owner and site. But with adequate regard for transitions
between periods and differences between places, some of the ideas generated hundreds of
years ago can fit well into the modern garden. The recent resurrection of the knot garden is
a case in point; and today, with new plants and materials available, we can delight in wholly
20th-century knots.

Practical limitations should encourage us to think hard before making or altering our
gardens, to ensure that we get the very best out of the site and budget available. Why spend
money on a dull garden, when, with a little more forethought, it could be a place of pure
delight? We should aim to capitalize on whatever resources we have – including our brains
and our imaginations. We should plant with care and examine our proposed relationships in
advance, and not after they have been built or planted, when the money has gone. We
should learn to look at the design as a whole, and not as so many individual events. We
should understand that changing a feature or group of plants at one end of the garden may
well have an effect over the whole site. All this is the concern of the second section of the
book, which is intended as an introduction to concepts and relationships that can make any
garden a better place. Examples drawn from all sorts of gardens, both great and small, serve
to illustrate design principles that can and should be applied to any site, whatever the
climate or scale. The coverage is far from exhaustive: each subject deserves a book in itself,
and indeed, for those who want to put these ideas into practice, there are many publications
available that can offer more help on concepts such as the use of colour in the garden.
Likewise, there are quite enough books devoted to the nuts and bolts of construction.

The third section of the book – the Catalogue – offers a wide-ranging selection of specific
design ideas from both historic and modern gardens around the world. These are there more
to excite the imagination than to offer solutions to particular problems. If they do no more
than encourage the reader to visit gardens at home and abroad for further inspiration, and
examine how garden ideas work in practice, they will have served their purpose.

GARDEN TRADITIONS

THE ANCIENT WORLD

Origins of the Western Garden

An Egyptian garden *(left)*

This fragment of an Egyptian wall painting shows a geometrically planned pool with ducks, fishes and lotus plants, surrounded by lines of fruit trees and date palms.

Varro's aviary *(above)*

This illustration of *c.* 1614 (J. Laurus, *Roma Vetus et Nuova*) interprets the aviary described by the Roman scholar Varro *(c.* 40 BC), who maintained his songbirds in architectural elegance.

The idea of a garden, a space set aside for the growing of plants, is probably as old as settled existence. However, it is likely that the garden designed purely for pleasure comes later as a luxury of power and wealth. Its development is nicely fogged, leaving plenty of room for speculation. What is astonishing is that, by the time of the Roman civilization, it was fully fledged, with most of the amenities that we would look for today. There were of course differences in layout and detail, and there was not the wealth of plants that confuses so many modern gardens. But to Pliny (*c.* AD 61-113) the garden was a place of ease and tranquillity and a refuge from the pressures of city life – a pleasure that has remained unaltered by the ensuing two thousand years of strife and revolution, of science and technology.

Evidence for the early development of the garden is scarce, but Egyptian tomb paintings depict enclosed areas for growing plants, with a highly developed layout and a strong aesthetic sense. In Babylon, between 604 and 562 BC, Nebuchadnezzar built the fabled hanging gardens, one of the Seven Wonders of the Ancient World. By the end of the 5th century the Greek historian Xenophon described the hunting park of the Persian King Cyrus at

Sardis; and at Persepolis, Cyrus and his successors created a massive complex of palaces with gardens and lakes, which perhaps later inspired Islamic garden designers.

Meanwhile, in Greece, shrines were set up in places which were felt to be propitious for the honour of particular deities. This might be a cave, or a glade in the trees, or perhaps a rocky promontory. In due course, a temple might be erected there. Such a place was the Grove of the Academy in Athens, where the philosopher Plato lived and discoursed.

Of private gardens in Greece, little is known. With Rome, however, we are on firmer ground, as there is evidence from both literary sources and from paintings. Varro (116-27 BC) noted in his treatise on agriculture ("De Agricultura") how much more elaborate the business of gardening had become, and Pliny's letters of the first century AD give us a detailed description of the gardens of a wealthy Roman: they were clearly sophisticated pleasure gardens that would appeal to anyone today.

The garden has always been imbued with symbolic meaning. Religion was a fundamental concept to the ancient civilizations of China, Persia and the Mediterranean, and found expression in the tradition of the Garden of Eden and in the Greek idea of the Garden of the Hesperides, whence Hercules collected the fabulous apples. Gardens have an obvious connection with fertility and growth, so it is understandable that the Romans should appoint Priapus, god of male procreative power, as their patron, or that Flora, when not looking after Spring and Flowers, should preside over a licentious festival, the Floralia.

The layout of gardens, or the provision of features such as sculpture, was often determined by considerations that went deeper than aesthetics or practical needs. In Egypt or Mesopotamia, the orientation of buildings and gardens, and the precise disposition of parts, may have had symbolic overtones. In Greece the grove containing a shrine acquired a sacred charge by association.

Water had a symbolic value. As a fundamental of life, the availability of water has determined settlement, and has sanctioned civilization. As the Nile held the key to the development of Egypt, so did Babylon depend on the Euphrates. To the Greeks the springs that issued from the many caves of the limestone hills were sacred to local deities, giving rise to the idea of the grotto, an important feature of Mediterranean gardens. In due course artificial caves, known as nymphaea, with springs and fountains, were constructed; they were used as settings for sculptures, as theatres and as dining places. The nymphaeum at Sperlonga must have been one of the most amazing. Inside were four groups of statues illustrating some scenes from the life of Odysseus, numerous pools and a floor paved in various marbles. It was used as a banqueting hall, and the roof collapsed while Tiberius was dining there in AD 26.

A different kind of grotto, the Serapium, can be seen at the end of the Canopus (a canal) at Hadrian's Villa in Tivoli. This is a huge semi-circular vault, half in and half out of the ground – a nymphaeum used for dining, with water gushing in complicated patterns and an abundance of statuary. At the time of its construction, Hero of Alexandria, in his *Pneumatica*, gives an interesting insight into Roman skills in hydraulics, which were employed to create virtuoso water effects in buildings. He describes fountains, both revealed and secret, and a vast range of hydraulic tricks, from balls balanced on jets to trilling model birds.

The writings of the Roman scholar Varro reveal that special garden buildings were commonplace. He describes at length a splendid aviary, in which a colonnade covered with a hemp net forms a huge birdcage around a rectangular court. In the same garden there were fishpools, and a dining area with a revolving table, and with hot and cold water laid on.

Pliny's garden at Tifurnum had a kind of garden bedroom: "the light inside is dimmed by the dense shade of a flourishing vine which climbs over the whole building up to the roof. There you can lie and imagine you are in a wood, but without the risk of rain." Green light in shade has always been a sensual refreshment in the Mediterranean sun, preferably taken with an afternoon glass of wine. How satisfying that both these luxuries are provided by a vine trained over a pergola.

An imperial palace

The Serapium, a nymphaeum at Hadrian's Villa at Tivoli, seen from the opposite end of the Canopus. Hadrian's mini-city was built *c.* AD 118-138. Pools, fountains, colonnades, grottoes and statuary were linked in a composition emblematic of the Empire. Around 1,800 years later, similar combinations of architecture and sculpture, though perhaps without the same degree of symbolic content, were still being built.

In the manner of the Athenian stoa, colonnades and pergolas were used as places to walk and philosophize. Of particular interest was Pliny's semi-underground arcade at Tifurnum, "which never loses its icy temperature in summer".

Seats doubtless had rough and ready origins, but by Pliny's time these too could be of marvellous complexity. At Tifurnum, at the upper end of the riding ground, Pliny had "a curved dining seat of white marble, shaded by a vine trained over four slender pillars of Carystian marble. Water gushes out through pipes from under the seat as if pressed out by the weight of people sitting there"; and "here and there, there are marble chairs which anyone tired of walking appreciates."

Not least among the ornamental effects contrived in ancient gardens was the training of plants. Egyptian tomb art shows plants that are more useful than ornamental, although their layout gives shape to the garden. Lining the paths and boundaries are date palms, pomegranate trees, fig trees and vines, together with shade trees; and around the pools there are beds of papyrus. With the Romans, ornamental horticulture became highly developed. Not only can we see a delight in flowers in the paintings at Pompeii, but both Plinys, Elder and Younger, describe at length the variety of designs to be found in contemporary topiary.

ORIENTAL GARDENS

Alternative Approaches

Colour and texture

In oriental gardens, there was a deeper understanding of the intrinsic colour, form and texture of natural objects than there was in the West. Surrounded by the beauty of the natural world, Man himself occupied a relatively insignificant place. However, in Japan, carefully drawn up rules regulated taste and artistic endeavour. In this Japanese garden, azaleas, clipped to resemble rocks on a mossy ground, are composed to present a minutely organized picture.

While geometry was establishing its rule in the West, in the East something entirely different was happening. People were inclined to view themselves as a part of nature, rather than as nature's masters. Accordingly, oriental garden-makers attempted, not only in their landscape creations but also in garden buildings and decoration, to reflect natural life forces, rather than to celebrate the achievements of mankind.

As Western civilization flowered in Greece in the 6th century BC, a similar process was under way in China. A pattern of customs and institutions was forged that was to last almost to the present day. Confucian philosophy had far-reaching effects on social relations, with an emphasis on the family. There evolved a paternalistic style of government based on tradition. A concurrent theme was Taoism – a more mystical approach to the world, which encouraged a belief in the unity and natural harmony of the universe, and the need to coexist with nature. Together with Buddhism (imported from India and subsequently passed on to Japan), these philosophies had implications for the design of buildings and gardens. Artists and gardeners attempted to distil the essence of nature, looking to mountains, lakes and plants for inspiration. Respect for tradition, antiquity and permanence led to forms of painting and gardening utterly remote in both spirit and technique from those of the West.

In the East as in the West, architecture was an expression of cultural vitality. But in the East there was never the same emphasis on buildings as great works of art: architecture remained a craft, essentially based on domestic techniques, rather than an art form. Individual creativity was limited by a traditional vocabulary of expression. Colour and decoration were treated as integral aspects of a building. There was much surface ornament, often incorporating symbolic motifs. Roofs were covered with glazed tiles in symbolic colours, their ridges and hips emphasized with dragons or other grotesque ornament.

Attitudes to space in Eastern gardens were, and still are, quite different from those in the West. Geometry was a necessary basis for architecture but external spaces, conceived as a contrast to buildings, were the domain of nature, which has its own way of

Garden architecture

The construction of buildings was not so inhibited by geometric considerations as it was in the West. Eaves soar upwards, roofs dip, flexed like the backs of dragons. Nor was there any embarrassment about the use of colour: reds enliven columns and railings, and roofs are turquoise-tiled. But the architecture would be nothing unless complemented, as in this Chinese garden, by ancient pines and gnarled rocks.

shaping the world. Gardens have tended to be a distillation of the varied and beautiful landscape all around, rather than the fleshing out of abstract human concepts.

There is early evidence of the creation in China (as in Assyria) of great hunting parks, which were also used for military exercises and displays. These became symbolic of the Empire, and reflected the splendour of the ruling house. Emperors began to give their parks vast lakes and artificial mountains. The mountains were designed to attract the Immortals – beneficent deities who were believed to prefer a cloud-capped residence. The same tradition of gigantic park-building was adopted by the Mongol invaders in the 13th century. When Kublai Khan moved his capital to Peking, he constructed huge lakes and an island covered in evergreen trees over a floor of lapis lazuli. As if this were not enough, there were two palaces rising out of the water, clad in crystal to resemble ice.

However, not all gardens were so extravagant. There was a parallel tradition of the "scholar's retreat", which satisfied the Taoist urge to throw off the cares of the world and become one with nature. From at least the 3rd century AD, poets and painters regarded the whole of nature as a garden, and built themselves pavilions in suitable places from which to observe it.

Japanese gardens developed in a rather different way. Early gardens tended to be attached to temples or palaces, and by the 11th century the art of gardening was codified in a set of rules, the *Sakuteiki*, which defined the acceptable types of gardens, how they could be laid out, how water should flow, types of rock and so on. Gardens were classed according to their elaboration, ranging from the meticulously planned simplicity of the garden of the Ryoanji temple in Kyoto (*c.* 1490) to the more sumptuous treatment of the Katsura Palace with its many tea-houses, constructed in the 17th century.

The invention of the tea ceremony was of lasting importance in Japan. It required its own pavilion and a garden designed to help the visitor shed the cares of the world. There were complex rules

The eye of the garden

A fan-shaped window frames the foliage of a palm in a soft courtyard beyond. Often in Chinese gardens, doors and windows are used to give an interestingly shaped surround to a carefully controlled composition. Windows were thought of as the "*eyes*" of a pavilion or dwelling-place: a vital ingredient of a building's life. They could be filled with intricate lattice designs, or even glazed, with decorative motifs painted on the glass. However, the design shown here is strong and simple. The use of grey softens the courtyard walls, making them recede, and diminishing any sense of claustrophobia. Sunlight falling onto the palm makes it seem to come forward. Such tricks with space and tantalizingly partial views through an architectural screen are a notable characteristic of Chinese garden design.

for setting out the entrance gate, the bench on which visitors sat, and the basin at which they washed. Stepping stones were carefully placed to control the speed of approach and the opportunities for pausing to enjoy the view.

Such painstaking attention to detail was an absolute necessity. An educated man could read a garden like a book. Nothing was contrived for purely visual reaons: there was was always an underlying rationale. Gardens were potent with symbolism, with every stone and shrub carrying a reference to something else. Just as the imperial park was a metaphor for the Empire itself, the scholar's retreat symbolized the aspirations of a cultivated man. It was no contradiction for a garden to symbolize the owner's life and character, while at the same time representing the universe. Even individual plants all had their meanings: the peony was a symbol of rank, the lotus represented purity and integrity, the venerable pine was associated with age, silence and solitude.

Water, also richly symbolic, was fundamental to both Chinese and Japanese gardens as the counterbalance to the mountain. According to Confucius, "the wise find joy in water; the benevolent find joy in mountains". All the great imperial parks of China incorporated lakes, as did many of the later urban gardens. Even the scholar's retreat more often than not had its own pool. Similarly, in Japan most of the great gardens were situated around lakes or pools, and even in the *kare sansui*, or dry gardens, the treatment of sand or gravel, so carefully raked, is such that it almost resembles water.

Although fountains were uncommon, Chinese imperial gardens sometimes had curious water devices, including dragons which breathed out mist and boats with moving mechanical figures. More often the natural movement of water was harnessed to produce interesting effects. The sound of water bubbling over rocks or rushing down cascades was much admired. Sometimes, dragon-headed springs were fashioned.

In both China and Japan, there was also a keen pleasure in still water, with pavilions placed at its edge. From the shelter of these little buildings, people enjoyed distant reflections, the gentle lap of waves, or the patter of morning rain.

In contrast were the rocks – the *yang* of the landscape, the male strength opposed to the female *yin* of placid water. Mountains were thought to represent supernatural power, and a single boulder embodied the local god. In a rock one could confront the elemental forces of nature: they were exhilarating, a catalyst for the poet's imagination.

The counterpart to water and rocks was the pavilion, a roof without walls, sited in a key position from which to view the garden, to "borrow" the surrounding landscape, or to muse upon associations.

Walls are important too, particularly in China. Where a variety of scenes was contrived, the wall makes a stabilizing and unifying element – perhaps a background for the intricate pattern of bamboo. Or it could be waxed to shine softly, or coloured to disappear beneath its tiled canopy, dipping and twisting along the hill like an agitated dragon.

Gates become moments of great invention. The moon gate, a circle and a symbol of perfection, concentrates the view through a dark wall to clear light beyond – or perhaps it is the wall that is clearly defined, with a dark mystery lying ahead. The business of stepping over its threshold enforces a pause, a drawing of breath, while you absorb the next scene.

Another divider of space is the gallery which zigzags across to a distant pavilion. Evil spirits were believed to travel only in straight

A garden bridge (*above*)

A marble bridge at the Summer Palace in Peking, with balusters and panels, offers a vantage point from which to take in views across the lake. When reflected in the water, the arch makes a circle – a symbol of the moon and of perfection, like the circular moon gate often used in China to pierce a wall.

A path mosaic (*below*)

Paths were sometimes elaborately decorated, particularly in China, with mosaics made up of different types of pebbles and broken stone or tiles, ranging in style from geometric to free-flowing. Fish, animals, birds and flowers appear underfoot, emphasizing a theme or introducing a new idea.

Essentials of the Chinese garden

This Famille Rose Canton dish, dated 1739, shows important elements of the Chinese garden – curiously shaped rocks, a pine symbolizing silence and solitude, a pavilion (or *t'ing*) from which the landscape is admired, and a zigzagging fence. Such fences were usually organized in rectangular patterns, as here. Sometimes they incorporated a swastika motif, which could be read as a symbol of prosperity and longevity.

lines, so the twisting path outwits them, and at every turn gives a changed view, a kaleidoscopic variety. The rippling texture of tiles above is balanced by intricately carved balustrades below. Beneath sheltering walls or across reflecting water, the rhythm of the columns draws the eye and extends the space. Paving provided yet more scope for inventive decoration. If something other than a calm stone-flagged path is required to suit the mood, then perhaps it is a pebble mosaic, illustrating a bat, bringer of luck. Or the path might appear as free-flowing forms hurrying along to a change of direction where an abstract mosaic of coloured tiles subtly alters the pace. In Japan, it is the stepping stones that perform this service, now confidently moving forward, now hesitating, here pausing for the view.

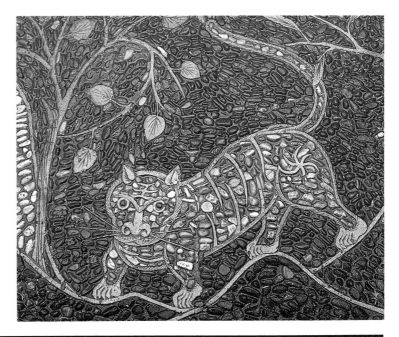

THE ISLAMIC WORLD

A Bridge with Antiquity

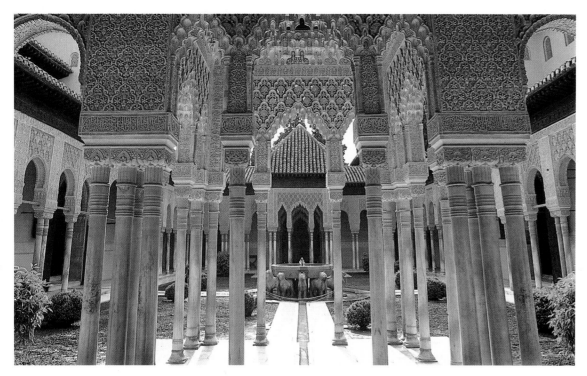

Islam is a faith that transcends geography and time. In the centuries after the death of Mohammed in AD 632, the Islamic faith penetrated Central Asia, North Africa, Spain and, later, northern India. Bridges were built between the classical world and the Renaissance, as well as between the East and the Mediterranean. The oasis garden, taken from Persia, eventually found its way via Islam into medieval Europe, ripe for evolution into the glories of the Renaissance. Although the Arabs imposed their simple faith as they swept across Asia and Africa, they were prepared to tolerate, to a degree, Judaism and Christianity. There was a rapid synthesis with existing civilizations, and architecture and the arts flourished.

The nomadic Arabs had no building tradition. Thus, Islamic architecture was an amalgam of styles absorbed from conquered regions and welded together by the inspiration of one philosophy. The direction of prayer, and the concept of balance and symmetry implied by the idea of perfect creation, determined the layout of buildings and spaces.

Buildings tended to be highly decorated, with carved and inlaid stone, mosaics, patterned brickwork, painting and inlaid timber-work. Motifs were derived from calligraphy, plants and complex interlacing geometric forms. But despite the brilliance of Islamic ornament, it was always subordinate to, and in harmony with, the greater concepts of space and structure.

The garden was particularly important to Islam. To the invading Arabs, the Persian garden must have seemed like a fulfilment of the promises of Paradise made in the *Koran*. Thus it served as a model that was transmitted to every part of the Islamic world. Climatic conditions were broadly similar throughout that world, so such a garden transplanted quite readily, provided that the sophisticated water engineering techniques of the Persians were taken too.

Unlike most Islamic gardens, those in Spain, such as the Alhambra (of which four courts remain), have an irregular layout, due to their hillside location. The Generalife, next door, is on many levels, with courts linked to each other along terraces or flights of steps. Another great medieval Spanish garden is the Alcazar at Seville, laid out by Pedro the Cruel in 1350 and heavily influenced by Moorish designs. Like other early Spanish gardens, it is overlaid with Renaissance work.

Comfort in a Mughal garden

An awning, a carpet and plump cushions made adequate garden furniture for the Mughal princes shown in this Indian miniature (*c.* 1680) discoursing in the moonlight by the side of a lotus-filled pool. Perhaps a distant reflection of nomadic ancestry, the use of such accessories as additional garden comforts was common in India and central Asia. Not only were carpets used outside to give shade and define space, but they often took the garden as a theme for embellishment, illustrating its tanks, canals and rows of trees.

A Mughal masterpiece

At the Taj Mahal in Agra, built by Shah Jahan in the 17th century in memory of his favourite wife Mumtaz Mahal, the harmony of building and garden reached a perfection rarely equalled. This view shows the entrance pavilion, with its vast central portal and a silhouette enlivened by 22 little kiosks and four larger corner pavilions. Steps descend to the canal that leads directly to the great white marble mausoleum.

The Mongols who made disruptive incursions into western and central Asia quickly succumbed to the pleasure of gardens. After Tamerlane had established his capital at Samarkand, numerous gardens were mentioned by visitors. They were terraced on the sides of hills, and they were formal, with many enclosures, pavilions and fountains. Trees of similar species were collected in blocks, and lawns were cultivated.

The other main area of garden building was India under the Mughals, where much remains intact. Gardens here were very large, often with a central pavilion. From a great tank flowed four canals which represented the rivers of Paradise and divided the garden into quarters. The canals were shaded by trees and often incorporated cascades and a succession of small fountains which delivered a fine cooling spray. The Emperor Babur (1483-1530) describes in his memoirs his garden near Kabul, and a later one in Agra. His successors were equally enthusiastic garden-makers, the best known of their creations being the Taj Mahal, where architecture and gardens combine to create a sublimely inspiring experience.

The idea of the garden as a symbol of Paradise has closely controlled its construction throughout the Islamic regions. For the sand-blown Arab, dried up with thirst, the image of a cool, shady place with fountains must have been wonderfully alluring:

And beside these shall be two other gardens:
Of a dark green:
With gushing fountains in each
In each fruits and the palm and the pomegranate:
In each, the fair, the beauteous ones:
With large dark eyeballs, kept close in their pavilions . . .

(The Koran)

If Paradise was like a garden, then conversely the garden was built to be like Paradise. Hence the four rivers flowing from the centre, the point at which God and Man meet, towards the four cardinal points. Hence also the division of some gardens into eight terraces, eight being the number of divisions within Paradise. The plants, too, made symbolic references: for example, the cypresses alluded to eternity and the beauty of women. And in decoration there were special meanings in numbers and geometry, references to the sun and moon, the planets and the signs of the zodiac. The ubiquitous patterns unified not only visually but also spiritually.

Water was symbolic not only of life itself but also of purity. It refreshed both body and soul. Without it, plants could not survive and the Islamic garden simply would not exist. Everything depended on its availability, and complex water-engineering techniques were used to transport it to cities and their gardens. Cisterns were built in gardens for water storage, and channels for

A garden in Kashmir

The Mughals made gardens in Kashmir to escape the stifling heat of the Indian plains. This view of the Shalamar Bagh, made by Jahangir in honour of his wife Nur Jahan, shows snow-capped mountains contrasting with the waters of Lake Dal. The three terraces of the garden exploit the movement of water, moistening the air with cascades and fountains.

Paving patterns

Mughal gardens, with their many terraces, displayed beautiful paving patterns. In a culture that placed a taboo on the representation of the human figure, geometric patterns became an important form of decoration. This rippling pavement of red sandstone stars and white marble diamonds makes a rich and strongly unified platform for the Taj Mahal.

The manipulation of water in Mughal gardens was superb. A garden in terraces permitted waterfalls – broad sheets of water rolling over from level to level – and the *chadar*, a water chute whose surface is carved to make the water foam and glisten as it slides down from beneath a pavilion on an upper terrace. The greatest refinement of all must have been the practice of having a niche behind a waterfall, in which pots of flowers were placed by day, and candles by night.

Shade was just as necessary as water. Pavilions became a notable element in Mughal gardens, often sited over water to help keep them cool. They could be small, elegant structures with deeply eaved roofs supported by arches, but sometimes they were huge, and destined to become their creator's mausoleum. Miniature pavilions were often placed over the corners of larger buildings as terminal emphases. And in the gardens of Kashmir, corner pavilions were built into the surrounding walls to give views of the spectacular mountains beyond.

Arcades to provide shade are also common throughout Islam, in both mosques and gardens. As part of a garden, they are particularly notable in Spain. At the Alcazar in Seville a fine example, with paired columns, supports, a confection of deeply cusped arches and high-relief lozenges that would make a *patissier* proud.

Paths between pavilions or arcades were invariably straight. In Spain they were sometimes built above the level of flower beds, so that the overall design appears flat, like a carpet. This was probably as a consequence of having to flood the beds periodically for irrigation. The paths were often tiled, or made in stone, brick or pebbles.

Balustrades around terraces were elements of great virtuosity in India. By ingenious workmanship, slabs of marble were transformed into a delicate filigree of repeated geometrical ornament. Similar in their impact were the superb lattice windows: seen from inside these stood out darkly against the bright sky, while from outside they gleamed white against the cool shade within.

Amidst all this stone and geometry, carpets were laid out to sit on, or suspended overhead for shade, and fat cushions of silk or velvet were brought to serve as chairs, just as they did indoors.

distribution. Pools provided coolness and moisture, supported aquatic plants and sometimes contained fish or ducks. Fountains and cascades sparkled in the light and soothed with their sound. Water could be light and playful or remain calmly still. Scarce though it was, it always made a focal point.

Every mosque court had its basin. Often this was designed to overflow at the brim, and was thus contained within a channel or larger pool. Some basins took the form of shallow depressions in the paving, with elaborately carved surrounds mimicking the swirl of water. Or sometimes a fluted bowl, set in a carpet of glittering tiles, was raised on a pedestal above a shallow octagonal pool. Wherever possible, there were fountains – simple jets to soften the air, to splash and tinkle, sparkling in the sun, bright against the deeply shaded wall beyond.

Plants, although arranged with geometric precision, helped to relieve the impression of almost overwhelming order. Trees were as important for their scale as for their shade. Planting them in rows not only accorded with the geometry of Islamic gardens but also facilitated irrigation. Set along canals, their foliage canopies reduced evaporation.

A curious theme in kingly circles was the fashion for artificial trees. Firdausi, in the *Shahnama*, describes one of gold, silver and rubies, whose hollow fruits were filled with musk; and Tamurlane was said to possess one six feet high in gold and silver, with leaves shaped like oak leaves, and studded with fruit made of pearls, diamonds, sapphires, rubies and emeralds – an interesting conceit, considering that the gardens themselves must have been like jewels glistening in the arid heat.

MEDIEVAL EUROPE

The Garden Enclosed

There were nearly a thousand years of chaos in Europe between the collapse of Rome and the beginning of the Renaissance. However, during these troubled times, the arts flourished spasmodically and, against all the odds, gardens were made and enjoyed. They were refuges of peace and beauty in utter contrast to the brutal world outside.

The monastic orders were the vital thread of continuity as Europe was torn apart by feuding warlords. They were repositories of learning, and provided a link with classical antiquity. Not only did they shape the philosophy of the Western world, but they monopolized the arts and kept alive the skills of horticulture.

Of particular interest is the development of the monastic cloister – a place for quiet and contemplation, with a central space frequently treated as a garden. A plan of the monastery of St Gallen in Switzerland, dating from *c*. AD 816, shows a central cloister divided into four quarters, remarkably like contemporary Islamic gardens. On the east side, three other spaces are shown: a herb garden, a vegetable garden and an orchard that doubles as a cemetery. Later illustrations of secular gardens generally show an enclosure of walls, fences or hedges. Inside were paths and rectangular or square beds, and often a fountain in the centre. There seems to have been a growing appreciation of landscape, and some of the later illustrations show well-cultivated parks lying outside the walls.

Gardens appear to have been symbolically important to medieval Christians, just as they were to the Muslims or Chinese. The cloister garden with its central fountain represented the Virgin Mary, a link encouraged by the famous lines in the *Song of Songs* of Solomon:

> *A garden enclosed is my sister, my spouse;*
> *a spring shut up, a fountain sealed.*

Straight paths symbolized the way of a true Christian, while the shade of a tree sheltered him from the wrath of God. The enclosed garden itself was a refuge from the deformed world outside, and a place of purification – again, a representation of Paradise.

One of the great symbolic medieval works of literature was the *Roman de la Rose*, a 13th-century allegory of courtly love in which the poet undergoes a series of adventures in pursuit of his love, the Rose. Not only does this poem throw light on the medieval mind, but through the several illustrated versions we can see, to a certain extent, how gardens evolved.

A palace garden in April

Much of our information about medieval gardens is derived from illuminated manuscripts, most of which date from the very end of the Middle Ages. This illustration from an early 16th-century Flemish calendar shows the garden in April, complete with lovers and a flowering apple tree. Typically, the space is enclosed by a trellis fence. There is a magnificent central fountain, with water issuing from a quadruple spout, tumbling via a lion's head into a hexagonal basin and thence into the pond below.

Admiring the Rose

Illustrations of the many editions of the *Roman de la Rose,* the great medieval love poem, offer insights into medieval garden design. In this vignette, a figure with a sword at his side savours the scent of a red rose grown in a circular raised bed contained by a wattle fence, while another figure looks on from behind a masonry wall. The two piles of stones are intriguing features.

A place for relaxation *(right)*

A characteristic feature of the medieval garden was the turf seat. Originally, this was probably a simple bank, but many illustrations show the turf retained below by timber boards or a wattle fence, with people seated either on the turf itself or on the ground, using the wall as a back rest. The charm of such a seat (which so often must have been unusable in northern climates) was partly in the little meadow flowers that grew on it.

In the Middle Ages, plants also were viewed symbolically. The iris represented Christ the King, the Madonna lily symbolized purity, the leaves of the strawberry alluded to the Trinity. Flowers that opened near a particular saint's day were thought to possess powers reflecting his or her attributes.

Water, of course, was also symbolic, but was not so lavishly used as in Roman or Islamic gardens, perhaps as much for climatic as for technical reasons. However, Albertus Magnus in the 13th century recommends that "a clear fountain of water in a stone basin should be in the midst, for its purity gives much pleasure". Wells and fountains are frequently illustrated, and in Spain and Italy there was a tradition of skilled hydraulics that was perhaps learned from the Muslims.

Perhaps also from Spain came the practice of building pavilions in gardens. There, a central pavilion, known as a *glorietta,* was common, and provided shade and a place from which to view the garden. In the garden at Tafalla in Navarre there were small pavilions on each side, as well as a pavilion with an open loggia in which to dine. Perhaps by way of Navarre, the idea of pavilions was eventually taken up in the north. In England they are known to have existed from the mid-14th century.

The walls surrounding a garden were most often extensions of the walls of the building to which the garden was attached. They were usually of brick or stone, and sometimes had a crenellated top. Alternatively, there might be just a fence of wattle, making a striking texture, or, less substantially, a railing above a diagonal trellis. Rough-picket fences and close-boarded fences were also used in the Middle Ages.

Within, the most striking ornamental feature must have been the arbour, a descendant of the simple pergola erected to spread out the fruiting vine. This appears in all shapes and sizes, including domes and tunnels. Good examples can be seen in Pol de Limbourg's *Très Riches Heures* of the Duc de Berry (1409-16) or the *Livre de Cuer d'Amours Espris* of *c.* 1465. The latter has elaborately detailed doors and windows, with rich mouldings and carved decoration. Carpenter's work, as such ornament was known, appeared even in Roman times in the form of trellises, but it reached great elaboration in the Middle Ages. Peter de Crescentiis, an author writing *c.* 1305, recommended the use of trelliswork to construct not only tunnels, but even tents and houses. Arbours were mostly illustrated with vines growing over them, but were sometimes clad in roses.

Although the garden was walled in, the mount gave a means of seeing out. Possibly descended from the motte on which early fortified buildings stood, the mount was an earth mound sited either in the middle or in the corner of a garden. It was certainly known in England by the middle of the 14th century, and became a feature of Tudor gardens. Sometimes it had an arbour or small building on top, and sometimes topiary.

Timber benches and stools were used, but more elaborate seats of stone were also made. These could be of quite complicated design, with arms and high, thronelike backs. Truncated figure-of-eight folding stools also appear in several illustrations.

A major category of ornament in the Middle Ages was the trained plant. Perhaps the most striking treatment was the *estrade* – a technique of pruning trees to create a series of diminishing discs of foliage at regular intervals up the trunk. Shrubs were also trained into complex shapes, and even herbaceous plants appear to have been trained on timber frames. More ambitiously, Peter de Crescentiis proposes a palace with rooms and towers entirely made out of trees. This may not be as far-fetched as it sounds: the technique is illustrated on the ceiling of the Sala delle Asse in the Castello Sforzesco in Milan.

RENAISSANCE italY

The Garden of the Intellect

The Villa d'Este

The exuberant use of water was a distinguishing feature of late Renaissance gardens. Perhaps the most impressive of all these creations is the Villa d'Este, built between 1550 and 1580, where water joyfully expresses the extrovert spirit of the age. Shown here is the great Organ Fountain, which alas no longer produces music – just as the Owl Fountain no longer emits screeches. Originally, the many-breasted Diana of the Ephesians, now sited at the bottom of the garden, stood at its centre in a celebration of fertility (illustrated on page 97).

With the Italian Renaissance, gardens were revolutionized. The treatment of water became wonderfully inventive and yet totally integrated into an all-embracing scheme of building, sculpture and planting. The gardens themselves were sculptural, stacked tier on tier up the hillsides, framed by their *boschi* (thickly planted groves of trees), regular yet happy to tolerate the odd wayward cypress. Sparkling water glinted against dark shadows, gleaming marble lightened the recesses. Such a revolution in gardening could only be brought about by a revolution in thought. Gardens served a central theme: Man at the centre of the Universe.

The ancient world had, in a quiet way, been kept alive in Italy. Roman buildings, although perhaps ruined, existed, as did the old Roman literature. Renaissance builders learnt to absorb their ancient inheritance and to fashion a new architecture controlled by rules of proportion. They sought to create order, stability and tranquillity – beauty flowing from Man's intellect. They revived the country villa and integrated it with the garden in an overall design which included the view. But their cool rationality soon gave way to the emotional appeal of the Baroque, which played upon dynamic movement and the illusion of infinite space.

In Florence in the mid-15th century a rich and independent merchant class married its prosperity to the new enlightenment. Led by the Medici family, they fostered the arts, built villas on hillsides, and invented a new garden. A painting of the Medici Villa at Cafaggiolo, which was refurbished *c.* 1456, shows a simple plan on a flat piece of ground. In one corner, in no particular relation to the building, is a topiary arbour and a fountain. To the rear are square beds and vine-pergolas. Seven years later, another Medici Villa, sited above Florence at Fiesole, is a whole world away. The garden is a series of rooms of different size and purpose, linked back to the house, but taking in the view of the city and hills beyond. It is a garden for walking in and conversing, a philosopher's garden perhaps – unlike those that developed in

The Villa Lante

At the Villa Lante, the treatment of water is subtle and refined, the flow giving energy and breadth to the design as it descends from level to level. The *cordonata (right)*, a scrolling chain fashioned to resemble the crayfish of Cardinal Gambara's coat of arms, ripples the water down to a semi-circular pool below. From there it wells up into the centre of a long stone table – a gigantic wine cooler, or perhaps dishes were floated down it as described by Pliny fourteen hundred years before. Then, by way of a circle of little jets, the flow finally reaches the great water parterre *(left)*. In the centre of the square pool, itself raised and urn-rhythmed, is Giovanni da Bologna's great fountain on a circular stone platform, linked to the surrounding terrace by four narrow balustraded causeways.

Rome a century later, which were definitely for show. The terraces still have a casual relationship to each other, unrestricted as yet by the dogmatic planning of the Baroque.

During the 15th century, Rome was still struggling out of its medieval confusion and dereliction. But with the accession of Pope Julius II in 1503, it was poised to become the cultural capital of Europe. Almost immediately, Julius commissioned the architect Donato Bramante to refashion the old Villa Belvedere as a setting for his collection of classical statuary, and to link it back to the Pontifical Palace. Thus was created the Cortile del Belvedere, which, with it axial plan, its terraces and staircases, was to influence the planning of Italian gardens for the rest of the century. It was at the Villa Lante, at Bagnaia, some sixty years later, that the Renaissance garden plan was perfected. The design exploits the flow of water down the hill: as it flows, so the terraces become more open, and the details progress from the rough grotto at the top down to the elaborate water parterre at the bottom. In acknowledgment of the all-embracing spatial order, the villa itself is split into two halves on either side of the central axis. The garden is a sublime exercise in geometry and proportion. But by the turn of the century, gardens tended to become more theatrical, a fusion of Art and Nature glorifying Man, reaching a climax in the Villa Aldobrandini, Frascati, where the villa lies at the focus of an entirely Baroque compositon.

The Renaissance garden was intended to provide food for the mind, and to this end was layered with learned allusions. Scenes of ancient mythology, especially those involving hunting adventures and pastoral figures such as shepherds, satyrs and wood nymphs, were profusely illustrated in statuary. At a time when classical literature and values were being rediscovered, when literature as much as the visual arts could be called upon to create a humanist Eden, it was natural to expect a garden to yield deep meanings through symbolic references.

Water was particularly symbolic, and held a central place in the Renaissance garden. It was associated with fertility and the abundance of Nature. More interestingly, perhaps, it was also associated with the Muses, the source of intellectual life. The garden of the Villa d'Este must be the most spectacular of all water gardens, putting water through a galaxy of tricks. The place is alive with the sound of gurgles and splashes, hisses and roarings. It is a sensual celebration of pleasure, from its quiet shady fish tanks to the crash of the water organ, from the all-fecund Diana of Ephesus to the powerfully restrained Terrace of the Hundred Fountains, now shrouded in antiquity, its eagles and lilies, its ships and stories from Ovid, dripping with moss.

The fountain was the hallmark of the Renaissance garden, expressing exuberance and joy at Man's new-found confidence. From the fountains of the great hillside villas to the giant Baroque fountains of Rome, the combination of stonework, sculpture and water everywhere gave delight and refreshment. As popular, it seems, as these great sculptural creations were the concealed jets built into many gardens, to give the unwary visitor a good soaking – Renaissance humour must have been a little more boisterous than today's.

Grottoes are another Renaissance feature which reappeared through the centuries. Generally, they took the form of a nymphaeum – a building above ground with stonework details mimicking stalactites or the drip of soggy weed; but alternatively, they could appear in more rustic guise as rockwork imitating a cave, deriving from the idea of the sacred cave set aside in classical times as a place to make offerings to the gods. Moist, cool and shady, such grottoes must have offered welcome relief from the hot Italian sun, as well as alluding to antiquity.

The Villa Aldobrandini

The garden of the Villa Aldobrandini, built at the end of the 16th century, epitomizes the idea of Man at the centre of the universe. The different levels are linked by the descent of water down a central axis towards the villa – from the grotto high up on a wooded slope, down a rocky cascade and channel, then shooting up the inside of a pair of stone pillars (shown in this photograph) and falling helterskelter down their spiralled sides, on down the water staircase and then through the fountains and grottoes of the water theatre at the bottom, where Atlas stands with the world on his shoulders.

A hundred fountains

Originally the Villa d'Este was approached from the bottom of the hill, and the Terrace of a Hundred Fountains made a magnificent level promenade across the axis – a breathtaking pause before the final steep ascent. It stretches all the way across the garden to the Rometta – a model of ancient Rome. Between the jets stand the eagles of the family and the lilies of France, where Ippolito d'Este had been papal *Nuncio* (ambassador). There was also a series of terracotta reliefs depicting scenes from Ovid's *Metamophoses*.

As important as the harnessing of water was the use of sculpture. It was known that the Romans had placed statues in their gardens. Boccaccio's *Visione Amorosa* describes the royal gardens at Castel Nuovo as being full of sculpture. Colonna, a 15th-century monk whose record of a vivid dream of a garden is a major source of evidence for this period, makes frequent mention of statues, herms (busts on pillars), altars and other sculptural pieces. Statuary provided a means for narrating a story or expressing symbolic meaning. At the garden of Castello, near Florence, laid out *c.* 1540, statues were used in an allegorical programme to celebrate the glory of the Medici and of Florence and Tuscany generally. At the symbolic heart of this garden was a grotto overflowing with sculpture, and at the rear was a pool containing Ammanati's huge figure of the Appenines, a man hugging himself with cold. It was at the Villa d'Este that the integration of sculpture and water reached its zenith. Many of the statues here were plundered from Hadrian's Villa a few miles away, but were incorporated in a garden fantasy of which even Colonna would have been proud.

The characteristic hillside location of so many of the great Italian gardens placed great emphasis on terraces and their balustrades, on the walls that support them, and on the steps that connect them. The rhythm of balusters repeating along the top of a wall gives a marked coherence to an elevation. For example, the balustrades connecting the terraces at the centre of the gardens of the Villa Garzoni at Collodi are locked together in a ladder-like ribbon. And the balusters themselves can be highly expressive. They can be fat and cheerful like those of the Villa Lante, or opulent in style like those at the Villa Borghese.

Below the balustrades are the retaining walls, either rusticated (that is, imitating heavy stonework with raked-out joints) or perhaps articulated in panels. Frequently an arch in the wall would frame the crumbling rock of a little grotto or cascade, as at Garzoni, where the cascade is surmounted by a statue of Fame. Another element in the composition is the steps, which link plane to plane. Again they set up a rapid repetition, but horizontally this time, drawing the eye upward. Sometimes it is their side view that we see, cross-bracing an elevation.

Just as the hillsides were sculpted into controlled forms, so were the plants. Colonna's garden is full of topiary in the most incredible shapes. There are complicated knots, in which the frames were made out of herbs, such as marjoram or rue, and the spaces filled with pansies, primroses, violets and the like. He advocated the use of shrubs such as santolina, box, juniper and small myrtles planted in antique pots or vases and clipped into curious shapes. Contemporary with his book was the topiary of the Villa Quaracchi, which was noted for its astonishing collection of figures ranging from apes to cardinals.

Trees in the Italian garden tended to be planted in regular rows, and then cut to form great blocks of green, like those overhanging the theatre at the Villa Aldobrandini. Or they were pleached and trained into arches, as the end of the main parterre at the Villa Gamberaia. Trees, as much as hillsides, were curbed by the rules of geometry. Cypress, box and bay were all trimmed into spheres, cones and cylinders, or sometimes spirals. Low hedges defined the edges of pools, made a complicated pattern across a terrace, or formed a little maze. It was an architecture in varying shades of green – more permanent than the ephemeral flowers, and perhaps more tranquil.

BAROQUE FRANCE

Nature Dressed by Geometry

France in the latter half of the 17th century was the most powerful state in Europe, centralized and controlled by one man – the Sun King Louis XIV, who ruled from 1661 to 1715, supported by a submissive church and nobility. For half a century Louis presided with unprecedented absolutism from his newly established court at Versailles. Circumstances were right for the Renaissance garden to reach a mighty celebration of Man at the centre of the universe, beyond which it could go no further. This involved a precise marshalling of the arts in the King's honour, under the guiding hands of Geometry and Allegory. The outstanding characteristics of his garden at Versailles were its manipulation of water, its sculpture, its parterres. But perhaps its chief ornament (alas, not easily imitated in today's gardens) must have been the richly clad courtiers promenading at their master's pleasure.

The 16th century had been a transition period in architecture and the making of gardens. There was much rebuilding in Paris, and along the Loire old châteaux were renovated and new ones created, making a romantic chain of great houses and castles running through Touraine. Buildings tended to remain essentially Gothic, but with grafted-on classical details inspired by the Italian Renaissance. In gardens the Italian influence was equally fitful initially. Drawings by Du Cerceau, in a book illustrating a selection of great French architecture, showed huge ornamental wooden galleries, quite Italian in inspiration, but surrounding knot gardens not much advanced on their medieval forbears.

With increasing Mannerist influence from Italy, a particularly French rendering of the Baroque developed. Its architecture was sober and dignified, favouring clearly logical layouts. The organization of space along geometric lines was extended to towns as much as to houses and gardens. The town of Richelieu, for example, was subsidiary to Cardinal Richelieu's château. This kind of planning prepared the way for great gardens such as Versailles, in which buildings were subordinated to a total spatial organization, which embraced the surrounding countryside.

It was André Mollet's *Jardin de Plaisir* (1651) that codified the concept of the French formal garden as a unified design intended to be seen from the principal windows of the house. Ten years later the magnificent garden at Vaux-le-Vicomte, the palace of the young King's Chancellor Nicolas Fouquet, was completed. In an utterly comprehensive scheme, the designer Andre Le Nôtre presented a huge compartment, in which everything from the entrance gates to the statue of Hercules at the summit of the distant slope was in its logical place. Yet although the garden rolls out from the house like a great carpet, it is full of surprises. The

A prototype for Versailles

The gardens of Vaux-le-Vicomte, laid out in 1657-61 for Louis XIV's chancellor Nicolas Fouquet, were an expression of total logical order. In August 1661 Fouquet held an extravagant fête here in honour of the young king, with fireworks, dances, open-air concerts and a new comedy by Molière. Louis, outraged at his chancellor's effrontery, ruined and imprisoned him and stole his garden designer, Andre Le Nôtre, whom he employed on the royal gardens at Versailles.

Water personified

A brilliant school of outdoor sculpture was generated by the works at Versailles. Coordinated by Charles Le Brun, sculptors such as Girardon, Coysevox, Le Gros, Tubi and Regnaudin created magnificent statues and fountains, following a comprehensive allegorical programme. Pictured here is Water, one of the four elements, carved by Pierre Le Gros. The features are those of Le Gros's favourite model, whose likeness appears elsewhere in the gardens. The damp hair bound with seaweed, the urn spilling water and the blunt-headed dolphin at her feet all reinforce the symbolic meaning.

Louis's symbol was the Sun, which linked him to Apollo, and so the palace and gardens are studded with references to this god, from the statues of Apollo and Diana set by the central window of the Hall of Mirrors to the group of Apollo and his chariot at the head of the canal. Other statues depict mythological figures from Ovid's *Metamorphoses* and various personified aspects of creation – the Elements, the Humours, the Four Parts of the World, the Seasons, Morning and Day, Evening and Night, and the four categories of Poetry. In addition, the theme of War and Peace is represented, as are the King's victories. The kingdom itself is symbolized in the water parterre, with bronze statues representing the rivers of France. Versailles was not only a theatre, but it was a temple, in which were united the symbols of Apollo and the Cosmos – the ultimate glorification of Man.

The King's triumph over Nature is symbolized more than adequately by the astonishing range of fountains, and the enormous extent of the various pools and canals – Versailles is, in fact, an enormous water garden. The French were quite familiar with garden schemes incorporating water. The great châteaux of the Loire generally overlooked a river or were moated for defence. At the Château de Ruel, Richelieu had indulged in an almost Italianate use of water in the water staircase, with its basins and fountains at regular intervals down the slope. Le Nôtre's water designs at Vaux-le-Vicomte were grander still, with massive fountains and cascades and complicated jets; and at Chantilly, he constructed a garden with gigantic water parterres and broad canals, where there is more water in the composition than dry land. His garden at Marly shows similar virtuosity: on the principal axis, a colossal water staircase with spectacular cascade effects sweeps down to broad-stepped pools at the bottom.

At Versailles the sheer scale of the water areas is awe-inspiring, and the diversity of tricks incredible. Many of the fountains have disappeared, some moved even during Louis's lifetime. In the Marais, where the Apollo fountain is now sited, was a tree whose branches spouted water, standing in a rectangular pool, contained by a "fence" of narrow jets arching into the centre. The Water Theatre, in one of the *bosquets* (groves) nearby, contained jets that could be turned on in different permutations. Most of the *bosquets* had fountains at their centres, as did the *bassins* (stone pools) at the intersections of the avenues. It may surprise us today that water was always in short supply, so the fountains could never be used all at once: they were turned on and off following the progress of the King and his retinue around the garden.

Of course, there was also a grotto, although it had to be dismantled when the palace was expanded. Used for entertainments and banquets, it was dedicated to Thetis, and had an interior encrusted with semi-precious stones, mirrors, mother-of-pearl, coral and the like. There had been a strong tradition of making grottoes in France, and Louis XIII was particularly keen on them. Le Nôtre had taken up the idea at Vaux-le-Vicomte, where he made a colossal wall with seven huge vaulted niches separated by gigantic Terms (busts on tapering pillars). Water gushed out over rocks into a pool below, while on the terrace above was a thick, flattish jet that appeared to form a pedestal for Hercules in the distance.

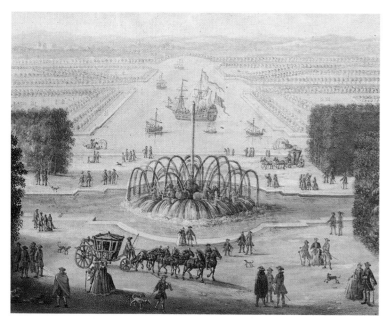

A giant playground

This 17th-century view of Versailles shows the Bassin d'Appollon, sited at the end of the Tapis Vert (great lawn) and at the beginning of the great Canal, which disappears to the far horizon. A full-size sailing ship on the Canal must have greatly satisfied Louis's sense of achievement.

canal on the cross-axis cannot be seen until one is on top of it. The Hercules, although it seems at first to mark the end of the scheme, is actually at the beginning of a long avenue that stretches out into the countryside. The garden has an heroic scale, quite unlike any garden design ever seen before. It is a total synthesis of the arts devised to celebrate the genius of Fouquet – much to the displeasure of the King.

Consumed with jealousy, one supposes, Louis took over Fouquet's team and set to work on a creation whose magnificence would show, without any doubt, who was the master of France. Versailles was to be the most splendid expression of absolute monarchy. The garden's central axis leads away to the west and into infinity, across the water parterre, the Latona fountain, along the grassy Allée Royale to the Apollo fountain, and on along the Grand Canal, which seems to dissolve into the light of the sky. Its boundaries are precisely defined by hedges which hold back the billowing greenery of the trees. In measured rhythm run the urns and statues, the planting cases and even the benches, all in subservience to the overall plan.

The gardens at Versailles were an immense theatre in which incredible events – balls, pageants, plays and tremendous firework displays – were organized, sometimes lasting several days. But Versailles must also be seen as the culmination of the use of symbolism and allegory in gardens. Few have been the instances when such a vast allegorical programme has been required, and seldom has there been such an opportunity for carrying one out.

The use of sculpture to reinforce both the layout and the allegory of the garden had been well established in Italy. But in France the production of outdoor sculpture took place on an unprecedented scale. Under the direction of Charles Le Brun, artists such as François Girardon, Antoine Coysevox and many others, worked in marble, gilded lead and bronze to the highest standards of invention and expression. Moreover the sculpture was integrated into the gardens as part of the overall design with a conviction that has never been achieved since. Not only are the pieces spatially correct, they are also thematically correct. However good the components of 19th- and 20th- century collections may be, and however well-placed, they remain collections. But at Versailles they are part of a story, and vital to the harmony of the whole.

While water and sculpture held pride of place at Versailles, treillage (or architectural trelliswork) had an important supporting role. The tradition of highly decorative carpenter's work, which appears so strong in Du Cerceau's drawings of Gaillon and Montargis, continued in the 17th and 18th centuries. Owing to the perishable nature of timber, treillage is more evident in paintings and engravings than in any surviving relics. But clearly by Le Nôtre's time the art had reached astonishing complexity. At the Hôtel de Condé he used treillage on a sumptuous scale to create domed pavilions linked by high fences, and an enormous central pavilion based on a triumphal arch. At Versailles treillage was used extensively in the *bosquets*, perhaps partly because of its ability to give an architectural effect more immediately than hedges and trees. Many *bosquets* are defined by high trellis fences, sometimes punctuated by apse-shaped niches, sometimes curved round the back of a fountain. Hedges were grown through the trellises, so that in time they became totally swathed in greenery. In some cases treillage appears to have been covered with a mantle of climbing plants.

With such strongly architectural attitudes governing the use of plants, pleaching and hedging assumed special importance. Bernard Palissy, who worked in the gardens of the Tuileries for Catherine de Médicis (1518-89), is said to have designed green halls, with branches entwined to make high sloping roofs and windowed walls. And the tree-weaving designed for the garden at Marly, laid out in the 1690s, shows an astonishing concept of an arcade roofed over with intersecting vaults, and punctuated with green urns.

Back at ground level, the parterre had developed as a characteristic feature of the 18th-century garden. The earlier knot garden had traditionally been set in an independent square framework and edged with aromatic sub-shrubs, such as thyme or lavender. Parterres, however, were not so framed, and were designed to relate to, or reflect, any adjacent parterres, as well as being closely linked with the building itself. By 1600, Olivier de Serres, in his *Théâtre d'Agriculture*, was recommending box as an edging plant for its greater durability. A little later, Boyceau and the Mollets were achieving some variety by the introduction of curves and arabesques. However, the spaces, as in previous centuries, were generally filled with sand or other coloured

Bacchus

The Fountain of Bacchus, or Autumn, by B. and G. Marsy in gilded lead from a drawing by Le Brun. Bacchus lies on the grape-covered island of Autumn clasping bunches between his hands while four satyrs loll sleepily, overcome with wine. The statue is located where the Avenue of Autumn intersects the Avenue of Bacchus and Saturn.

materials, and it was only in the gardens of the Trianon at Versailles that they were embellished with flowers; these were grown in pots – two million of them by Le Nôtre's reckoning – so that they could be changed daily, or even twice a day should the King so desire.

On a larger scale were the *caisses de Versailles*. These boxes containing small tender trees were generally kept in the Orangery in the winter, and were lined out on the nearby parterres during the summer. Alternatively, in some were grown small standard trees pruned to a neat spherical head and disposed in suitably architectural arrangements.

AFTER VERSAILLES

Ornament for Autocrats

The greatness of Versailles lies in it ruthless application of a logical order, from which no deviation was permitted: it was a work of art commanding obedience. Such a work can be conceived and executed only once in a culture. It leaves its participants exhausted and needful of more frivolous things. Relief was found in imitations of the idea of the English garden (the *jardin anglais*), in rococo details, and in mock-Chinese ornament *(chinoiserie)*. Meanwhile, throughout Europe, aspiring princes attempted their own Versailles. Few of these autocrats had the vision, and none had the wealth, of Louis XIV. Nevertheless, they made their mark, and took their pleasure, in princely gardens of fantastic extravagance.

At the same time the religious principles that underpinned the idea of absolute monarchy were increasingly questioned. A moral rationale was sought rather than a religious dogma. In architecture and gardens, this trend was expressed by throwing off the straightjacket of logical geometry. Where philosophers and artists led, princes followed, creating gardens in bizarre mixtures of rigid planning overlaid with whimsical layouts that deferred to the idea of Nature or to the exotic. Symptomatic was the pagoda dressed in tinkling bells – a product of the strange marriage of Chinese and English influences mingled to create the *jardin anglo-chinois*. Symbolic of the change in attitude was the Petit Trianon at Versailles, where Louis XV's formal gardens were flanked by Louis XVI's more "natural" layout, with a serpentine river and tree-fringed glades.

The frivolity of *chinoiserie* made a welcome fantasy to relieve the stiffness of court life: however, devoid of symbolic content, it bore little relation to its Chinese model. It was manifested principally in upturned eaves, complicated timber railings and hump-backed bridges.

The rococo style was similarly whimsical – a frenzied accumulation of exotic scenes and allusions, from the hermitages of Graf von Sporck's Bethlehem, near Kuskus, with its saints carved in the living rock, to the looking-glass grotto of Prince Potemkin at Taurida near St Petersburg. As the clouds of revolution piled high over Europe, gardens became more and more extravagant and lighthearted. In Spain, Philip V's garden of La Granja at San Ildefonso, made in the 1720s, had fountains, *jets d'eau*, canals, temples, covered seats, cabinets, bowers, grottoes, labyrinths, pastures, and hedges of myrtle and laurel. Philip's son Charles III commissioned a cascade at Caserta near Naples, so vast that the water had to be collected over a distance of thirty miles, conveyed over aqueducts and tunnelled through mountains. The cascade and water staircase have an overwhelming magnificence out of all proportion with the palace, the composition as a whole, or indeed with Charles's real importance.

German gardens of the 18th century were crammed full of ornament. In Munich were the Nymphenburg and Schlessheim, both worked on by Dominique Girard, with enormous *parterres de broderie*, elaborate canal systems, fountains, statues and urns. Herrenhausen, built for the Duke of Hanover by Charles Charbonnier, a pupil of Le Nôtre, had an enormous parterre divided into triangles by paths, with pools, fountains, pavilions, *bosquets* and a circular lake, all contained by canals bordered by avenues of limes. Schwetzingen, likewise, planned by Nicolas de Pigage (1723-96), had all the fountains, statues and *bosquets* necessary for the dignity of the Elector Palatine.

Frederick the Great's garden near Potsdam, started in 1744, was exceptional in being planned round six terraces, each 10 feet high, on which vines were grown; in winter the sides of the terraces had to be glazed. Above rose the palace of Sans Souci, while below there were large French parterres, a *parterre d'émail* (made of glass beads and Dutch faïence), a variety of individual gardens in different styles and, in the distance, a hill of windmills.

Most extraordinary of all was Wilhelmshohe, laid out from 1701 by the Landgrave of Hesse. An avenue, four miles long, stretched from the centre of Kassel to the Habichtswald escarpment. There, a huge octagon was built, surmounted by a steep pyramid on whose pinnacle stood Hercules, 33 feet (10 metres) high. Below was the grotto of Pan, a confection of rocks and water-jets, contained by curving staircases with watery balustrades. The grotto was the start of a gigantic cascade, of which only a part was completed, although the result is still awe-inspiring. In the middle of the century, this site was overlaid with a garden in the English style, with temples and grottoes and even a Chinese village.

Peter the Great of Russia, after a sojourn in England, lodged at the Trianon and fell under the spell of Versailles. Near his new city of St Petersburg he built the Peterhof, with gardens designed by Le Blond, another pupil of Le Nôtre. Sited on an escarpment, impressive cascades, flanked by vertical jets and gilded statues, lead down from the terrace. Below this a canal stretches out to the Baltic and, marching with it, an avenue of circular pools, each with its own fountain.

To the south of St Petersburg, Tsarskoe Selo was laid out for Catherine the Great in a mixture of styles, including French gardens near the palace, a *jardin anglais*, a Turkish bath, and a Palladian bridge. *Chinoiserie* was much in evidence: there was a "creaking" pavilion and the strange "Bolshoi Kapriz", a pagoda

Caserta

At the foot of the vast rocky cascade descending from the woods above Caserta, near Naples, are groups of sculpture celebrating Diana and the chase – a theme that recurs throughout the gardens. To the right of the great waterfall, the group of nymphs surrounding Diana are pointing in agitation to the group on the left (not shown) where Actaeon, who has been transformed into a stag, is attacked by his own hounds. From this point the water continues to flow as a gigantic water staircase extending through more than a mile of landscape.

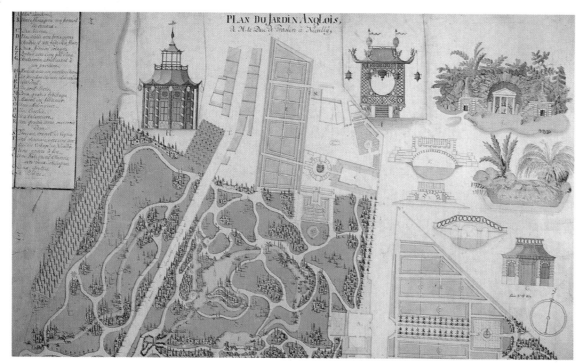

A jardin anglo-chinois

This illustration for G.L.Le Rouge's *Détails des Nouveaux Jardins à la Mode* (1776-87) shows a plan for a "Jardin Anglois" at Neuilly. Among the serpentine paths and watercourses is an array of "Chinese" confections, pavilions, temples, bridges, cascades and grottoes, all designed to present a sequence of fantastic events. The creation of varied scenes of make-believe costs the garden its overall unity: it has become a series of isolated incidents.

with Ionic columns; beyond was a Chinese village designed by a Scot. There were picturesque ruins, pyramids and obelisks, and a temple housing a sculpture collection.

The symbolic aspects of the garden, so important in the preceding centuries, were becoming more diffused. Classical allusions still prevailed. Wilhelmshohe had a Virgil's tomb, an Apollo's temple, a Pluto's grotto. Girardin's revolutionary garden at Ermenonville had a Temple of Philosophy, dedicated to Montaigne, each of its columns serving as a memorial to a philosopher. Caserta indulged Charles III's love of hunting through sculptural references, particularly to Diana and Actaeon. But as fashions followed each other, governing themes fell apart, and allusions tended to be restricted to isolated groups of ornament. In any case, a serious allegorical programme perhaps no longer appeared necessary. At Weikersheim, near Würzburg, the statuary, by Johann Jakob Sommer, may be thematic, but it is altogether light-hearted, with portraits of servants as dwarves, and the gods lounging about.

Sculpture continued as a vital element in gardens, providing focal points, making allusions, or quietly attending the cycle of seasons. Ferdinand Tietz's work at Veitshochsheim was humorous, almost caricature-like. At Peterhof, the gilded bronze figures of Coysevox's pupil, Nicholas Pineau, shimmer in the spray. But in an age of bizarre effects, few can have been so droll as the statuary in the Polish garden of Lazienki, laid out for Stanislas Augustus in 1764. Here, as J.C. Loudon observed, "pedestals, as if for placing statues, were ranged. . .particularly along the broad walk leading from palace to amphitheatre. On these pedestals, on extraordinary occasions, selected living figures, male and female, dressed in character, were placed, and taught to maintain certain attitudes."

Rococo levity

The central sculpture of the garden at Weikersheim depicts Hercules struggling with a dragon-like Hydra, lifting it off the ground by its neck. Carved by J.J.Sommer in 1712, it has a light touch that reflects rococo attitudes, and is quite different from the more dignified statuary at Versailles.

Many of Sommer's other sculptures in the garden depict court personalities and servants as dwarves. The garden is designed to be friendly in the Renaissance manner rather than awe-inspiring, as in the Baroque.

THE ENGLISH LANDSCAPE

Expressions of Freedom

As the Baroque garden, with its allegorical programme and statement of autocratic power, came to a magnificent dead end in France, new concepts were stirring in England. The French style, though significant, had the briefest of flowerings before a new attitude to nature developed, culminating in the vast landscaped parks of "Capability" Brown, whose magnificent sweeping views needed ornament the size of buildings – an expense in land and construction that few could undertake. This style flourished for half a century before the inevitable reaction set in, demanding a smaller, more intimate scale with greater emphasis on horticulture and a more versatile use of ornament.

Until the end of the 17th century, England remained far behind the rest of Europe in garden development. Certainly, the Tudors, particularly Henry VIII, indulged in garden-making, but they never introduced any radically new ideas. Henry VIII's garden at

Manipulating the landscape

The landscapes of "Capability" Brown, encompassing large-scale elements such as belts of trees and spreading lakes, brought to a climax the radical English approach to design in the 18th century. At Petworth (Sussex), the sward reaches right to the house, and beasts are kept out by a ha-ha (sunken wall).

Hampton Court was essentially medieval, and the gardens of Elizabeth's reign were not very different. However, towards the end of her reign, houses were beginning to be built in a grand, outward-looking style, requiring a formal setting for each front, with decorative gateways, corner pavilions and elaborate gardens. French influence finally made an impression during the later 17th century, partly through the court of Charles II, and partly through Sir Christopher Wren, who, with Sir John Vanbrugh and Nicholas Hawksmoor, presided over a brief spell of English Baroque.

Most famous of all the gardens designed before the Civil War

The classical style

At his villa at Chiswick, based on Palladio's Villa Rotonda near Vicenza, Lord Burlington, aided by Charles Bridgeman and William Kent, sought to conjure up a feeling of antiquity. The Amphitheatre, shown here in a painting by Peter Rysbrack (c. 1730), had an obelisk in the central pool, and small trees in tubs were laid out around the steps.

was that at Wilton House, near Salisbury, made for the fourth Earl of Pembroke between 1632 and 1635. Near the house was a broad path flanked by parterres, beyond which was a wilderness, and then an arrangement of trees along formal walks. Through the wilderness, the River Nadder took a course unrelated to the geometry of the garden, with a waywardness that could only be English. At the end of the garden, on the central axis, was a grotto with an impressive array of hydraulic effects.

After the Restoration, there was a preoccupation with axial planning, and the integration of water, *allées* (rides cutting through massed trees) and parterres. André Mollet's *Jardin de Plaisir* (1651) provided the model, but the English were only ever half-hearted about the application of French logic. Typical was the work at Longleat by London and Wise, where the garden, even though axially planned, was set at right angles to the main entry axis. An interesting survival of the time is Melbourne Hall in Derbyshire, with a parterre running down to the Great Basin and iron arbour (by Robert Bakewell), and with intersecting avenues leading off to the south. This sort of anglicized French style continued well into the 18th century, receiving encouragement from books like John James's *Theory and Practice of Gardening*, a translation of a French work by Dezcallier D'Argenvilles, published in 1714.

However, there was a growing urge to relax the formality. Already, in the first decade of the 18th century, Vanbrugh was treating the landscape in a completely idiosyncratic way at Castle Howard in North Yorkshire. Perhaps being a playwright, he could see the landscape as a stage upon which to mount architectural "scenery". It was the land form itself, not an artificially imposed geometry, that determined where his temples and obelisks should be placed.

The need to shake off French doctrines was expressed in print by Stephen Switzer, Joseph Addison and, most effectively, Alexander Pope. Pope admired the irregularity of nature, but felt that the role of art was to discover and enhance its hidden order. The composed and relaxed landscapes painted in Italy by Claude and Poussin provided models for a new concept of garden-making. This kind of landscape was felt to heighten the effect of buildings in the Palladian style (inspired by the Renaissance architect Andrea Palladio) which was favoured by Lord Burlington and his circle, arbiters of taste for their whole generation. A great patron, Burlington was to have considerable influence on the direction taken by English architecture and gardening during the 18th century. His protégé William Kent (*c.* 1685-1748), who had painted in Rome, understood the idea of landscape composition, both on canvas and on the ground. He became the most successful garden designer of his day, paving the way for "Capability" Brown and the classic English park landscape.

Kent's Elysian Fields at Stowe in Buckinghamshire were in complete contrast to the French manner of the work recently completed there by Charles Bridgeman. His buildings were set in a flowing landscape, in combination with a lake and clumps of trees, the whole fashioned to create a series of unfolding views composed like paintings. At Rousham House we are fortunate in having a mature example of Kent's style still extant. Buildings and sculpture, subtly linked to the curving river, lead one through a landscape of deep peace and serenity.

Other current ideas, such as that of the *ferme ornée* (ornamental farm) which transformed a utilitarian scheme into an artistic scheme, helped to relax the grip of the geometric plan. Individuals such as Charles Hamilton at Painshill, Henry Hoare at Stourhead, William Shenstone at The Leasowes, produced romantic land-

Dominating Charles Hamilton's 18th-century park at Painshill, Surrey, is the recently restored Gothic temple, sited as a gateway between the vast green amphitheatre on the higher ground and the lake and valley extending to the west. Seen from below, the temple hangs above the lake like a crown.

A sculptural masterpiece

Kent's greatest surviving work is the garden at Rousham House, Oxfordshire. At the end of the Bowling Green, where the land falls away to the River Cherwell, is this brilliantly sited Horse and Lion by Peter Scheemakers, a magnificently vigorous sculpture carved *c.* 1740.

scapes which accepted the excitement of nature in its changing moods, seeking a variety of landscape pictures rather than a heavy-handed domination by Man.

Lancelot "Capability" Brown (1716-83), who had worked under Kent at Stowe, became the professional sweeper-away of geometric order. His parks consisted essentially of rolling ground with greensward running right up to the house, clumps and belts of trees, large sheets of water, and strategically placed architectural features to guide the eye.

The sheer scale and simplicity of these landscapes often gives them great beauty. However, not only did they substitute a new formula for an old one, but they also excluded the interest of horticulture. The Picturesque school found the Brown landscape all too smooth and easy, and lacking in excitement, while Sir William Chambers and others wanted more variety and fantasy as well as the possibility of taking some pleasure in flowers.

Alongside the landscaped garden, formal gardens also seem to have flourished as a parallel line of development all through the 18th century. Moreover, it is likely that flowers played an increasingly important role. Thomas Robins's paintings of Richard Bateman's house at Old Windsor show flowers set in large circular beds; there are also seats, arbours and temples, a variety of sculptures and shrubs grown in pots. Around mid-century, Thomas Wright was recommending that decaying parterres be

restored and flower beds and rose gardens be laid out. Chambers, working at Kew Gardens from 1757, created an ornamental garden in which the diversity of plants was as important as the inventive quality of the buildings. Practising at the turn of the century, Humphry Repton, while thoroughly absorbing the strengths of Brown's designs, also appreciated flowering plants, generally positioning them either near the house or in special enclosures.

In the fluidly organized landscapes of Kent and Brown, the need for an allegorical programme was probably less apparent than it was in the formal French garden. However, there were certainly symbolic meanings at work. In Kent's Elysian Fields at Stowe, the Temple of the British Worthies lies in sight of the Temple of Ancient Virtue across the River Styx. The landscape at Stourhead is said to have been based on Virgil's *Aeneid*, as an allegory of Man's passage through the world. From birth at the Temple of Flora the visitor passes through the grotto of the Underworld to glory in the Pantheon; and from there the route takes him under a rock arch, where he shakes off his mortal coil, heavenwards to the Temple of Apollo. How many other 18th-century gardens were laid out with this type of programme, only diligent research will tell. Certainly, there were plenty of temples dedicated to Venus or Fame or the like, with ancient deities doing service in aid of the Genius of the Place.

Buildings in the landscape were not only important for the moral virtue they might evoke, or for their classical (or sometimes Gothic) allusions. Where a composition consisted solely of grass, trees and water, a classical or Gothic building (like a *t'ing* in a Chinese landscape) made a necessary focal point, its calculated form contrasting with the swelling ground or the sky-reflecting sheet of water. The ponds at Studley Royal in Yorkshire would be

nothing without their little temple reflected in the water. In the manner of the Arcadian landscapes of Claude, the ancient temples and ruins framed the view. At Castle Howard, the scene is contained by the Temple of the Four Winds (standing square at the end of the Grass Walk) and the drum-shaped Mausoleum seen in the distance over copse and field. At Painshill the Gothic temple, suddenly perceived, hangs distant over the lake, a sublime apparition. Similar effects could work equally well on a smaller scale, as at Nuneham Courtenay where the little temple of Flora makes a fitting end to the flower garden.

In older gardens, small buildings had been used as part of the formal plan. Sometimes they reinforced corners, as at Montacute in Somerset. Frequently such pavilions housed a banqueting room. But alternatively they might house a grotto, like de Caus's three-arched grotto on the axis of the garden at Wilton, containing suitably watery effects, whistling nightingales and the like. Of similar date was the grotto built by Thomas Bushell at Enstone, containing a ball-balancing fountain and rocks that continually dripped water.

The great grottoes of the 18th century were made to seem underground. Pope's grotto at Twickenham was an underground passage connecting his garden to a lawn on the bank of the River Thames. Formed into a series of rooms, the walls and ceiling were lined with shells, mirrors and luminous and semi-precious stones. It was a sort of philosopher's cave. The grotto at Stourhead, however, with its allusions to the Underworld, is a place of dramatic lighting effects, with a statue of the River God seen eerily bright through the gloom, and a wonderful view at water-level across the lake, craggily framed. The Painshill grotto, likewise,

once sheathed in spar and topped with tufa, is down at water-level with views across the lake, but is now sadly decayed. Its creator, Charles Hamilton, also advised on the construction of the Cascade at Bowood, a magnificent cliff of rocks piled dramatically onto the end of Brown's dam, over which the water makes, from time to time, a local Niagara.

As a principal element of the great 18th-century landscapes, such as Bowood or Blenheim, the lakes give life and variety in a way more subtle than the gushings of a thousand fountains. The use of water in gardens is as desirable in England as anywhere else. In a damp climate, with soft atmosphere, and the sky often overcast, the cooling effect of moving water, its sparkle caught in a shaft of sunlight, has less immediate appeal. However, the broad expanse of water, levelling in gentle valleys, reflecting silhouettes of trees against the sky, is a dreamy mirror in which the seasons change, ruffled by the wind or smooth like glass. A more local focus might be permitted in a cascade, broad and frothing like Charlecote's, or that between the Fishing Lodges at Studley. At Wilton and Stowe that happy invention, the Palladian Bridge, draws the eye over the rippling water. Water also looked well in the more formal layouts of Studley, with its canal and moon ponds, and at Wrest Park, Hall Barn, Westbury Court, Erdigg and many other canal schemes. Basins were popular in the French-inspired gardens – they were shallow, circular or at least regularly shaped, with a fountain in the centre, as at Melbourne. Kent produced a pretty effect with his version of an octagonal basin and rill at Rousham. More spectacular water displays were also attempted. There was a tradition of making freestanding fountains that had continued from medieval times. A description of Chatsworth, Derbyshire, in

One of the most satisfactory garden buildings conceived during the 18th century was the Palladian bridge, of which there are two notable examples. The Bridge at Stowe *(left)* was modelled on that at Wilton House (Wiltshire), which was designed by Roger Morris in 1736. Essentially, the bridge consists of a colonnaded gallery with pedimented arches at each end, surmounting a deeply rusticated three-arched structure. The Stowe bridge, with woods behind, contains the view along the lake to the east, its gallery giving it sufficient height to serve effectively as an eyecatcher.

1700 notes a Neptune fountain and a copper tree like a willow, with water dropping from the leaves. And the great Cascade there must always have been a thrilling spectacle, even with grey clouds scudding overhead.

Statuary began to be popular in gardens from the latter half of the 17th century, continuing into the 18th century. Talented artists included Gabriel Cibber, who worked at Chatsworth and Hampton Court Palace. Among the skilled Dutch craftsmen who came to England in this period was John van Nost, expert in lead; he executed statues such as the kneeling Blackamoor at Melbourne Hall, Derbyshire, of which many casts were made. Peter Scheemakers, his contemporary, did many important works at Stowe, including the great equestrian statue of George II. The Cheere brothers, also linked with van Nost, furnished many great gardens of the time. Michael Rysbrack was responsible for Flora and other pieces at Stowe, and for the nymph in the grotto at Stourhead. But this school, though prolific, flourished relatively briefly: their services were not much in demand for the sweeping scenes composed by "Capability" Brown, where buildings and mighty columns took the place of sculpture.

THE NINETEENTH CENTURY

The Age of Eclecticism

A rare survival

The enormous parterre at Drummond Castle in Scotland is one of the rare instances of a 19th-century bedding scheme that has been kept going, even though in reduced form. Viewed from the castle high above, the parterre reveals a construction of cross-axes and diagonal axes framed in low hedges of box and punctuated with clipped hollies and yews. Golden-leaved conifers and purple broadleaved trees play an important part in the scheme, which was laid out by Lewis Kennedy from about 1838.

The 19th century was one of unprecedented social change. The economies of many Western nations developed from an agricultural to an industrial base, and their populations increased sometimes as much as tenfold. A significant feature was the emergence of an ambitious and educated middle class, particularly in Britain. As the population expanded, towns burst at the seams, creating the suburbs in which the middle classes sought to emulate the gardens of the aristocracy. A busy horticultural press directed itself towards their needs with gardening periodicals such as *The Gardener's Magazine* and *The Floricultural Magazine* and with books such as J.C. Loudon's *The Suburban Gardener and Villa Companion* (1838).

In the midst of such turmoil, it is perhaps hardly surprising that there was no overriding style of garden design. Certainly the great parks of Brown, of maximum extent and minimum content, had had their day. The work of Humphry Repton, around the turn of the century, and his invaluable writings, show an increasing interest in the zone between the house and the green sheep-mown lawns beyond.

Not only did Repton devise agreeable foregrounds with flowers and ornament, but he planned gardens around horticultural themes such as the growing of roses, and he also generated designs from historical precedents. He accepted that gardens were manmade, and that they could and should appear so – a theme taken up by both Loudon and Hibberd as the century progressed.

A profound influence on the course of European gardening was the rapid increase in the number of plant species available. This was aided by the development of the greenhouse. Originally the greenhouse was a large-windowed building into which tender plants might be retired for the winter. But in the 19th century, with improvements in glass and iron technology, it became technically feasible to glaze the structure all over and heat it to maintain high winter temperatures. Sir Joseph Paxton's greenhouse at Chatsworth – the Great Stove – was a radically new departure in building design, and paved the way for his marvellous Crystal Palace, erected for the Great Exhibition in London in 1851. The improved greenhouse enabled tender herbaceous plants from sub-tropical climates to be over-wintered and propagated, and to be incorporated into exotic bedding schemes. The other major invention of the time was the lawnmower, which permitted the maintenance of greater areas of neat, close-mown sward, requiring for its upkeep neither excessive labour nor cattle.

J.C. Loudon wrote prolifically about all aspects of gardens. He distinguished between the geometric (or formal) style and the irregular (or English) style; the latter he further categorized as picturesque, gardenesque or rustic. He believed that the use of different styles in the same garden was desirable, given sufficient screening or transition areas. Much influenced by Repton and Loudon was the work of Andrew Downing in the USA, whose writings appealed to a comparable middle-class readership. He in turn may have influenced F.L. Olmstead, who to some extent carried on the Repton tradition in the public realm of town parks.

Britain led the way in garden planning in the 19th century. In both France and Germany, English-style gardens appeared, often alongside or around earlier, more formal layouts. At the same time, however, Britain borrowed themes from historic European traditions. During the 1830s the Italianate style was emerging, in the hands of the architect Sir Charles Barry with horticultural assistance from W.A. Nesfield. Although there had been an early essay in the genre at Wilton, it was at Trentham in Staffordshire, in 1833, that the style was truly established. It was characterized by geometric beds laid out on terraces and interspersed with fountains, sculpture and neatly trimmed evergreens. A little later, Paxton was carrying out alterations at Chatsworth in a similar manner. Shrubland Park near Ipswich (by Barry and Nesfield, started 1848) and George Kennedy's terraces at Bowood (1851) are both thoroughly Italianate. The formality of the style was particularly suited to bedding schemes, which looked better in a strong architectural framework.

At the same time, eclectic gardens in a kind of Picturesque style were made. At Biddulph Grange in Staffordshire (started 1842) a series of carefully separated areas of differing historical or geographical character was laid out in a free-flowing plan attached to the formal layout around the house. A tunnel leading from "Egypt", a monumental topiary construction lined with sphinxes, emerges through a half-timbered cottage into an arboretum. Another tunnel leads through a pavilion to "China", which has lakes, bridges, a tower and a Great Wall. Biddulph is a romantic garden, full of surprises and exotic ornament, and richly planted.

Bedding out in the 19th century became incredibly complex. The parterres at Castle Ashby, near Northampton (dating from 1865), contained monograms, heraldic devices, huge fan shapes and interlocking hearts, all illustrated with bedding plants and edged with white gravel. There was an increasing demand for historically accurate imitations: for example, Elizabethan gardens were built, with mounts and mazes, and designers such as Blomfield, Sitwell and Peto looked directly at Italian precedents, rather than following the hybrid style of Barry.

As new plants flooded into Europe and America, decorative horticultural techniques became as important as water and sculpture had been in preceding centuries. Loudon aptly described

bedding, in 1824, as "the changeable flower garden, in which all the plants are kept in pots, and reared in the flower nursery or reserve-ground". He recommended that identical plants be grouped together in carefully worked out colour schemes, and that any plants which began to flag be immediately replaced to maintain the pristine freshness of the composition. By 1856, Shirley Hibberd, in *Rustic Adornments*, was emphasizing the need for dwarf plants. He also described the fashion for lining a grass walk with pincushion beds – circular beds of identical size, each with a standard rose in the middle and an edging of bricks or stones or perhaps stumps of larch poles about three inches high in each bed; inside were planted flowers such as geraniums, lobelia or calceolaria. Another style he described was ribbon gardening, which consisted of lines of plants, all in one colour (or a series of blended colours), ranging up in size towards the rear, and backed by a climber-covered wall or fence.

Edging was particularly important in bedding displays. Box was commonly used, as well as other plants such as thrift. Ivy, closely trimmed, was also very popular. Edgings were sometimes made of timber, despite its short life. More durable were bricks set on edge or slanted in a herringbone pattern. Also common were ornamental clay tiles fashioned to resemble rope or in geometric forms. Cast-iron edging was manufactured in a number of repeating patterns. In some architectural gardens, stone edgings were used, with a variety of mouldings.

Bedding schemes were widespread in France, where they were particularly favoured by Edouard André, who referred to them as *jardins fleuristes*. They also became popular in Germany: there was an important example at Sans Souci, and several were made by Peter Lenne, director of the Potsdam gardens. In due course, changing fashions and the high costs of maintenance were to relegate bedding schemes to the municipal park. But they can still

A rosary by Humphry Repton

Repton was important for his ability to design not only great parks but also gardens for the flowering plants that were beginning to be imported from all over the world. This was his rosary at Ashridge, Hertfordshire.

be seen in innovative combinations at gardens such as the Royal Botanic Gardens, Kew, or in the dry moat at Angers in France. There is an interesting survival at Drummond Castle in Scotland, where the vast parterre, although it has been greatly simplified, shows clearly the intricacy of such schemes and the intensive labour demanded for their upkeep (see illustration, page 40).

The flower garden increased in popularity throughout the century to the point at which it virtually displaced all other forms. An early herbaceous border at Arley Hall in Cheshire, laid out in 1846, foreshadowed the more relaxed, less regimented effects that were to be sought by the end of the century. William Robinson fiercely criticized the formality of the Italianate style and the unnatural practice of bedding out, urging a closer appreciation of plants in their natural state. The great designer Gertrude Jekyll, with her painter's eye, albeit a myopic one, was able to dispose her plants like paint on a canvas, carefully selecting them to harmonize colours at various times of flowering. Unlike Robinson, she understood the need to create a balanced relationship between different parts of the garden, and between the garden and the house. She raised the border to a sophisticated art form, creating subtle interplays of carefully shaped plant groups, balancing and blending colours and exploring the many shades of green, always taking fully into account the soft English light. Moreover, Jekyll appreciated the advantage of a strong architectural framework to bind the composition together. Her collaboration with many architects, but particularly Sir Edwin Lutyens, produced a method of organizing gardens that was to dominate the 20th century.

Topiary came back into vogue during the 19th century. Trees were cut or clipped into animal shapes, mushrooms, geometric forms such as triangles, globes, cones, walls, columns, arcades, vases, arbours, temples and theatres. The garden at Packwood in Warwickshire, with its stylized topiary representation of the Sermon on the Mount, was planted out in the 1850s. In the same county, the impressive topiary of the garden of Compton Wynyates was created in the 1870s. At Biddulph, clipped ilex formed the Egyptian temple, while at Rous Lench the topiary took the form of towers and battlemented walks. A particularly popular topiary motif was the peacock standing on top of a hedge. Other birds and animals also provided inspiration. In the United States, the famous topiary menagerie made by Thomas Brayton at Green Animals, Rhode Island, included camels, giraffes, elephants and bears. Topiary satisfied the Victorians' desire for fantasy.

An influential idea that gained ground in the 19th century was the division of a garden into compartments in an effort to prevent disparate styles and dissimilar planting schemes from visually interfering with each other. This practice gave prominence to hedges. Yew was always the most favoured hedging plant, its fine texture and dark green colour providing an ideal background for flowers. Other evergreens, such as holly, privet and *Pyracantha*, and deciduous trees such as beech, hornbeam and thorn, were also included in the repertoire. Sometimes, different species were mixed in one hedge, together with roses, to make a tapestry hedge. When an exceptionally tall hedge was required, palisade- or pole-hedges of lime, elm or hornbeam were grown; unlike yew hedges, these do not fall apart at a great height. Sometimes the pole-hedge was clipped bare up to a height of ten feet or so, with a subsidiary hedge of yew or box filling in the lower portion. Alternatively, the lower part was left open to form an arcade.

Although Robinson disapproved of what he called "the tonsile arts", clipping, pruning and training of trees and shrubs had long been practised for practical as well as ornamental reasons, particularly in the production of fruit. There were dozens of ways of training fruit trees, including the herringbone, irregular fan, stellate (star-shaped) fan, drooping fan, wavy fan, and many more. Shoots were even grafted back onto themselves to produce circular forms. Such feats of training were mostly confined to kitchen gardens, but despite the utilitarian purpose, some highly ornamental shapes were created. In smaller gardens (particularly

A bedding scheme

This bedding-out scheme at Manderston, Berwickshire, is part of the formal gardens laid out by John Kinross at the end of the 19th century. Regular clumps of white allyssum and blue lobelia frame carpets of red and pink begonias. The plants are arranged within a pattern of circular, heart-shaped and elongated-lozenge-shaped beds disposed around a central balustraded fountain. A stone pergola with climbing roses trained up the columns divides this garden from the sunken garden to the south.

The Italianate style

Sir Charles Barry's layout for an Italianate garden at Shrubland Park, near Ipswich in Suffolk, was conceived around 1848 for Sir William Middleton. It covered some 65 acres of ground and was maintained by 40 gardeners. Shrubland has been described as a garden of "great yet depressingly mechanical grandeur". This painting by Adveno Brooke shows the amply balustraded steps descending from the terrace in front of the house down to a lower terrace containing a circular pool. The terraces were embellished with parterres of box scrolls framing coloured sands and gravel and with bedding-out schemes in the brightest colours.

in France where such pruning became highly sophisticated), horizontal espaliers or diagonal cordons of apple or pear were often used in place of a hedge at the back of a border.

Alongside the vigorous pursuit of horticulture, there was a burgeoning of mass-produced ornament, generated by the needs of the expanding suburbs. Several firms produced ranges of cast-iron vases, seats and the like. For gates and railings, cast ironwork replaced wrought iron. Seldom was the grace of 18th-century ironwork achieved, the details being characteristically coarser and chunkier, but an astonishing range of patterns was produced, from simple spear-headed railings to complicated honeycomb-like work. At the Great Exhibition of 1851 a prodigious variety of cast-iron ornament was displayed, including vases, flower pots, flower stands, seats, tables, and even fountains. The designs were frequently modelled on existing works in stone or imitated currently fashionable forms such as rustic work.

Wirework became popular for baskets and tiered plant stands. The baskets, either suspended or placed on a pedestal, were filled with a variety of trailing plants. Many beds were edged with wirework, sometimes with spokes attached to a frame in the centre along which plants could be trained. Wirework was also curved in simple arches over paths and covered with climbers.

Even sculpture was mass-produced. The earliest substitute for stone was Coade ware, which was invented in the latter part of the 18th century. This consisted principally of clay with various additives cast in a mould to make a vitrified substance of great durability. A wide range of statuary, armorial devices and architectural ornaments was produced until the Coade firm was wound up in 1840. Both contemporary and antique sculpture was copied in Coade stone for important architects such as John Nash, John Soane and William Wilkins, as well as for private patrons in Britain and America.

Other artificial stones were made during the 19th century, notably by Cottam and Hallen. Ransome's "Siliceous Stone" was well-known. Another material was Pulhamite stone, from which fake rocks were made, piled up into huge outcrops. Pulhamite rockeries were made at Battersea Park (1866), Waddesdon (1874), Madresfield Court in Worcestershire and elsewhere. A process similar to that used for Coade stone yielded terracotta ornaments such as balustrades and urns.

Rockeries enjoyed a considerable vogue, and were sometimes of enormous dimensions. One at Hoole House, near Chester, which took eight years to complete, was modelled on the Chamonix valley in Savoy; it was made of red sandstone, with additions of spar and white marble to represent snow, and was planted with creeping and alpine plants. Such extravagances were not universally admired. Shirley Hibberd observed: "it really makes one feel melancholy to reflect upon the waste of money, time and ingenuity involved in the construction of many of these accessories".

Cast iron *(right)*

The development of cast iron was of particular importance in the garden ornament market. Its strength made it suitable for seats, tables, railings and gates. It was resistant to rust, and, once the mould was made, a cast-iron ornament was relatively inexpensive to reproduce. However, the details tended to be much coarser than in wrought iron, creating a more chunky and angular appearance.

Artificial stone

With the burgeoning of the middle-class suburbs, garden ornament was industrialized to satisfy the expanding market. Artificial stones such as Coade stone, which could be moulded and carved before firing, made it possible to reproduce a wide range of statuary, fountains, keystones, heraldic devices and other architectural and garden accessories. The firm was closed down in 1840, but similar processes were continued throughout the century.

However, he acknowledged that rockwork had a function to perform in setting off "the beauties of other objects" or in creating "light and shadow" effects. Hibberd in fact devoted a whole chapter to rockwork, such was its importance. Today it is well worth visiting the great rock garden of Kew, home of a wonderful plant collection; the rockwork was started in 1882 as a miniature Pyrenean valley and developed over the next fifty years to reach its present size of just over an acre.

A curiosity of the period was the stumpery – a collection of tree stumps. There was an example at Biddulph Grange, where the old stumps, artfully disposed on the ground, were planted with a variety of woodland plants, and surrounded by yews. To Hibberd, stumps looked particularly attractive when interspersed with ferns, which were becoming so popular.

Rustic ornament was considered quite appropriate for areas outside the flower garden. The rustic style was defined by Loudon as "what is commonly found accompanying the rudest description of labourer's cottages in the country". He thought the style suitable for gardens in towns, "in order that the scene created may contrast the more advantageously with everything around it". It was characterized by straggly, grass-covered paths, rickety gates and ruinous hovels. Such ornament required the most careful construction. One type of rustic seat recommended by Loudon has log-like columns, a rear wall sheathed in rough bark set in parallel strips, and a neatly thatched roof. A polygonal rustic summer house has "nine pillars, each of a young fir tree...with capitals formed of square boards", an entablature of rustic boards and a roof of "heath or reeds, or of larch, birch, or oak bark". All manner of garden accessories were made in rustic work, with suitably gnarled and contorted appearance: summer houses, arches, and seats of intense discomfort. A coat of varnish was often applied to allay any fears of contact with a rustic labourer.

A variation on the rustic summerhouse was the moss house. A timber frame supported laths through which varieties of moss or lichen were pushed to form patterns in various colours; the roof was thatched or covered in bark. Root houses, incorporating tree roots and stumps, were another eccentric feature of the period, although their origins lie with the ornamental hermitages of the previous century.

A wide variety of pavilions and other garden buildings, ranging from pigeon-houses to pagodas, continued to be built throughout the period. The amazing collection of structures erected at Alton Towers for the Earl of Shrewsbury included a fountain in the form of a Chinese pagoda, a Chinese watchtower, a circular temple based on the monument of Lysicrates, a Swiss cottage, a terrace of the Muses, a Gothic temple and even a Stonehenge. There were also huge conservatories designed by Loudon.

In his *Encyclopaedia*, Loudon describes innumerable types of building "introduced more for their picturesque effect as parts of the external scenery, than as absolutely necessary". He goes on to describe not only Grecian, Gothic and Chinese cottages, but also "The Bengal Cottage" of mud and bamboo and a roof of palm leaves, Scotch, Italian, Polish and Russian cottages, and the primitive hut. Also included are prospect-towers, kiosks, temples, alcoves, arbours and roofed seats. Being so often in perishable wood, few such structures survive today. However, there is little doubt that many were built: fertile invention transformed the garden into a world of fantasy, remote from the industrial squalor that made it all possible.

THE TWENTIETH CENTURY

Continuing Traditions

In the 20th century, the lack of visual appeal, of comprehensible style and detail in the built environment, makes much of our surroundings deadening. In this context, a re-establishment of our affinity with nature is vital for our spiritual health. Public parks and private gardens have a vital role to play. It is thus hardly surprising that, whereas the appreciation of modern art and architecture has become an intellectual exercise understood by a small minority, gardens have remained essentially traditional and always popular – a refuge from material and technological progress, and a way of preserving identity in an age of collective decision-making. Generally, gardens in the 20th century have either reworked themes established during the preceding two thousand years, or dispensed with a theme altogether, existing solely as a collection of plants. Some modern garden designs are radically innovatory, but only a few.

At the turn of the century, Gertrude Jekyll, inspired partly by William Robinson, created some beautiful gardens, using her rare combination of painter's eye and planting skills to create a time-controlled burst of carefully graded colour. Her most frequent partner was Sir Edwin Lutyens, who provided inventive and interesting architectural frameworks, for example at Folly Farm, Hestercombe, and Bois de Moutiers, near Dieppe. Influenced by the Arts and Crafts movement, Lutyens demonstrated a fine understanding of traditional materials, and a mastery of scale. But he looked to the past for inspiration, as did so many other designers and patrons of the time.

Another garden-maker of the period was Harold Peto, who in his own garden at Iford Manor in Wiltshire carved terraces out of the hillside following the Italian Renaissance practice. The idea was reinforced with all the necessary colonnades, flights of steps, pavilions and sculpture. At Renishaw in Derbyshire, Sir George Sitwell also created an Italian-inspired garden, combining a profound knowledge of the originals together with fruitful experiment.

In 1905, Lawrence Johnston began his work at Hidcote in Gloucestershire. Framing the garden in substantial hedges, he drew upon the concept of a series of "rooms", each of which was crammed with horticultural delights. In a similar spirit, Nathaniel Lloyd surrounded the house of Great Dixter in Sussex with a ring

of spaces, which exploited the slope across the site to great advantage. At Sissinghurst Castle in Kent, Harold Nicholson and Vita Sackville-West created a series of regular spaces off an axial spine, combining a plantsman's knowledge with a fine sense of colour. Many other compartmented gardens, domestic in scale, were made in the years before and after the First World War.

At the same time, many gardens were being made merely as casual spaces defined principally by trees and large shrubs. There was no geometry, and often little attention to the quality of space. The texture and colour of the trees were supplemented by flowering shrubs, some herbaceous plants and masses of bulbs. This was the kind of garden that virtually created itself with the gradual accumulation of plants. With their lack of architectural structure, such gardens are liable to uncontrolled changes of shape and content, and are hard to grasp in their entirety.

America in the early part of the century was still dominated by the Beaux Arts tradition, with the emphasis on classical features treated in an eclectic manner. There is an interesting example at Vizcaya near Miami, started in 1912. Essentially an Italian-inspired stone-and-water garden, making use of the lush flora available in Florida, it is laid out on a central axis with buildings at each end, and with an appropriate arrangement of stairs, balustrades, urns, obelisks and grottoes. The garden is edged by the sea, where a stone barque has been built – a reminiscence of Isola Bella in Lago di Maggiore.

Dumbarton Oaks, near Washington D.C., is one of the most famous compartmented gardens in America. Laid out in the 1920s by Beatrix Farrand, it consists of "rooms" enclosed by stone walls and hedges, and there is a magnificent example of carpenter's work. There is a beautiful water parterre, shallow, with pebble-lined pools and an oval sculptural fountain. Another garden which draws on European tradition is Longwood in Pennsylvania, built for Pierre du Pont – an enormous complex of fountains and waterworks liberally scattered with sculpture.

The most significant innovations in garden-making at this time were being carried out in Brazil by Roberto Burle Marx, a painter who began designing gardens in the late 1930s. He used the luxuriant flora of the country to make three-dimensional groups in swirling abstract patterns of strong colour and varying texture. His was a method of design that demanded great skill and experience, but it was peculiarly appropriate to his time and place.

As the 20th century progressed, it became apparent that large-scale gardens would be a luxury possible only for well-funded institutions and wealthy individuals. Even where large gardens were already well-established, rising labour costs and other financial burdens all too often rang the death knell. And yet, gardens continued to be made, on a modest scale with modest expenditure. A new breed of self-helping gardener emerged, well-informed and quick to learn more. There was a growing reliance on plants and a diminished use of properly organized structure or high-quality ornament.

Against this general background, there were some gardens that were planned according to an integrated design, rather than left to

A compartmented garden *(above)*

The gardens of Great Dixter in East Sussex were laid out by Nathaniel Lloyd from about 1910, when Sir Edwin Lutyens recreated the house. With a sustained family input culminating in Christopher Lloyd's deep knowledge of plants, Great Dixter has become one of the most important gardens of this century. Within its firm architectural layout, it nurtures a wide range of plants in imaginative combinations.

An Italian-inspired garden *(below)*

The gardens at Vizcaya, near Miami, started in 1912, celebrate water and sculpture in the tradition of Renaissance Italy, but modified to accommodate the mangrove swamp vegetation of Florida. Laid out along an axis that runs between the house and a garden pavilion, the gardens include grottoes, a grand water staircase and fountain, together with lawns and Italian-style parterres.

An abstract garden *(left)*

One of the few landscape architects to find entirely new modes of expression is Roberto Burle Marx, a painter who started making gardens in Brazil in the 1930s. He translated abstract concepts into landscape by using the luxuriant native plants of Brazil either repetitively for their texture and colour, rather in the manner of bedding plants, or singly for their sculptural form.

Dumbarton Oaks *(above)*

The garden at Dumbarton Oaks, near Washington D.C., is one of the most important of those created in the interwar years. The designer Beatrix Farrand converted a farm into a series of complex spaces, with delicate plantings and some ravishing architectural details. The shallow pond illustrated here is lined with a pebble mosaic, sometimes showing bright through the water, sometimes obscured by reflections.

evolve haphazardly. In California an important and influential school of design sprang up in the 1930s and 1940s, based around the work of Thomas Church (d. 1978). In its pursuit of functionally appropriate solutions, it perhaps owed something to Frank Lloyd Wright and other modern architects. The garden was treated essentially as part of the accommodation. It catered for family functions, and the barbecue was as important as the choice of plants. Great attention was paid to privacy, to appropriate materials and to plants that were both interesting all the year round and tolerant of some neglect. Gardens were moulded by their topography, and were kept simple and uncluttered. There was a satisfying directness that dispensed with illusion or symbolic content. Church himself wrote: "Landscaping is not a complex and difficult art to be practised only by high priests. It is logical, down to earth, and aimed at making your plot of ground produce exactly what you want and need from it... Yet it must also perform its primary function of being a garden in the true sense of providing trees and flowers, fruits and vegetables; a place where man can recapture his affinity with the soil..."

Other themes in 20th-century gardens can be traced back to 19th-century precedents. At the turn of the century, the rock garden was still enjoying a considerable vogue. Sir Frank Crisp's great garden at Henley, Oxfordshire, with its scale model of the Matterhorn, consumed over 7,000 tons of stone, topped with grated alabaster to simulate snow, and supported over 4,000 plants. Reginald Farrer, who plant-hunted in China and northern Burma and gardened at Ingleborough in Yorkshire, did much to popularize the rock garden. An excellent example of a rock garden of the 20th century can be seen at Sizergh Castle, near Kendal in Cumbria. This was laid out in 1926 with Lakeland stone, a little watercourse gently running through, and a wide variety of dwarfish plants.

Japanese gardens continued to be made. They sometimes come to light in the undergrowth of a long-neglected site, marked by a toppled stone lantern. The nearest to an authentic example must have been Miss Christie's garden at Cowden in Scotland, laid out by a Japanese artist and tended by a Japanese gardener. It was unusual among Japanese-inspired gardens in that there the symbolic aspects were taken seriously. At Heale House in Wiltshire, a thatched tea-house was brought over from Japan and erected over the stream by Japanese craftsmen (see page 136). It was accompanied by a red Japanese bridge and stone lanterns, and planted around with Japanese maples.

With the pressure on urban land and the development of the balcony and the flat roof, a type of garden that has come into its own in the 20th century is the roof garden. Often these creations nestle secretly, high among city buildings. Lacking space and access for quantities of earth, they rely on trellis screening, planting cases, pots, paving and sculpture. Furnished with a selection of wind- and heat-tolerant plants, these are the oasis-gardens of the modern age.

The production of interesting sculpture in the 20th century has been as copious as ever before. However, freed from prescribed convention, sculpture has been much more diverse than in previous eras. Although academic work typical of the 19th century continued to be done well into the 20th, sculptors like Constantin Brancusi had a radical approach, exploring the material as much as the subject, and tending to reduce forms to simple abstractions. The Constructivists Antoine Pevsner, Naum Gabo and Laszlo Moholgy-Nagy considered that time and space were as much their concern as were mass and volume. The Surrealist movement likewise had its influence on sculpture, particularly through the works of Jean Arp.

Like architecture, sculpture of this calibre demanded considerable application of the intellect. Yet, removed from the built environment of everyday activities and located in parks and gardens, it is remarkable how easily even the wildest of sculptural notions can be accommodated. Notable among sculptors whose works have a strong affinity with the landscape are Henry Moore and Barbara Hepworth. However difficult it may be to understand an inner meaning in their creations, there is an undoubted visual satisfaction in the contrast of swelling bronze forms against the texture of green leaves.

The garden dedicated to a collection of sculpture, as distinct from one supported by a sculptural theme, is a 20th-century phenomenon. A typical example is the Pepsico Sculpture Garden north of New York City, where an astonishing collection of works by Auguste Rodin, Max Ernst, Arnoldo Pomodoro, George Segal, Henry Moore and others has been put together by the Pepsico Corporation in a landscape worked by E.D. Stone and later by Russell Page. Another example is the Hakone Open-Air Museum in Japan, where there are works by Arp, Brancusi, Gabo, Dubuffet and by Japanese sculptors less well-known in the West.

Sometimes just two or three large sculptures have been sufficient to give impetus to a garden design. For example, Sutton Place, in Surrey, is planned around two great sculptures by Ben Nicholson and Henry Moore. In a skilful revitalization by Geoffrey Jellicoe, the gardens, dominated by the warm brick and chimney-stacked outline of the substantial Tudor House, have been planned to support these two colossal works. Sutton Place is particularly interesting in that it re-introduces the idea of a programme, or at least a philosophical rationale to justify the re-creation of the garden in more than merely visual terms. Jellicoe has stated that his purpose there is to explore the invisible world through abstract art, to communicate by and through the subconscious. Another British sculpture garden that specifically attempts to go beyond purely visual concerns is Ian Hamilton Finlay's garden and temple at Little Sparta, Stonypath, in Scotland, where his work, together with that of a number of collaborating artists, is linked to poetic themes.

For the most part, garden ornament in the 20th century has tended to rely on the past for its inspiration. Many gardeners have collected antique sculptural pieces, and many have improvised with architectural fragments. There is also a thriving reproduction industry, making classically inspired urns, fountains, and similar pieces. However, so much modern sculpture looks towards the future, exploring ideas dimly perceived and understood, and ironically it is the garden, a preserve of tradition, that somehow provides the least prejudiced forum for this work – an environment in which one is relaxed and receptive, where one can readily delight in a sculptor's discoveries.

The beauty of function

Thomas Church has been one of the most influential garden designers of the century. Much of his work has been involved with smaller houses whose gardens he planned to respond to functional needs as much as aesthetic effects. A marriage of the main characteristics of the site to a rigorously analysed brief has produced gardens that make a virtue of the pressures of limited time and space that beset the modern family. This San Francisco garden by Church has been given over to a large seating area. The lines of the seat make the primary statement, and the planting is reduced to ivy sprawling over the ground and up the fences. It is an exercise in simplicity. Although doing little to delight the horticulturally minded, the garden remains a well-thought-out and valid use of exterior space, appropriate to the inclinations and requirements of the owner.

CREATIVE CONSERVATION

Restoration and Regeneration

While the small domestic garden has proliferated in the 20th century, the larger garden has suffered a major decline, in Europe if not in America. Gardens have been early casualties of high taxation and soaring labour costs. They are inevitably given a lower priority than the house they ornament; and, in any case, fashions have moved away from the more elaborate concepts of Victorian and Edwardian gardening. The reduction in the labour available for upkeep has had a dramatic effect. Before the First World War, there were many large gardens which supported between twenty and thirty gardeners: today the same houses struggle to maintain the vestige of a former glory with three or four. This has inevitably meant that there is time only for horticultural drudgery such as grass cutting, hedge clipping and (inadequate) weeding, and that insufficient new and replacement plants are being propagated, as old ones wither and die. Moreover, gravel and paved areas deteriorate, and without regular upkeep the accumulating effects of frost and thermal expansion are destroying statuary, urns, steps, balustrades and other stonework. Many gardens have been greatly simplified, with beds grassed over or their edges straightened to accommodate larger mowers, and their annual plants replaced by shrubs. Some gardens have been sold off to accommodate new residential development. Sometimes, large houses are turned into offices, and the gardens given over to the motor car.

It is only with the greatest dedication that historic gardens are kept going, and it is only in the last decade that there has been any official recognition of their importance. Yet important they certainly are. The conservation of historic houses and gardens is crucial in an age that has countenanced such a severe destruction of its inheritance by war, economic attrition or mere indifference. And clearly, the setting of a historic house – its park or garden – is as vital to its character as the furniture or paintings inside. Through its plants and ornaments, if they are properly maintained, a garden can impart a period flavour. If the garden has deteriorated or disappeared it may be necessary to recreate it.

One of the earliest and best-known of such recreations is Villandry in France. When Dr Joachim Cavallo bought the château in 1906, there was no trace of its former garden, so he made a new one using typical features from Du Cerceau's drawings of the 1570s. Purists may question some of the details, particularly in the choice of modern plants. However, there is no doubt that the garden gives a splendid period flavour to the château.

Another important recreation, made in the 1930s, is at Edzell in Scotland, a delightful early 17th-century enclosed garden, medieval in concept but Renaissance in its vigour, and now a wonderfully

A historic French garden

The gardens of Villandry, near Tours, are not an exact restoration but an educated guess at what the gardens might have been like, based on the designs of Du Cerceau in *Les Plus Excellents Bastiments de France* (1576-9).

serene place. Many excellent restorations were carried out in Germany after 1945. The Zwinger at Dresden, the Residenz at Würzburg, the gardens of the Herrenhausen in Hanover, the parterres of Schloss Bruhl near Cologne, have all been returned to their former glory.

Attempts to restore gardens to a particular period very much depend on the availability of good contemporary evidence, written or pictorial. Sometimes there has to be an element of guesswork, but garden history is attracting increasing attention today, and valuable research is being carried out on all aspects of gardens by academic institutions both in Europe and in the United States, as well as by independent individuals. Meticulous research allows us to penetrate the minds of the original creators and to probe long-forgotten concepts. The restoration of the gardens at Williamsburg, the colonial capital of Virginia, in the style of the early 1700s, is a triumph of painstaking archaeological research, not only into contemporary documents but also into plant remains found on site. In both the planting and the ornaments, this is a most convincing recreation of a colonial garden.

In Britain the National Trust has played an important role in the restoration of gardens. Under its auspices, the gardens of Ham House, Surrey, have been restored in a style appropriate to the 1670s, when the house was in its heyday. Likewise, the gardens of Erdigg in north Wales have been brought back from almost terminal decay. The canals have been dredged, lawns resown, and old varieties of fruit planted. With Victorian elements still extant, this may not be an exact restoration, but it certainly gives a convincing idea of an 18th-century formal garden.

Other restorations are being carried out by a variety of patrons, including local authorities. Painshill in Surrey is currently being returned from an overgrown, derelict condition to something approaching its 18th-century appearance, and a similar scheme has been devised for the gardens of the Royal Pavilion at Brighton, with serpentine paths and mixed shrubs and flower borders in accordance with Sir John Nash's plan and "Views" of the 1820s.

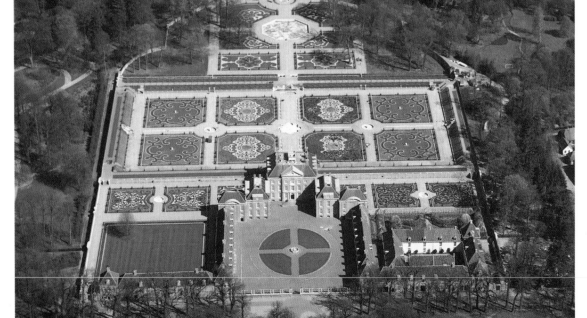

Garden archaeology *(above)*

The gardens at Williamsburg, former colonial capital of Virginia, are an important restoration based not only on documentary evidence relating to structure and planting, but also on thorough archaeological searches for identifiable plant remains. The small-scale formal layout outlined in box is typical of the late 17th and early 18th century.

A royal garden in the Netherlands *(left)*

One of the most spectacular of recent restorations is the garden of Het Loo in the Netherlands, originally laid out in the late 17th century for Prince William of Orange and his English wife Mary by the French designer Daniel Marot. The reconstruction was completed in 1984. The principal element is a superb example of a sunken garden surrounded by a broad terrace walk from which one can look down on the beautifully laid out parterres. The beds were planted out with the plant varieties that existed in the 17th century. Where possible the original statuary has been restored or, if necessary, faithfully copied.

As part of the garden restoration movement, more attention is being focused on construction and ornament. Researchers are studying a diversity of subjects, ranging from mounts and follies to chemical reactions between stone and cement. The deterioration of garden sculpture is a matter of increasing concern, and experts are exploring ways to protect existing statuary or to make convincing reproductions so that the originals can be removed to safety. Moulded cement-based reproductions have long been a poor substitute for carved stone; but today not only are there more interesting compounds available, but work in cement has also improved remarkably.

Despite the good intentions and often excellent results of the conservation movement, it is a fashion, and like most fashions it sometimes verges on the fanatical. There is a danger of misplaced emphasis: new creative work may be stifled in the effort to preserve historic gardens or individual artefacts of indifferent merit. An apt definition of conservation is making the best use of resources available, both naturally occurring and manmade. But human creativity – the ability shown by garden-makers past and present to resolve a range of difficult problems, to find a compromise between conflicting needs – is also a resource, and must not be wasted. Gardens of any age are mostly a conglomeration of work by different hands at different times. Part of their charm lies in such historical diversity. Fixing a garden in a particular period creates a museum-piece, often beautiful, but not alive as a garden should be.

For the most part, garden-making in the 20th-century has been quietly carrying on the tradition whereby each generation repaints part or all of the canvas. The genius of the place is summoned and a new creation forged. The outlines stay the same but the details develop to suit new needs and new tastes. Work on this basis will often produce a creation that is just as rewarding as any garden considered to be historically important.

In Britain, there are many historic gardens that have changed over the centuries without a lowering of standards or loss of interest. For example, at Powis Castle in Powys, Wales, the National Trust has worked onto the frame of terraces and mighty yew hedges a new scheme of borders with shrubs, climbers and herbaceous plants, taking advantage of an especially benevolent microclimate. At Cranbourne, in Dorset, the garden is still divided by old hedges and avenues but in many areas is newly planted: drawing upon a sure knowledge of historical precedent, Lady Salisbury has built on a firm foundation to make a delightful garden with new compositions and colour schemes skilfully worked out and executed. And at Tyninghame in Scotland another of the great gardeners of this century has created sumptuous effects that contrast with William Burns's great red stone turrets. Soaring costs have prompted Lady Haddington to paint here with a new palette, replacing the more ephemeral plants with longer-lasting shrubs – and in the process she has made the garden better than ever.

This pattern of regeneration, selective improvement and adaptation to the needs of our time is very like what the great garden designer Sir Geoffrey Jellicoe has described as "creative conservation". Quoting the American landscape architect Grady Clay's question "Whose time is this place?", he concluded that it has to be today. At Hartwell House, Buckinghamshire, he attempted a design that reveals all the successive phases of landscape composition that contribute to Hartwell's present character and beauty, adding them together in a single coherent composition that unites time and place. It is an idea that requires great depth of understanding and knowledge to carry out, but one which both respects our heritage and gives scope for relevant artistic expression. To explore new ideas in a garden does not demand wholesale renewal. The ability to appreciate a sculpture by, say, Henry Moore is as much a part of our cultural baggage as is a recognition of historical values. The two are not mutually exclusive, and the garden makes the perfect arena in which unfamiliar forms and textures can happily confront and coexist with a traditional layout of brick or stone, flower and foliage, opening our minds to new ideas and sensations. And if modern sculpture can lead us towards new experiences, why not modern pavilions, chromium pergolas, mirror cascades, holographic grottoes? As the Renaissance garden was an expression of an age in ferment, so too the modern garden, remoulding ancient forms onto new gardens and architecture, is a place of creative ideas fed by tradition – a seedbed for the future, nurtured by the past.

New gardens in old places

Sir Geoffrey Jellicoe's work at Sutton Place, Surrey, is justly acclaimed. Drawing upon both historical knowledge and artistic imagination, he has breathed new life into the old gardens, celebrating modern creativity, not merely relying on a revival of old ideas.

GARDEN STRUCTURE AND ORNAMENT

THE POTENTIAL TODAY

Every garden is quite different from the next, even if they lie on the same side of the street. The overlooking buildings will be different, the overhanging trees will be different. Some gardens are affected by the proximity of a noisy road or the sound of a difficult neighbour. The views within and out of the garden will be unique to a particular site. Most of all, the owners will each have their own family, lifestyle and aspirations, and their own different ideas of what the garden should be like. It is the owner who has to persist in turning a plan into reality, who has to live with the decisions made about the construction of an arbour or the position of a seat or sculpture. And, of course, it is the owner who foots the bill, whatever is done and however well it is done.

But in making gardens today it is surely a help to know a little of what has been achieved elsewhere, in the past and by one's contemporaries – by whom, with what means and under what conditions. History is brimming over with ideas, many of which can, with careful thought, be adapted to our new requirements. We still need shelter from the sun and rain, we still need enclosure for privacy and security, and we still require a garden to be a place of delight. While an indiscriminate plundering of the past is likely to lead to difficulties, not least financial, we can all learn much from historic precedents.

Equally, it is a help to think about modern design processes – to make lists of functional requirements, to plot your spaces on paper. Unless you think carefully about combinations of colours and textures, the weathering of materials and the flowering periods of plants, then you will rely on chance, which may favour you or it may not. The three-dimensional form of your site may make a perfect place for a truly exciting garden, but only by consciously taking advantage of what the site offers will you achieve it. At every stage, you will need to make a creative decision. What is the optimum type of enclosure? Where is the best place to site your pergola? Is it worth trying to exploit water for life and movement? Can anything be gained by investing in a sculpture, or will topiary suffice to contribute sculptural form? A good design will take nothing for granted, giving each element its proper place and its proper value within the clear rationale of an overall scheme.

Today, we are often faced with the overriding limitations of space and money. For most of us, there is not room for acres of magnificence, even if the budget were to be available. For our long views, we have to borrow other people's landscapes. To make ourselves feel comfortable within our allotted boundaries, we need to summon all sorts of illusions. The cost of construction has risen prohibitively over the last few decades; a new terrace or a cascade is an expensive undertaking. The prices of sculpture and other specially commissioned works climbs yearly higher, and antique sculpture has become not only dear, but scarce. The better-quality garden furniture is likewise keeping pace with price increases in other fields. Only the most skimpily mass-produced items in the poorest quality materials remain inexpensive.

This argues strongly for making the best of what limited means we have. If space is restricted, we should take the greatest care to ensure that it is used effectively. We must look at precedents, both historical and contemporary, to see how other people have solved problems, and we must use the principles of design to discover how the layout and details can be improved. Everything in the garden should lead to delight – there can be no room for waste. Relationships should be thought out with care: poor construction, unsatisfactory colour groups and tatty ornament will irritate to distraction if they fill our only view.

Most gardens are made, and doubtless will continue to be made, by the unaided effort of their owners – without professional designers and with a great deal of well-intentioned, albeit conflicting, advice from friends and neighbours. Usually, horticultural expertise is developed disproportionately in relation to architectural and sculptural considerations. And yet an appreciation of these aspects can undoubtedly lead to a better planned and more exciting garden. If you can develop an eye for the whole design, rather than for individual plants, and if you can create interesting relationships between plants and structure, plants and ornament, as well as between the plants themselves, then the garden may become more than the sum of its parts. It may be a place in which mind and body can linger at pleasure, enjoying the achievements of a human creation, yet absorbed too in the cycle of natural delights.

FUNCTIONAL REQUIREMENTS

One of the more important design ideas to emerge this century is the consideration of function. The concept of the fitness of an artefact or building for its purpose is a mainspring of the design process. To satisfy this criterion, you need to analyse intensively what the artefact is supposed to be able to do. The plan of a successful modern garden is almost wholly generated from a marriage between its performance and its environment.

Small urban gardens are areas of sorely needed additional space, to be used whenever possible, particularly by children. Thus, a clear functional analysis and design are essential. Children's play, adult relaxation, mobility for the elderly and handicapped – all these functions need careful consideration. Aspects of the site also come into play – the direction of view, the prevailing wind, areas of sun and shade, overhanging trees. Some areas must be left open, others must be screened. The neighbours will make their demands – through planning restrictions, or in a more direct way if they overlook your site. Or perhaps your garden needs to respond to a communal space where the children can play.

Equally important is the question of image. Often visitors arrive through the garden: perhaps a small area in front of the house or, in more spacious circumstances, by way of an avenued drive. As they approach they inevitably receive impressions of the occupant – little signals conveyed by unkempt plants or by neatly trimmed hedges. The space in which visitors get out of a car and approach the front door gives away a great deal. Is it generous in scale, allowing time to stop and admire, or is it a mean, narrow, sideways entrance, better passed through as quickly as possible? The image can be adjusted to show ease and affluence, a cottage-garden riot or eccentric foibles; it will give away the owner's taste in colour, plants and decoration – in many ways, it is like a flag.

The garden is a jigsaw of conflicting requirements that is only resolved by careful thought, a drawing or two, or experiments with posts and string to simulate walls, lawns, planting or any other necessary elements. Such requirements must be defined and a strategy or plan worked out. More often than not there is inadequate finance to execute the plan all at once, but at least it provides goals to be pursued as time and money permit. The plan reduces the possibility of abortive work – all too often, in the unplanned garden, last year's work has to be undone to accommodate next year's ideas.

You must give a thoughtful eye to the future. Nothing is straightforward in gardening, as the element of time must be taken into account. Children grow up, sandpits and slides become redundant. Labour undertaken cheerfully in our youth will be impossible as we creak into old age. Plants die, leaving a view of the neighbour's drains; or they grow, obliterating a carefully planned sun-trap. In an age when many home-owners seem to be living in reduced circumstances, the functional garden requires foresight and flexibility, and must be as well-planned as a life assurance scheme or an old age pension.

The plainness, or lack of decoration, that is associated with the functional school is, perhaps, a hangover from the architectural thought of the first part of this century. Despite this prejudice, functional needs can give rise to all sorts of ornamental possibilities. Not only can paving, walls, seats, pergolas and so on look good by answering their purpose with grace and economy, but they can all be enlivened with abstract or perhaps figurative decoration. Executed with discrimination, the functional artefact will transcend its prime objective and add to the overall flavour of the garden. It might harmonize with other aspects to create a family of decorative motifs; or it appear in opposition to its surroundings, thus drawing attention to itself. It may work in sympathy with the planting or introduce a contrasting texture. Though primarily employed for a special purpose, the functional element can contribute so much more, imparting a mood, summoning an idea, or even making a joke.

Around the house, on the terrace or timber deck, the business of relaxing, eating and entertaining can all become a matter of visual satisfaction as much as of convenience. Timber, stone, even plastic seats and tables can be designed to be more than purely utilitarian. A timber seat can make a focal point in a layout, or it can be modest, retiring into the background. A table may be solid and four-square for serious eating with a throne at either end; or it might be in delicate wirework, just right to support a glass of white wine, the bottle cooled in a convenient ice-packed urn. And nearby, the edge of the space is defined by a colourful hammock, ready for the afternoon nap. The paving itself gives pattern, texture and scale that fundamentally affects the use of the terrace. And if the appearance of so many constructed elements offends your taste, and if the climate is favourable, make a turf seat for taking your ease and enjoying, as you do so, the scent of crushed chamomile or thyme.

Perhaps the most difficult matter to reconcile with other garden needs is the area in which children can play. When they are small, a hard paved area, a sandpit and perhaps a paddling pool may suffice. Portable, disposable containers for sand and water may be a better investment than a permanent structure that will have to be taken down as the children grow. But if something more substantial is required, consider how it can be changed to a bed or a lily tank in later years. Play equipment, such as slides or swings, is so often awkwardly shaped, unpleasantly coloured and visually intrusive in a composed garden scene. If space permits, some kind of screening may be desirable, which takes us into the world of pergolas and trellis-work, of walls and hedges. If you think that your screen will be permanently useful in that position, a hedge or wall may be the answer, but if you propose to restore the garden to its former shape after the children have grown up, then a split-cane fence, inexpensive and not particularly durable, might be more suitable. Footballs and bicycles are very disruptive, and incompatible with any but the toughest of plants. Even so, such needs can be turned to advantage with sculptured goal-posts or a turf maze designed for bicycles. If space permits, turn part of the garden over to being an adult and plant reserve, protected by really stout fencing or hedging. Once you have opted for permanent enclosure, there are many opportunities for interesting and beautiful work – for example, tapestry hedges, topiary, fruit hedges or pleached work, serpentine walls, trellis panels, rose-clad pergolas

Recreation (*above*)

The provision of space for children to let off steam can be a vexing problem in the smaller garden. Play equipment often looks intrusive. A rope ladder in a tree may well be quite as much fun for the children, and much less disruptive for the adults, than complicated climbing machines.

Pool and pool-house (*left*)

A function commonly integrated into gardens is the swimming pool. Designed as a self-conscious (often bow-ended) rectangle, bright blue and isolated in grass, it so often looks uncomfortable, unprotected and out of place, and frequently it is accompanied by a poorly sited changing room and a shed for ancillary equipment. Yet pools offer such opportunities for interesting designs. They can be of all shapes and sizes, with a variety of edgings – you can even have planting and rockwork coming down to the "shore". With a dark internal lining, the blueness, attractive in sunny climes but so foreign in northern light, can be eliminated. The pool house can be designed in conjunction with the enclosure to give privacy and protection from the wind, and to suit the mood of the garden.

Function and pattern (*page 55*)

Gardens may be planned to satisfy functional needs and aesthetic urges with equal success. In this kitchen garden, vegetables are neatly lined out so that they are easy to cultivate; but at the same time there is thought for visual pleasure, with contrasting colours and textures of purple cabbage and green spinach and parsley.

or shady arcades. How satisfactory to make the garden beautiful by keeping the children under control.

Some gardens may be large enough to accommodate croquet or tennis. The smooth flat lawn needed for croquet may generate a formal area, enclosed by hedges or borders, an elegant attribute to the garden. A tennis court, however, is more problematic. The scale and colour of a hard court are seldom sympathetic with the surrounding area, and things are only made worse by the standard fencing that so often surrounds the court. Some kind of enclosure is essential, with trees, hedges or climbers – an opportunity for a tunnel, perhaps of apples trained to metal arches, or of vines trained on a timber arcade – a chance not to be missed.

If horticulture finds its way into this garden that seems so little concerned with plants, it too makes its demands. Beds must have room for plants to grow, and yet not be so big as to make access difficult. Their layout will be determined by the kind of spaces that you want to make, yet they must take account of access and views, of the pattern of sun and shade, wind and drainage. In a garden with little construction or ornament, plants will be the principal decoration, so choose them with care and site your beds well. The horticultural back-up may include greenhouses, tool and machinery sheds, compost heaps and a bonfire. Attention to their layout and enclosure will promote convenience and a better microclimate. You may want them plain and workmanlike, but equally well you can introduce an arbour in the centre of your vegetable garden, thick with jasmine, or space your paths with standard viburnums or spiral-trained box. Finish your rows against a pear espalier, edge your herbs with lavender. Every move should lead to delight.

Even the dreadful but necessary motor car, which eats up space with its garage, its turning circles and area to spare for visiting friends, can be turned to advantage. A skin of doors and windows might be applied to the garage to disguise it as an elegant pavilion. Or it may make a support for a mass of roses, or wisteria. The drive need not necessarily be an endless sea of tarmac. Gravel, given a neat edge, can look quite satisfactory. Or patterned with setts or narrowed strategically to diminish the area exposed to view, and edged with a regular succession of stone or box balls, a drive can become a pleasure to look at.

The functional requirements of a garden should be welcomed as providing a sensible guide for both its development and its ornament. There will inevitably be compromises if you want to impose a powerful aesthetic idea, such as a symmetrical layout or the need to keep open a distant view. But alternative arrangements will present themselves, with different advantages. As opportunities arise for creating something new, remember the unity of the garden: you can be sure that however imaginative and beautiful a new feature might be, it will be even better if it acknowledges the overall character of the garden, by harmony or by contrast. Few things succeed in isolation: they are nearly always tempered by their surroundings.

Inside-outside

The conservatory serves as a useful weatherproof zone between inside and outside. Like its traditional Victorian forbear, it is an extension of the house in which we can enjoy the exotic scents and colours of tender plants. It often makes an eating place off the kitchen, with light pouring in from above and doors that can be thrown open. Decorated to the same standards as the house, with cane or perhaps perforated metal chairs and tables, with an abundance of flowers and foliage in clay pots or painted containers, conservatories can be magical places – a change from routine experience where lush nature rubs with the paraphernalia of elegant living.

SPACE AND SCALE

The concept of space is fundamental to the layout and success of the garden. Space is either apparently infinite, a limitless prairie, or it is defined by some sort of boundary or enclosure. Space – that which lies between – is the converse of mass and volume. It has shape and proportion and a dimensional relationship with other spaces and volumes.

A garden, almost inevitably, is enclosed, weakly or strongly, by distant trees or by nearby walls and fences. The house, though it has spaces within it, normally appears from the garden as a volume. The play between space and volume admits of enormous variation, and determines the way in which we perceive both house and garden, not only as an overall composition, but also in their details. However fascinating a garden may be for its plants, its character is chiefly determined by its spaces and the way they are contained. A space, of course, does not exist until something is put round it, and for most gardens the defining limits have generally been determined by the history of the site. Normally, there is a house and boundaries, perhaps walls or other structures. With luck, there might be trees or at least some reasonably sized shrubs. Between these there is rudimentary space – space that feels wide open or confined, barrenly empty or fussily cluttered, or perhaps balanced and serene. Such reactions depend almost entirely on the quality of the surrounding enclosure, its dimensions, texture, colour or opacity. It is largely the successful manipulation of space and enclosure that can make a garden a pleasure to be in, as well as one that is functionally convenient.

Faced with a small urban plot, a gardener may feel that the space within his or her garden is predetermined by the proximity of boundaries and of neighbours, and that it is unalterable. The country gardener, perhaps girt about with sheltering trees, may also think that little can or need be done to improve the size and quality of the space.

So often this attitude of resignation is unnecessary. Adjustments carried out with a view to making better spaces (rather than just incorporating more plants) can dramatically improve the feel of the garden, introducing a sense of distance or of breadth, creating surprises or a feeling of intimacy. It is the thoughtful use of structural or ornamental elements that can bring about such radical transformations. A trellis or a balustrade not only makes a division but also gives an edge to the new spaces. An area may be defined by as little as four large pots placed at its corners. Or, again, a visual boundary might be suggested by something as temporary as a hammock slung between two trees. Moreover, structure and ornament used in this way have an instant effect, an immediate definition of the new space, whereas if you use plants for the same purpose you must wait for them to grow.

Organizing space can be a puzzling task, but often the *genius loci*, the essential character of the site, together with your own clear idea of functional requirements, offer strong guidelines. Even so, you will need a basic understanding of what might happen in the process of making or adjusting spaces. The enclosure, trees, walls, pots, or whatever it is that marks the edges of the space, are paramount in determining how the space feels. A small area strongly enclosed by tall trees or buildings may feel claustrophobic. However, a large area weakly surrounded by a low fence may not feel like a space at all. A tall, closely-trimmed hedge around the area will give a much stronger sense of containment than will an open pergola. A broken texture of leaves seems to enclose a space more gently than does the rugged masonry of a high stone wall. An enclosure of regularly spaced trees or columns is visually much stronger than one that is formed by the same elements but without the regular spacing to create an effect of unifying rhythm.

A general rule (and rules may often be broken to great advantage) is that a comfortable space will be one where its width is not less than the height of the surrounding enclosure, nor more than three times the height. At the same time, it is important to relate to human dimensions, for beyond a distance of about 25 yards, it becomes difficult to discern facial expressions and successfully communicate with other people; whereas in very small spaces, people may seem uncomfortably close. The shape of the space on the ground also affects comfort. A long, narrow slot may seem fit only to hurry through, and if its sides are tall you will wish to pass through faster still. A circular or square space encourages pausing and repose, but again, if its sides are too tall in relation to its ground dimensions, you may only want to escape. Remember always that such general rules can be turned on their heads. If, in a small circular space, surrounded by tall, dark hedges, you put at the centre a statue, you will powerfully concentrate all attention on the statue, and you might forget your claustrophobia. But be warned, if you do that, the statue must be excellent, meriting all the interest that is focused on it.

The relative levels of the ground within the space also affect its feel. A depression in the middle of the space will tend to concentrate the feeling of enclosure. A mound, however, falling away to the edges of the space, dissipates the feeling. The most interesting results occur when a depression is located to one side, or in a corner, thus giving a formerly static space a direction and a dynamism.

A garden platform *(page 59)*

Space may be marked out in a variety of ways. Here, it is a great white umbrella that clearly makes a *place* of a part of this verdant hillside, looking over valley and town below. An encircling wall of stone robustly protects this outpost, and a convenient tree of heaven *(Ailanthus altissima)* reinforces it from behind. Strongly defined, this tiny platform commands the greater space of the valley.

A garden in compartments *(left)*

In compartment gardens, it is the progression from space to space that is exciting. In the historic English garden at Sissinghurst, Kent, shown here, each space is notable for its proportions and for the texture of its enclosure – perhaps on one side the crumbly old wall of Tudor brickwork, or perhaps the mighty yew hedge, dark and fine-textured. In this view, through a door over-arched with tumbling clematis, a brick path leads to a pool of light. The space that we are in is firmly defined and comprehensible, but through the door is an indication of a mystery that as yet lacks space or definition – a promise of further pleasures to come.

A point of arrival *(right)*

Even a small space can have an enormous impact – and here, at the entrance to a house, impact is just what is needed. It is here that you state your style, what your house is like, your own taste and preferences. With colour and pattern, flower and foliage, you welcome your visitor into an ambience of pleasure. In this entrance area, the pattern on the floor and step forms a break between the paving of the street and the carpet inside, distinguishing the point of arrival. The fuschia adds to the impact, softening the geometrical lines and offering an attractive colour contrast.

Spaces relate to the world outside their enclosure. The surrounding wall or hedge gives privacy and shuts out distractions. It shelters us from wind or sun and may improve growing conditions. Or if the enclosure is open, it can draw attention to spaces outside. You can throw a frame round a view, as though it were a painting, or highlight a focal point. The enclosure may lead the eye outwards to a space beyond, and to another beyond that.

Spaces may be linked in so many different ways. A light filigree of ironwork, almost transparent, will bring separate spaces so close together that they almost fuse. But if you have to pass down a long tunnel or through a thick mass of planting, the connection between the spaces is more tenuous, permitting a greater change of colour or mood. This transition, smooth and quick, or to be undertaken with care as over stepping stones, is a preparation for the space to come. It can work in opposition to the space beyond, or it can enhance the space by anticipation.

A further consideration is scale – the comparative size of spaces, the elements that enclose them, and the objects within them. We tend to compare a space with the size of a human being, and there are always elements that support such comparison. Steps, for example, tend to have risers of roughly the same height in gardens both great and small. Doorways are sometimes vast, but on the whole give a consistent clue to the size of the enclosure or building. Another critical comparison in most gardens is the relationship between the walls of the house and the gardens that surround it. There must be room to stand back from the house, or the space will feel cramped and uncomfortable. But if you are faced with a long narrow slot, stretching along the front or the side of the house, try treating it as a series of tiny spaces, each with its own focus and its own interest: it might then become rather fascinating.

Scale is complicated by the need to compensate for an altered perception of size out-of-doors. Perhaps because of an unavoidable comparison with the huge vault of sky, objects that might appear rather large indoors seem quite insignificant outdoors. Dimensions on the ground are much greater than we are used to in the house, and perspective makes large objects diminish to mere specks over the length of a couple of tennis courts. Consequently, when creating structures, or placing ornaments, it is all too easy to make them too small. Because the rules of perspective work in any direction, you must take account of the vertical dimension as well as the horizontal. A pitched roof, particularly when viewed from a restricted space below, will appear to recede. Make sure that it is steep enough, or it will disappear behind its own eaves, producing an unsettling effect.

A circle of stillness

In this area of a garden in Adel, West Yorkshire, the principal enclosure is provided by the tall yew hedges which make a long passage. But within that, there is an area of stillness, where the narrow path becomes a more open circle. The transition from path to circle is reinforced by the balls of box which transform the area into a coherent space. Although the path seems to speed us on toward the gap in the distant hedge, the circle modulates the rhythm, checking our momentum so that we can briefly pause and absorb what we see.

Not only do spaces have scale, but so too do materials and plants. Intricate, small-scale patterns can seldom be satisfactorily executed in large-scale paving materials such as stone flags. On the other hand, large-scale patterns often look good in small-scale pavings such as cobbles or bricks, provided that individual patterns are all subservient to an overall scheme and not used to create endless separate incidents. These principles are perhaps more obvious in planting, where large groupings of small-scale plants in a large space are always far more satisfactory than a collection of different individual plants, each vying for attention. Structure and ornament, likewise, have their own scale and you must plan them carefully in relation to surrounding spaces.

There has always been a tendency to reduce the scale of the great outdoors to an area of defensible space – unless, of course, you are Louis XIV. However, gardens are places of leisure, and to be comfortable, spaces must be as ample as possible. They must certainly be adequate for normal human activities. Paths must be wide enough, preferably for two people walking side by side, and arches high enough for you to pass through without stooping, unless there is a good reason to have them otherwise.

It may, of course, be necessary to make a small area appear larger, particularly in town gardens. A visual filter in the foreground, a pergola maybe, or even just an arch, provides foreground detail but partly obscures the space beyond. Thereby the boundaries become unclear, and the distant space seems to extend much further than it really does. *Trompe l'oeil* treillage designs can allude to space, and false perspective, with trees or pots appearing to diminish towards a vanishing point, creates greater depth. But use this trick with care, for a false perspective viewed from the wrong end can look peculiar. Stripes of light and shade created by openings on the flanks will make a garden appear wider, as will paving patterns running from side to side. Where there are smooth walls or hedges, or lines of paving, that lead away into the distance, the garden will appear longer. In very small gardens, or in conservatories, large mirrors can be useful to give the appearance of more space, but you must frame them with vegetation or a trellis some distance in front to disguise the edges, or the illusion will be spoiled.

However you adjust appearances, your decisions about scale must be positive. Either the spaces and the objects within them must work together as part of a greater composition, or one element must be chosen as the most important, with everything else subservient. It is a question of seeing beyond the individual space to its position within the larger scheme. Where such relationships are clearly worked out, the garden will be memorable; where there is a muddle, it will remain a muddle in your visitor's mind, and will be soon forgotten.

Movable items, too, can be used to reinforce your spatial ideas. A view of a handsome seat can draw the eye along an axis around which the garden is planned. A pair of urns can form a gate through which you pass into the next space. A sequence of large pots ranged round a space will emphasize its shape, and perhaps define an outer path around. Timber seats can be grouped in pairs or threes to make an intimate area within a larger space. Large planting cases, perhaps planted with standard roses or honeysuck-

A trick of the eye

The perspective effect of *trompe l'oeil* trelliswork, with battens all pointing towards a single vanishing point, creates a sense of depth. This example is unadorned with plants; but if the edges were obscured with climbers, the illusion of extra space would be even more convincing.

les, can make a useful filter, partly obscuring the space beyond, yet providing occasional glimpses through. Create a sense of distance with the sparkle of light and the sound of a fountain. Or position a statue to lure the visitor on, remembering that if the statue is too small, or too distant, it will be lost. Keep a small statue in a small space, or at least, by the lie of the path and partial screening, make sure that it can be seen only from relatively close-to. Pots, too, are invaluable for giving a lift to a composition, at either end of a bench, or at the foot of a statue, or on steps or lining a path. If only small pots are available, group them to make a big collection. Be bold in what you do: it never pays to be timid in a garden.

Unfolding spaces *(left)*

The central staircase up the side of a hill at Iford Manor, Wiltshire, its landing emphasized with piers and columns capped by urns and statues, gives a promise of unfolding spaces. The piers in the foreground are sharply defined with dressed stone, while the next pair of urns have less strongly articulated bases in the corners of the retaining walls. Further up these walls, columns topped by little statues, looking rather slender in comparison with the piers at the bottom, accentuate the gateway on the third level. Together, the vertical elements create an impression of depth and spaciousness, suggesting that the staircase crosses wide horizontal spaces. But in fact, on this steep hillside, space is quite restricted.

Towards a focal point *(right)*

In the late Sir Frederick Gibberd's garden at Harlow, Essex, this sculpture forms a compelling feature at the end of an avenue of coppiced limes. The texture of the branches, pushing up to the sky, increases the sense of distance along what is actually quite a short path. The branches also create a unified space, in which the statue is not included: it lies beyond, in the next space. The linking of one area with another, and the suggestion of more to come, draw on the visitor irresistibly. It is a deft manipulation, making the garden a place that has to be explored.

Ambiguous space

To attempt a serious modification of the
restricted area of an urban garden
might seem at first a futile exercise. The
site may seem too small ever to appear
spacious. And, anyway, your first
inclination may be to keep the area as
open as possible: openness and
spaciousness might strike you as being
the same thing. But look at this garden.
The already small space is divided into
smaller spaces, marked by a change of
level, a raised bed dividing a staircase,
and a greenhouse. Only from the upper
window (where the photograph was
taken) can the garden be seen all at
once. From ground level, from the area
closest to the house, you can see that
there is space beyond, behind the
greenhouse, but how much is far from
clear. The back wall is mostly obscured,
so maybe the boundary is somewhere
among the trees. Or are the trees within
the garden itself? Deliberately, the
space has been made ambiguous.

Colour and Texture

Our perception of the garden and its contents is conditioned by colour and texture. Different surfaces reflect either white light or selected wavelengths which we interpret as individual colours. If there is no reflection at all, they appear black. Texture also is a function of reflection, in that a textured surface appears as a pattern of highlights (where light is reflected) and shadows (where light is absorbed). The coarser the texture, the larger the areas of light and shade. Texture informs us about "feel": a visual stimulus is confirmed by a tactile memory. While space and form determine our perception of the garden as a three-dimensional reality, colour and texture tell us about its surfaces.

Useful analogies may be drawn between garden-making and interior decoration. Whenever we go into a room that seems particularly agreeable, in which everything belongs and fits well together, the chances are that it is decorated with a relatively limited palette of colours. These may be chosen to harmonize around one dominant colour, or they may contrast to give emphasis to one particular aspect of the room. It is unlikely that a room decorated indiscriminately with many colours, in which no one colour dominates, will be in any way memorable. So in gardens – although there is so much potential for colour, ruthless control is needed for the garden to become anything more than a mere collection of plants and ornament, however beautiful each individual item.

In the more fertile parts of the world, the predominant garden colour tends to be green, but that in itself comes in many shades, varying from yellow-green to dark blue-green. Its intensity will change with the light from a misty, soft sage green to a vibrant, extravagant jungle green. The foliage greens already make a major impact in a garden, and any further colour must take account of them. Plants, of course, also have a vast array of flower colours, and often these colours are far from happy together. Rhododendrons *en masse*, for example, frequently stand and shriek at each other. Other elements of the garden, apart from the planting, also make their contributions. Large ares of structure may introduce whites, greys, browns, oranges, reds – even green or blue. Water may appear as a silvery-white non-colour, or reflect other colours around. Sculpture and furniture may come in a wild variety of unrelated hues. Now, if you are able to bring all these elements into harmony, the garden could be as thrilling as the beautifully decorated room.

Certain groups of colours mix well together, while others look unpleasant. Fashion to some extent influences our taste in colour, but there are also more fundamental relationships that have been objectively and exhaustively analysed. A basic theory of colour was formulated by Michel Chevreul in the 19th century, and has influenced discussions about the use of colour ever since. He was important to the Impressionists in painting, and to Gertrude Jekyll in gardening. In Jekyll's book *Colour in the Flower Garden*, she strongly emphasizes the necessity for colour control, and gives many practical examples of successful colour combinations, using plants as the principal medium.

However, the application to the flower garden of complicated theories appropriate to the work of physicists, chemists or even painters is fraught with difficulty. Conditions in a laboratory or a studio may be relatively stable: light, pigment, viewing distance, surrounding colours, and so on, may be predetermined. But in the garden there are so many variable factors quite outside the control of the gardener or the visitor. As you walk through the garden, viewpoints change constantly, so that colours are seen in all sorts of combinations with each other. The sun alters its position and intensity, throwing a deepening shadow, yellowing the garden at midday, reddening it towards dusk. The humidity of the atmosphere may soften colours that appear sharp and bright on a dry day. As the season advances, bright young leaves become dull and frequently turn a totally different colour before falling off. Flowers appear, then disappear, perhaps to be replaced by berries of quite a different colour. Despite such difficulties, scientific colour theories may offer a broad guide that can help in the choice of palette. For example, by combining hues that are closely related to each other in the spectrum (such as red, orange and yellow), you can achieve an harmonious scheme. Another way to create such

harmony is to combine a hue with its tint (the colour lightened with white) or its shade (the colour darkened with black): red, pink and crimson would thus work well together. In dealing with other simple relationships, such as the complementary (opposed) colours red and green, you can again obtain satisfactory results provided that one or the other dominates.

More sophisticated colour schemes can be built around triads. This notion depends on the concept of the colour circle – an arrangement of the spectrum in a continuous wheel, with complementaries opposite each other and harmonizing colours adjacent. A triad is found by rotating a triangle round the circle. The three primary colours – red, yellow and blue – make a triad, but produce the least satisfactory results when combined. However, by shifting round the colour circle to less fierce colours, you can obtain more subtle and interesting combinations: citrus, russet and slate, or buff, plum and sage, are commonly recommended. Remember, though, that green must form part of the group – unless, of course, it is a garden in which green is eliminated.

The colours of leaves *(page 67)*

The colours of the plant world are astonishingly rich and require careful handling to make an integrated, colour-coordinated picture. The bluey-purple centres and red edges of these leaves of *Cotinus coggygria* 'Foliis Purpureis' will inevitably draw attention to themselves within a general planting of green. While they may be worthy of such attention, you need to ask yourself if they reinforce the colour scheme in which they are planted, or if they fragment it by being so obviously different.

A carpet of colour *(left)*

This sumptuous drift of *Narcissus* at Threave Garden in Scotland, making a unified carpet of palest cream, is radiantly beautiful. The success of this planting is in its simplicity and lack of distraction. Bright yellow daffodils may have their merits, but they would spoil this scene. Gardeners who love plants may be tempted to add more and more intrinsically interesting species and varieties. The artist must resist this temptation, and ensure that each plant makes a positive contribution to the overall picture.

A vibrant combination *(right)*

Strange plant colours can be added together in ravishing combinations. Here, the large leaves of red-stemmed ruby chard rise above purple *Setcreasia*, with its distinctive pointed leaves. Together, they are set off by the wispy filigree of *Artemisia schmidtiana*. Such a startling combination needs to be contained by an intermediate planting or enclosure which will permit it to coexist with the quieter greens of the rest of the garden.

Choosing a mixture of colours is further bedevilled by the
variable ways in which we perceive them. Most important is the
way in which certain colours appear to advance or recede. The
colours of the spectrum all have differing wavelengths, and the eye
has to refocus as it traverses from, say, the long wavelength of red
to the short wavelength of blue. It most easily focuses on the
greens of the middle wavelengths, which is why green is perceived
as restful. Objects at the red end of the spectrum tend to appear
closer, while those at the blue end appear to be farther away. As
colours become less intense, they also appear to recede; however,
the reds keep a crisp form, while the blues begin to blur.

The quality of colour is affected by other colours seen nearby or
seen moments before. If red and orange are placed together, the
red will appear more blue, while the orange appears more yellow.
Moreover, our perception of brightness alters with the quality of
the light: in the intense, high sunlight of tropical and sub-tropical
regions, gardens appear as areas of bright light and deep shadow,
and colours tend to appear faded, so that only the most vivid hues,
together with white, have any weight. In cooler climates, however,
relatively dull greens, such as the greens of grass in winter, appear
quite strong, and pastel shades seem bright. Any bright colour, or
white, will draw attention to itself, and vivid scarlets or oranges
may appear almost painful to look at.

With the immense range of flower colours that is available to us,
the colour planning of a garden can be quite a daunting task, and
the problem is aggravated by the difficulty of coordinating the
flowering times of different plants. But when we turn to the
architecture and sculpture of the garden, things are less complicated. Inert materials do not change to the same extent as plants:
by their nature, they tend to be static. The only colour change to
be wary of is that due to weathering when materials are bleached
in the sun or pick up growths of algae, lichen or moss. When
weathered, natural materials such as brick, stone and timber tend
to have subdued colours. Most lie on the warm side of the
spectrum, among the natural earth colours – the reds, greys and
browns – and thus contrast well with the foliage greens. It is worth
remembering that if you use local materials for the structure and
ornament of your garden, it is likely to harmonize with the
surroundings and look completely appropriate, as if it could have
been built in no other way. There are, of course, stones that can be
quite yellow or blue, and much of the marble that finds its way into
the garden is white. This must be considered with care. In the
virtually monochrome gardens of the Mediterranean, dark with
cypresses and ilex, where the sun glares off the paving and water,
the white of a marble sculpture is needed to stand up to the
dramatic lighting. But in duller light, marble will create an
eye-catching focal point – which is fine only if it is a wonderful
piece placed in exactly the right spot.

More difficult is the use of applied colour or of artificially coloured
materials. Paints and stains offer the opportunity to make almost
any inert material whatever colour we like. But think carefully: in
a soft light, a pavilion painted a Chinese red will contrast happily
against the foliage greens. A bluey-grey pavilion will seem to draw
back among the leaves, while a yellowy-green one will seem to

come forward a little. A scarlet pavilion will come right forward and its position will seem uncertain. A white one will draw the eye like a magnet. If the building has large painted surfaces, they will seem hard and lacking in subtlety in comparison with the everchanging leaves nearby, unless you can find a way to temper the effect. In a hard, bright light, however, a different set of criteria applies: the bright reds and oranges are needed if the structure is not to look insipid, and white can look good against a bright blue sky or sea.

Garden furniture, similarly, can be made to stand out brazenly or to serve its purpose without too much fuss. Unfortunately, so much that is available today is of a poor design in which structure and materials are reduced to a minimum for the sake of economy. To proclaim the presence of such items in strident colours is clearly unwise. If, however, your garden chair is a throne, a beautiful piece of furniture of which you are particularly proud, then by all means paint it to stand out.

Bright sunlight tends to flatten surfaces and make subtleties of colour imperceptible. Consequently, in the Mediterranean there grew up a tradition of using moulded projections that throw shadows to outline those surfaces – a technique fundamental in the formulation of classical architecture. In bright sun, strong shadow lines define, for example, the mouldings of a cornice or the form of a box parterre. Such lines will only be confused by a prominent texture. However, under grey skies, where shadows are more subdued, linear definition weaker and colour variations more distinct, we rely more on the texture of surfaces to inform us of their nature.

Texture is augmented by cast shadows. In the low slanting sunlight of the north, or in the early morning or late afternoon, the bold pattern of highlights and shadows creates an obvious texture, which can give life and interest to a paving design. Smooth slabs can be contrasted with knobbly cobbles to emphasize a route or create a significant area. More subtly, the dynamic texture of herringbone brickwork can be contrasted with the static texture of bricks laid in a rectilinear basketweave pattern. Similarly, the texture of vertical elements can be exploited to give emphasis to a particular area within the garden, to induce stronger or weaker feelings of enclosure, or to make an element appear closer or further away. A smooth-surfaced wall, of mud or ashlar masonry, will not impinge so strongly as one of craggy stones, or of wattle. A coarse hedge of laurel, with its deep shadows and highlights on the leaves, will appear more robust and agitated than the fine restful texture of yew. And then there is trellis, which makes yet another kind of texture – both strong and transparent.

The textures of polished materials, so smooth that they reflect, are especially interesting. They contrast powerfully with plants and with most natural materials suitable for structure, and they draw attention to themselves in the same way that bright colours do. Thus, polished surfaces are frequently used for sculptural pieces. The more reflective materials such as stainless steel have, in some ways, the same quality and appeal as water, bringing the sky down to the earth, creating visual ambiguities, making us pause to think.

Woodland reds and pinks

A woodland planting of azaleas making a felicitous composition. Here, the colours concentrate on various shades of pink. White fits naturally into the range, as do the coppery reds of the purple *Acers*. For such a scheme to succeed, you must ruthlessly eliminate any leaf or flower colour that does not fit. A group of orange azaleas, for example, would totally destroy this composition.

Green and white *(above)*

The stems of these trees have been painted with white limewash. Their branches reaching up and out from the trunks stand out beautifully between the greens in the box parterre below and the leafy canopy above. Such simple colour combinations are often the most striking.

Colours under northern light *(right)*

Blotches of orange and brown lichen give this beautiful old stone seat a patina of age. Colours in northern light tend to appear more subtle, so even slight variations can be perceived and enjoyed. In bright light, with hard reflections, such minute variations would be lost.

A welcoming gateway

A decorated gateway giving onto the street in a Mediterranean hillside town is painted in colours strong enough to stand up to the intensity of light. In the north this contrasting scheme of orange and green would look garish, but here the paintwork brings the gateway into prominence without making it seem too obtrusive. The crowning pots further reinforce the impact of the entrance.

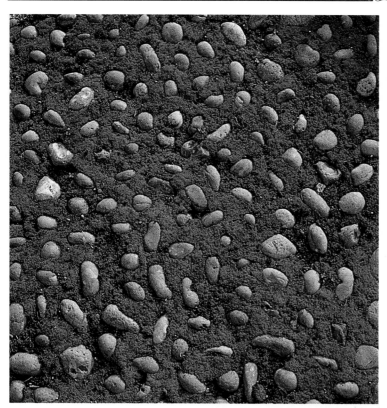

Paving textures *(above)*

Pavings often show wonderful texture.
The cobbles in the paving shown above
have been colonized by a moss growing
in the earth that has accumulated in the
valleys between the stones. Above right
is the more subtle texture of
herringbone brickwork, which gives a
sense of movement to a path. The
subtle colour variations in the bricks
also give the path life.

Sculptural greenery *(above)*

The habit of clipping evergreens into rounded forms like this seems to have originated in Japan, and from there its popularity has spread to America. These conifers clipped as balls make a strong statement in the garden through both their form and their texture, introducing a somewhat bizarre element.

The textures of grasses

Grasses are excellent for introducing a textural variation into a planting scheme. Their slender upright stalks, topped by a great variety of flower heads, depending on the species, have a fineness of texture that is seldom found in other plant forms. Also, in the autumn, many grasses change to an attractive papery brown that stays throughout the winter. Illustrated here is a composition of grasses in Washington D.C.

An artful use of shrubs

A strange and beautiful combination of colours and textures. The red-purple of *Berberis thunbergii* 'Rose Glow' is put with the pale blue of the spruce *Picea pungens* 'Glauca'. In the middle is the darker green of *Pinus mugo* and in the foreground the pale green of *Juniperus x media* 'Pfitzerana'. The stiffish needles of the pine and the spruce contrast well with the softer foliage of the juniper and the broader leaves of the *Berberis*.

The texture of a trellis

A different kind of texture is provided by this lozenge trellis. Standing close to the trellis you can easily see through to the garden beyond. However, step a few yards back and the diagonal timberwork becomes a veil that stops the eye. Removing the distraction of the view, the texture of the trellis concentrates our attention on the plants in front.

GROUND FORM AND SURFACE

The three-dimensional form of the ground on which a garden is made has a profound influence upon its character, the spaces within its boundaries and its views of the world outside. It is the base on which the garden composition is built, influencing access, circulation and the structure and surfacing materials required. The steep hillsides of Italy have generated a totally different kind of garden from those of the flat polders of the Netherlands, even though in each case the same kinds of geometric principles have been applied.

The lie of the land, which influences drainage, microclimate and the views that are offered, will suggest a layout for the garden. Certain functional elements, such as a kitchen garden or swimming pool, may best be sited where the ground gives shelter from the prevailing wind or freedom from frost. A naturally flat area may be just right for a croquet lawn or tennis court.

The shape of the ground and changes in its level evoke particular optical and psychological responses. A hill has a visual advantage over the spaces below, and thus appears to be a special place. A hollow, too, seems to have its own magnetism, concentrating attention towards its centre. The eye is naturally drawn along a valley, so that a building sited at the end of the valley gains in importance. Rising ground tends to foreshorten distances: buildings or sculptures appear taller and more impressive as you look up towards them. Falling ground, however, seems to lengthen the view, so that vertical features are diminished in impact, appearing shorter, and perhaps less important, than they would when seen across level ground.

Ground form also introduces an element of surprise. A winding path will open up a series of different views, each concealed until you are round the next bend. And, as you ascend a flight of stairs, the view ahead is restricted until, as you reach the top, a whole new scene appears.

You may need to change the ground form, perhaps to conceal an unsatisfactory boundary, to modify the previous excavations, to correct the impression that the garden slips away to one side, or to give sculptural interest to an otherwise flat site. However, altering the lie of the land is feasible only if you have enough space to grade gently into the flat at the top and bottom of the slope. To appear natural, a slope must not be too steep: even an incline of 1:2 (25 degrees) is too sharp for comfortable walking and may result in erosion by rainwater run-off.

It is important to relate slopes to the principal views. A view at right-angles to the contour lines is always more comfortable than a view across ground falling away to the right or left – that is, unless the incline is counterbalanced by a slope the opposite way or by a strong vertical to contain the eye. By canalizing a view between gentle mounds, reinforced by their planting, you can make a series of pictures that unfold as you progress; this is possible even on a small scale with rocks and banks of scree, small trees and alpine plants. Manipulating the land form allows you to make secret romantic places or open up sudden views.

In some gardens, more formal constructions will be appropriate – perhaps a grass amphitheatre, a series of terraces or a mound divided by a deep cleft. Earth-moving is not such an expensive operation as it once was, and with modern mowing machines grass slopes can be easily maintained. However, for economy's sake, you should try to balance the cut and fill: the volume of the hole you require should be the same as that of the hill you are constructing. Carting away excess earth, or bringing new topsoil to the site, can be costly. For the centre of your mound use subsoil or piles of rubble left over from building operations: be sure not to bury precious topsoil. Take drainage into account: a waterlogged slope will tend to slip, and rain will drain down rapidly to make a bog at the bottom.

Banks and slopes may not be appropriate to the style of your garden, or may not be practicable if the space is cramped. The retaining wall offers an alternative way to create a change in level, without taking up so much horizontal space. By introducing a constructed element, it offers opportunities to exploit texture and colour, give a unity to a series of spaces, or create rhythms with a surmounting balustrade. Such walls can conceal pipework, allowing water to cascade down their surface or spout out of masks. They create a special microclimate, retaining heat so that tender fruits can be grown. They also provide a background for the decorative training of a wisteria or magnolia. Alternatively, a low retaining wall can provide a seat or raise a bed for the convenience of an elderly or disabled gardener.

Retaining walls, however, are expensive; and if a large one is envisaged you may need an engineer to ensure that the weight of earth behind will not make it unstable. Drainage must be included, with a land-drain behind or weepholes through the front.

A change in level usually implies steps. Visually powerful by their repetition of horizontal lines, they may underline the house, making a podium, or they may climb a slope. Even when twisting and turning in steep descent, they draw the eye down, like falling water. They can look dramatically imposing or they can appear rather secretive, leading to an adventure. By their breadth they can unite spaces above and below, or by their narrowness they can emphasize separateness. Shallow steps draw you on at a leisurely pace, while steep ones encourage a purposeful ascent. They can take the place of a retaining wall, providing a continuous seat, or surfaces on which to display a range of pots.

Of course, the principal purpose of steps is to allow you to move easily from one level to the next. They must therefore be related to the human scale, with correctly sized treads and risers. A traditional formula suggests that twice the height of the riser measured in inches, plus the length of the tread, should equal 26 (although some authorities say 24). Thus, a comfortable tread length of a 4-inch riser is 18 inches, while a 7-inch riser requires a 12-inch tread. Risers are normally most comfortable between 4 and 7 inches.

If the steps are part of the main access to the house, frequently used, you will need to construct them well in bricks or stone. But if their use is intermittent, you could make them from timber risers and grass treads, or in a woodland setting from logs with gravel or even earth and bark flakes built up from behind to form a rudimentary tread. If they gather routes from many parts of the garden, you might make them semicircular, or three-sided. Normally, they should be broad enough to suit the external scale,

Banks of grass (right)

The grass terraces at Dartington Hall, Devon, originally formed the side of a 14th-century tiltyard, which was reshaped in the early part of this century. The terraces are set off by a wayward pine leaning out from the bank and the Pfitzer's juniper in the foreground. The bands of light and shade created by the step formation give the bank great sculptural strength.

Sculpting the land (page 77)

Shaping the ground can be like making a giant sculpture. These terraces in Bali are formed to keep the topsoil in place as an anchorage for rice plants, as well as for keeping the plants permanently wet. Although here the terraces are purely functional, you can create similar earth sculptures in a garden, given a basic understanding of soil mechanics and a sympathy for the site.

The lure of steps

Like a door, steps bid you forward, inviting you to ascend or descend. This impressive flight draws the eye up to a massive beech tree at the top of the hill. On any steps, the pattern of treads, which catch the light, and risers, which appear in shadow, creates a powerful image. This idea can be used in a composition to accentuate space if the steps are broad, or height if the flight is long. Here, the steps make a strong forward and upward movement that divides the fiery autumn colours of the planting. A ramp, lacking the bands of light and dark, could never have created such a surging sense of movement.

A hilltop arbour

This mount – a specially built mound which serves as a viewing platform – provides a base for a splendid black and gilded wrought-iron arbour. Fine though the arbour is, it is made even more magnificent by its elevated position. The sides of the mount are clad in box, which is kept trimmed at a constant height above the ground, thus creating a unified colour and texture. A shadow marks the line of the path spiralling up to the arbour, which offers views inwards over the garden and out over the surrounding landscape.

but not wider than the path that leads to them. With a broad flight, an easy-going ascent generally looks better than a steep one. Consider also the relation of the steps to the slope. Steps that cut into the bank between small retaining walls are less obtrusive than steps built outwards from the bank. They can be emphasized by the lines of their balustrades, or played down with planting spilling over the edges. Safety is a crucial factor: avoid slippery treads or an uneven pitch. Steep steps are tiring to climb and potentially dangerous. You should slope the treads a fraction so that water cannot lie and turn to ice on a frosty night. On a long flight, introduce a landing or two to give a pause or break a fall. Treads should also have a nosing, a slight projection over the riser that throws a shadow, making them more easily visible.

An alternative method of changing level is by ramp, which has advantages for moving machinery and barrows, or for the disabled, provided that its surface gives a good grip. However, ramps are impracticable if the slope is more than about 1:10 (6 degrees), which means that they take up a lot of space. The stepped ramp is an interesting space-saving hybrid with some of the visual attractions of a stair. Steps alternating with ramped sections will still allow you to manoeuvre machinery successfully.

Much of the garden will need to be paved to afford dry-shod access, to control wear, or to modify a microclimate. The pattern of hard materials on the ground is a basic way to decorate the garden, and normally provides a transition between the hard construction of the house and the softer spaces and volumes of the garden. It may be understated – a passive platform for other features, both temporary and permanent – or it may use pattern and direction to draw together the different parts of the garden. Paving patterns may reinforce the spaces that you have made, echoing the shape of the enclosure. Alternatively, a path may cut through a space without disrupting it, perhaps even slightly sunk below the surface so that it can scarcely be seen. It can draw the eye through a space, leading to a focal point, or perhaps hinting at a further space to come. Depending on its texture, it can hurry you through or make you linger.

Often, most of the paving is around the house, providing a foil to the architecture, a visual platform from which it rises. On the entrance side, the paving should be generous, yet in scale with the front of the building; it should help the visitor to the front door and should outline a space in which he or she can wait at ease before being admitted. To the rear of the house, you will perhaps need additional paving as a private place for sitting in the sun, eating or entertaining. This should not be merely an ill-paved rectangle sited off the living room, but a place that recognizes or improves upon the lie of the land, that complements the materials of the house and that satisfies a variety of functional requirements. This might be an intimate area, a sheltered place from which you can admire greater spaces beyond; or it might be large, incorporating beds or

A garden hollow

A view at the Villa Taranto in Italy shows how our eye is drawn along a valley. The space under the bridge claims our attention more than anywhere else. There is a dynamic line of force through the bridge which contrasts perfectly with the upright form of the cypress. To give the scheme unity, the planting should strategically accentuate the space of a hollow, rather than fill it indiscriminately. Similarly, tall plants or trees should be located towards the tops of hills to emphasize their height. Tiered planting on the slopes, introducing bands of light and shade, will also serve to reinforce height.

an arbour laden with roses. It should be a transitional space, relating to the dimensions and formality of the house as well as to the larger spaces and informality of the garden.

Paved areas may be introduced elsewhere in the garden to enhance a special character. If there is a view from a particular place, paving may be required to accommodate the wear. Sometimes, it is better to set off plants with the colour and smooth texture of paving than with grass. Furthermore, paving reduces the burden of maintenance and in small gardens often provides a more suitable ground surface than grass. Where paving predominates, the few plants that there are gain more value by their scarcity, and probably more attention than they would in a garden brimming with countless varieties.

Paths are essentially lines of communication around the garden. Either they should make for a worthwhile goal or they should lead back onto themselves, making a continuous walk. Consider their width carefully: 18 inches may be adequate for a lightly used access path, but paths for strolling around the garden should take two people abreast, so they need to be at least four feet wide. Ensure that you have left enough room for your garden machinery. At the same time be careful that such areas do not get out of scale with the house or with the rest of the garden. Make sure that your pavings will dry quickly, that water cannot stand on them, making a treacherous patch of mud or ice. Give paths a slight fall into the drainage system or, if they are small in scale, into a nearby bed. Take care that they do not merely conduct moisture into the walls of the buildings.

Materials such as brick and stone, which are enlivened by minute variations in colour and texture, tend to be more sympathetic in gardens than uniform, dull-coloured concrete pavings. Indigenous materials will never look out of place in their locality, though where concrete predominates they may draw too much attention to themselves by their excellence. Consider the inherent scale and pattern of the paving materials. Bricks can give a sense of direction, whereas gravel cannot (unless raked in the Japanese fashion). Avoid too many different types of paving which might destroy the unity of the garden, or over-fussy patterns which might conflict with plants.

Gravel, being derived from natural stone, makes an excellent paving material despite its low cost. The shape of the pebbles and

A formal staircase *(below left)*

The design of steps conditions our
sensations as we change level. If they
are broad and generous, with long
treads and shallow risers, an ascent will
seem easy, almost unnoticed. If they
are steep and narrow, the ascent must
be done quickly. These steps leading
down from a terrace cut into the upper
level but at the same time project in
front of the retaining wall. There is a
sense of width and ease, and the
pleasure of a pausing place half way up;
and yet, built around a central ellipse,
the steps are economical in that they
need no additional retaining structure
or balustrading.

A swirl of textures *(left)*

This interesting exercise in textural
design includes a path of simple square
tiles over a bridge, breaking into an
agitation of cobble fans. The cobbles
are selected for their elongated shape,
and laid with the greatest care. In
contrast are the parapet walls made
from large round flints, which from a
distance look almost like the scales of a
lizard's skin. The flints are set off in
their turn by the waterside vegetation
of rushes and ferns.

their small colour variations can make it look quite lively. Used
loose, gravel needs periodic raking as it tends to move under
traffic. It can also be used bound with clay but still needs to be
retained by timber or concrete edgings or it will spread over the
years. A camber is necessary to drain off rainwater.

Cobbles have a coarser texture. Laid in lines, they can create a
directional pattern. Granite setts are more regular, sometimes
square, sometimes rectangular. They tend to be grey or brown,
sometimes speckled, and are durable enough to take vehicles.
They too can be laid in a pattern, one of the most satisfactory, for
large areas, being the fan-shaped designs common in France.

Large paving slabs are often more economic to lay than smaller
units. Rectangular stone flags with riven faces, or sawn into
regular smooth slabs, make the best garden paving of all. They are
normally bedded on sand, and their joints are either left open so
that plants can colonize the cracks, or filled with mortar for a
smooth finish. The pattern and scale are determined by the stone
available; sometimes the slabs are coursed, sometimes laid in a
more random fashion. Sawn stone can be laid into very precise
patterns, as can regular slabs of reconstituted stone.

Another excellent material is brick. The less well-fired varieties
tend to flake in frost, although this can be quite acceptable next to
old buildings. However, more durable bricks are obtainable.
Depending on their function and loading, they can be bedded on
concrete or on sand, in which case they may move slightly,
acquiring a well-worn look. On the whole, brick paving looks
better on paths or smaller areas: acres of unrelieved brickwork can
become tedious.

Concrete in various forms can be used, but it is liable to
monotony. You can achieve a better texture if you choose a good
pebble aggregate and then brush it to expose the pebbles before
the concrete sets. Alternatively, you can make interesting paths by
pressing other materials into the newly cast concrete, such as tile
fragments or pebbles. Precast concrete slabs can be greatly
improved by being laid in combination with other materials such as
bricks or cobbles, or by having wide cracks with plants growing
through. Avoid, at all costs, the precast slab that tries to mimic
real stone – it never succeeds.

In dry climates where wood is abundant, timber decking makes
a good surface. One of the most exciting terraces for a house is
that cantilevered over the side of a hill, with trees growing up
through the decking, so that you sit among the branches, as in a
tree-house. A timber such as western red cedar needs no
preservative and will weather to a beautiful silvery grey. It is
important to choose a timber that is durable and does not warp or
splinter easily. Only non-corrosive fixings should be used.

You should also consider plants as part of the ground surface.
Some, such as thyme or chamomile, do not suffer from the
occasional footstep and can be used in the paving. Others, for
example box, can be worked into marvellous patterns of low
hedges with gravel or other small plants for infilling. Masses of
small shrubs or herbaceous plants can be used to emphasize the
ground form, in the manner of Burle Marx (see page 47), or in
flat patterns like the Victorian bedding-out schemes. Trees can be
used to add a crown to a hilltop. Use plants and paving to work
with and enhance the shape of the ground.

Crazy paving *(above)*

A variation on the theme of stone paving, "crazy paving" is a perfectly sensible use of surplus broken stone. Well-laid, with carefully meshed pieces, it makes an adequate paving surface but unfortunately it has been misused in pursuit of a cottage-garden sentimentality, and is often made from broken concrete slabs, which lack the pleasant variations of stone. Here, an attractive effect is produced by grey stones with subtle brown stainings. Plants in the cracks improve the overall effect. In this case they happen to be dandelions, but neater plants such as thrift or one of the many suitable saxifrages could equally well have been encouraged.

Movement through a static space *(right)*

This courtyard in Charleston, South Carolina, also serves as a passage. The central path of irregularly shaped stone flags emphasizes the route towards the entrance. To underline the shape of the enclosure and the static character of the outer area, the rectangular granite setts are laid in circles around the central point. The contrasting textures of path and paved space create a fascinating ambiguity that corresponds to the dual purpose of the space.

Geometric contrasts *(above)*

This fine-texture paving exploits the juxtaposition of an area of triangles and an area of circles, separated by a dividing line. The use of pebbles of a uniform colour, shape and size has given the paved area coherence. However, adjusting the direction of the pebbles has set up rich patterns that add variety and life. These kinds of geometric patterns can equally well be set up with bricks, with rectangular setts or with tiles laid on edge.

Measured progression *(below)*

A suggestion of speed can be used to reinforce the character of a space. A uniform grain along the length of a path will tend to hurry you on, while a less directional pattern will encourage you to linger. This paving consists of large, irregularly shaped stones set in a matrix of medium- and smaller-sized stones. The path thus has a sense of calm, gentle movement: it neither rushes headlong towards its objective, nor does it appear altogether without purpose.

A pattern of plants (above)

Parterres make a ground surface in high relief. Here, the basic pattern is worked in box. Large pebbles are laid around the standard shrubs, and smaller, purple-grey pebbles in the beds. The paths are finished with a brown gravel. Together, these materials make a satisfying and unified composition with subtle colour variations.

Shades of green and blue (right)

A more colourful but still restrained parterre, with beds outlined in box and containing blue scillas. The simple shapes, the choice of a single infilling plant and the warmth of the brickwork make this a restful composition.

ENCLOSURE AND BUILDINGS

Enclosure is as important in gardens as it is in buildings. It is needed to define spaces and give them an identity. It lends a sense of security from the pressures of the outside world, and allows freedom of action within. It is the continuation of the structure and spaces of the house out into the open air. The character of an enclosure can vary from a defensive wall that shuts out the world to an open ha-ha that allows the garden to take in part of the surrounding country.

There are certain practical reasons for making an enclosure – for example, to define the boundaries of the site and to establish a territory. Historically, walls, fences or hedges provided a degree of protection from intruders, human or animal. Today they may be more useful in keeping children and pets in. Within the garden, enclosures help in modifying the microclimate, creating shelter from the wind, or warming up a particular corner. They also help to make the garden more private, screening it from passers-by or from the overlooking windows of neighbours.

Vertical surfaces present themselves strongly to the eye, with the result that the provision of an enclosure, or a change in its nature, radically affects the feel of the space. It is important to take a positive attitude. Either let enclosure assert itself as part of the design, or treat it as a discreet background element. Judge the height carefully to satisfy the functional requirements and to provide the right feeling for the space. Take care that the enclosure does not merely emphasize the smallness of your garden, or make it claustrophobic.

Enclosure is most commonly provided by trees and shrubs, hedges, fences or walls. Alternatively, more complex structures such as pergolas, tunnels or parts of buildings may determine the edges of an area. Often, space is defined by a combination of elements, which need to be carefully related to each other in terms of height, colour and texture. The choice of materials will depend on the locality, the overall character of the garden and adjoining spaces, as well as any definite functions that the enclosure must perform. If it is a question of improving the microclimate, a stone wall will absorb and retain heat better than a hedge or fence. However, if a filtered view is required, then a pergola may be more appropriate.

Using plants to form a space will always be less expensive than using a structure or building. However, plants take a long time to grow, whereas a constructed screen has an instant effect. Plant forms are normally in utter contrast to the lines of the house, unless you trim them to the geometry of a hedge. If you can wait long enough, hedges will give you a fine architectural framework, and they are not too difficult to maintain. They also provide an opportunity for green sculpture or topiary, which you can grow into new shapes if you become bored with the old ones. Alternatively, you can make a quick hedge with climbers such as roses or honeysuckle, by growing them over a wire or light timber fence, which will rapidly disappear under their vigorous growth.

Fences are normally used for boundary enclosure, and sometimes for internal divisions. Although often made with a light, open structure, they can also be solid for maximum privacy, although not as physically solid as a wall. Their colour and pattern may draw the eye, or they may merge into their surroundings. Traditionally constructed in timber or iron, they appear in a great variety of patterns, including the horizontal lines of post-and-rail fences, the repetitive vertical timbers of the picket fence, the smooth surface of close boards and the rough texture of wattle. Sometimes they are made in highly decorative styles, with diagonal latticework or a *chinoiserie* pattern. They may consist of close vertical boards on a timber frame, or horizontal boards nailed on opposite sides of the posts. High fences may do service for a wall, while low "trip-fences" merely denote the boundary in an otherwise open space. The choice of fence must ultimately depend on what it has to do, how long it has to last, and what is appropriate to the locality and garden. The simpler the fence, the more easily it will coexist with other elements. The more complicated it is, the more it will intrude visually and dominate the space; this may be your intention, but if so, manage the paving and plants to support that intention.

Softwoods used in fencing must be treated against decay, and hardwoods are frequently treated as well, even though they are generally more durable. However, the vapour of some preservatives is harmful to plants and must be used with care. Paint can be used to protect timber as well as to continue a colour scheme, but impervious paints can trap moisture inside the timber, starting rot from within. The most satisfactory timbers for their durability are oak and chestnut, as well as western red cedar. A further cause of trouble is the deterioration of metal used for fixing the parts of a fence together. Iron rusts and should be galvanised, and some metals are subject to attack from acids within the timber.

In the same way, metal and wire fences require protection from corrosion by galvanizing or other suitable treatments. They have traditionally been made in a variety of styles. Spear-headed railings are still seen, and so are stout drawn-wire fences that bolt together in sections. However, most metal railings now consist of simple vertical bars spanning between top and bottom horizontal rails – crisp, elegant, but all too often slightly boring. The tradition of using decorative ironwork in gardens, for balconies, stair railings, arbours and tunnels, deserves more encouragement. Wire mesh used in fencing tends to have a relatively short life, but plastic-coating enhances its durability. Although plastic-coated chain-link fencing around a tennis court may look unpleasant, it provides an excellent support for climbing plants, provided that the roots can be prevented from breaking up the playing surface.

The posts that support a timber or metal fence must be firmly fixed into the ground, or the fence will blow over in the wind. They are often concreted in, although this can accelerate rotting at ground level. Dropping the posts into sockets formed by drain-pipes on end will ensure that any moisture will always drain away.

Walls tend to be altogether more durable than fences, creating a stronger, more imposing boundary. Ideally they are constructed in the indigenous materials, be they stone, brickwork or even mud, as they will then belong to the character of the locality. Like fences, they offer a range of visual possibilities. The combination of brick and flint, typical of English chalk country, can be built with the flint in long horizontal bands or in a rhythm of small panels. Drystone walls (built without mortar) may have a fine texture of closely laid flat stones or a more rugged appearance of round boulders; they provide an excellent habitat for small plants that appreciate the good drainage and can tumble down the face of the wall in decorative abandon. The brick of clayey lowlands may be bonded in a variety of ways, each with its own subtleties of texture; or you can introduce a colour varation by creating a pattern of differently coloured bricks.

A living fence (*left*)

A pretty fence of trees trained as cordons along a framework of bamboos, with arms crossing to form an open diagonal pattern. As the flowers and leaves emerge, the fence changes colour and density.

A covered walk (*right*)

This laburnum tunnel creates a long thin enclosure over the path round a sunken herb garden. The laburnum trees are trained on simple metal arches fixed in the ground. For two glorious weeks in summer, the structure lets down its bright yellow flowers.

A boundary of box (*page 87*)

Enclosures can be made with plants as well as with buildings. Here, at Tyrconnell, Maryland, the enclosure, aligned on an axis through the trees, is defined by box with has developed a characteristic billowing shape.

The top of a wall lends itself to decoration. Copings to shed the rain may introduce a change of materials or an ornamental detailing with interesting shadow lines. Where appropriate to the character of the garden, they may support busts, statues or urns, and a change in level may be the occasion for a curve or scroll. A hedge might be grown along the back of the wall to form an extension of the wall upwards, keeping it dry below.

However, walls can take up a surprising amount of space. A drystone wall may need to be between two and three feet across at its base, and a tall brick wall may also need to be as much as two feet across. This is for structural reasons: walls can be easily blown over in a strong wind if they are not thick enough. Another approach is to support a wall with buttresses, which divide it into bays and give it a rhythm. Or the wall can be zigzagged, or made to curve sinuously as in the crinkle-crankle or serpentine wall. Although such walls take up even more space, they provide interesting possibilities for arrangements of beds or sheltered sitting areas within their recesses.

Apertures in walls need particular attention as they permit a selective view of the space beyond. They lend a certain excitement to the garden as you catch distant glimpses or speculate on what lies on the other side of a door. Whereas a door blocks both access and view when shut, a gate may prevent access but entice with the view. Being allowed in then becomes especially pleasing; and to intensify the event, a gateway can be highly decorated, particularly if it passes through a high wall. However, its elaboration should accord with the character of the space that is to come. A virtuoso wrought-iron gate could, by being over-ornate, actually spoil the view through. It is always important to consider the relative values of foreground and middle distance.

Gates obviously must be functionally appropriate, particularly if access is required for vehicles. They may need to be wide enough to admit a furniture truck. If a heavy gate is required, the piers must be stout enough to support it and the hinges strong enough not to let it sag. If the gate is only for pedestrian use, determine whether or not you require a view through it. The criteria for choosing timber and metal apply to gates as much as they do to fences. If wrought or cast iron is available, remember that more delicate shapes are possible in wrought iron, and that cast iron will be more chunky and more angular. Steel, a common substitute, is limited by production sizes, and even when galvanized is liable to rust quickly if the galvanizing is chipped. Because they are on circulation routes and seen at close quarters, gates tend to be particularly prominent in the garden, so you should always make sure that they are of excellent quality.

Enclosure may be provided wholly or in part by a structure such as a colonnade, a pergola or an arbour. While revealing the view beyond, these features also establish an internal division, as well as providing support for climbing plants. The pergola originated either as a means of spreading out vines to improve their fruiting, or to provide an area of shade. It developed into a structure for shading a path, with a roof of beams or wires supported on vertical posts at regular intervals. Pergolas are useful in the modern garden as frameworks for quick-growing climbers which can provide a

A tunnel of roses (*above*)

Compare this pergola with the structure shown on page 89. Here, the enclosure is formed by a succession of hoops rather than by a continuous tunnel. The shadows striping the path increase the apparent distance of the walk. The roses are trained on light metal arches, and by dint of good pruning fill out with abundant flowers in summer.

A walled garden (*right*)

This unusual garden in South Carolina is made from the shell of an old building – an extreme example of improvisation. With upper windows letting in light, the garden is ambiguous – a garden in a room, or a room in a garden. The walls are lined with well-chosen shrubs, and the old fireplace decorated attractively with pot plants.

degree of privacy and define spaces more quickly than hedges and at less cost than walls. They can be used to frame views or block out eyesores, or to provide an open roof over an outdoor room.

When making a pergola, decide which should predominate: the structure or the planting. There is little point in erecting a wonderfully complicated and expensive timber structure only to submerge it in a cloud of greenery. Metal or light timber structures will be lost in the foliage soon enough and thus are frequently used in making tunnels of apple, pear or lime. Brick or stone supports, however, will always be visible and perhaps are most suitable for climbers that flower high up in the roof. Ensure that the verticals are stout enough for the superstructure and that the beams are in proportion with the supports. Beam sizes will generally be restricted to the lengths of timber readily available and in section should be large enough to counteract any tendency to warp. The proportion of the height of the roof to the breadth of the walk will radically affect the sense of enclosure within the pergola, and will also be partly determined by the proportions of the space you are trying to make outside. However, there should be enough height to permit some festooning by the climbers.

An arbour is essentially a short pergola, and is normally built in the same way. It may be used as a focal point in a scheme, wreathed in flowering climbers, or sometimes it appears as a local focus in a more secluded part of the garden. Occasionally an arbour is made by training plants such as yew or holly, clipped to make an apsidal arch or cylindrical house. As with pergolas, metal structures are soon lost in the foliage, so that the plants appear to be self-supporting.

A roofed-over version of the arbour is the summer house. Traditionally, this was built to give a degree of protection from the elements while remaining relatively open-sided. Often summer houses had crude timber posts with a thatched or tiled roof above. Sometimes they were made so that they could be rotated with the sun, or moved to another part of the garden. Today they usefully serve as a permanent decorative focus in a garden and can roof over an outdoor dining area or cover a seat from which a fine view can be enjoyed. Although they are most commonly made out of timber, you could equally well use steel or aluminium, and such materials might encourage new and adventurous designs.

Of greater functional immediacy is the conservatory. This tends to be purchased ready-made, but in the long term, a purpose-made structure may well be worth the additional cost. Because most conservatories are made in treated softwood, they will require frequent painting, which, on a glazed structure, is difficult and time-consuming. Timber may, however, be the most suitable material for the style of the house. Cedar can be used unpainted and will weather to an agreeable silver-grey. Perhaps the best modern material is aluminium, which is expensive but relatively maintenance-free. The choice of materials inside will largely depend on the functions to be satisfied and the accommodation of plants, which may be grown directly in the ground or in pots or other containers. It is important to remember that water must be easily available and that you must be able to hose down floor finishes and fittings.

There is a whole range of utility buildings, including garage, machinery and tool store, fuel store, storage for outdoor furniture and barbecues, greenhouse and cold frames, that need to be integrated into the garden efficiently and unobtrusively. If possible, you should group such structures to make them more in scale with the external spaces, to limit the number of paths, to facilitate the provision of water and electricity, and to lessen the need for screening. You could perhaps create a service area for the garden, containing these buildings as well as the compost heap, storage for pots, bins for soil mixes and other ancillary features. Better still, make use of an old outbuilding.

Whatever the options, always try to avoid having utility buildings dotted all over the place, and use them if you can to make a positive contribution to the pleasure of the garden. Grow a climber over the garden shed, give it an elegant window or a classical porch, exploit its walls to support a closely trimmed shed-shaped yew. Give your fruitcage a lift with elegant posts and a graceful timber roof. Provide your greenhouse with a fretted bargeboard or ridge, and add decorative finials. Build the garage as a positive feature, an eyecatcher, with a generous roof and in

Classical temples (which are available in reproduction from several manufacturers of landscape ornament) make useful focal points. This one, a temple of Aeolus originally designed by Sir William Chambers in the early 19th century, rises as a high accent in a woodland garden, drawing curious visitors towards it. The hill, planted with *Magnolia x soulangiana,* is a pretty feature in itself. But with this simple temple on top, it becomes more – a presiding feature, a place of account in the garden.

A ring of water (*right*)

In this robust enclosure, in the Generalife garden, Spain, walls and paving focus on the central fountain, which itself is aligned with the steps and fountain beyond. The enclosure is further reinforced by the trees arching overhead. Note the way in which the walls have channels along their tops conveying water – an interesting device that could be used in a garden on a much smaller scale.

A garden in a passage *(right)*

Enclosures can be formed with a minimum of means. Although this tiled passageway is enclosed by the structure of the building, the small conifers in pots make a secondary enclosure, a focus within the overall space in which to pause and look to either side.

materials sympathetic to the house. Or, if it must be the cheapest possible shed, screen it with a fine hedge. Surround the oil-tank with trelliswork laden with honeysuckle. Unite the structures with coordinated paintwork in a colour that blends well with the background and harmonizes with the colours of nearby flowers. Turn utility into beauty and banish all ugliness.

A building for a seat (right)

Seats make an excellent excuse for a fine building. This pavilion at Old Westbury Gardens on Long Island, New York, is well-proportioned and beautifully built in brick with stucco dressings and a tiled roof. It makes a quiet and dignified accent within the space, and a secluded vantage point from which to view the garden. Note the subtlety of the roof line and the steep slope to compensate for a diminishing perspective.

Rustic elegance (below)

This thatched garden house is a stylistic hybrid. Thoroughly rustic are the supporting columns, which are made of tree trunks, and the thatched roof. In complete contrast is the more polite style of the windows, with their pointed Gothic glazing bars. The combination is superb, creating a fantasy under the flowering pear trees in the orchard. The building admirably serves its dual purpose of garden room and eyecatcher.

A trelliswork arbour

A magnificent octagonal arbour at Charleston, South Carolina, provides both focus and pausing place on a path that would otherwise seem too long. The structure is beautifully detailed, the rail at the top of the diagonal trelliswork corresponding neatly with the lower level of the arches. This design eloquently demonstrates the importance of the roof: the lightly curved ribs give it a spring, creating much more life and interest than straight ribs would have done.

The glasshouse revival

Since the mid-1970s there has been a revival in the building of ornamental conservatories. No longer does a conservatory have to be a crudely assembled glazed lean-to, nor do you have to have an expensive custom-built structure to achieve something more elegant. This example is a pre-fabricated low-maintenance structure with an ogee section roof. Such conservatories can be freestanding or, if space demands and structure permits, attached to the side of the house.

A place of relaxation

This Victorian alcove arbour shows another way of giving shelter to a seat and at the same time creating an attractive focus. First, an alcove was built in durable brick, which was then rendered and painted. A trellis was constructed on the inside to form a backing to a semi-circular seat. Around the opening of the alcove is a wire structure beautifully fashioned, which supports climbing roses. It may not be easy to obtain such high-quality wirework today, but you could use a trellis arch as a satisfactory alternative. The rest of the structure would be simple enough to construct.

WATER

The ability of water to support life and to cleanse away dirt or waste has made it a symbol of spiritual life and purification in every religion. Even though we may not care to give much weight to such ideas today, water has a deep cultural and philosophical hold on us. Its aesthetic attraction is also immensely strong. Still water disposes the mind to contemplation. Water in movement, tumbling in cascades, eddying, surging or broadening in concentric ripples, stimulates the eye with a flash of light or a dancing sparkle. Water helps us get closer to nature – a current and necessary preoccupation of urban society. Even the smallest garden pond can support a microcosm of the natural world which we can observe with fascination, season after season.

In the garden, water draws attention to itself as no other feature can. Reflections in still water bring the brightness of the sky down to ground level, inverting the image of the opposite bank. Or there may be no reflection, just a mysterious blackness, in which only the darting glint of a fish is seen, or where an opening waterlily stands out in vivid contrast. Moving water, however, refracts and reflects light with such rapidity that although the form of a cascade or jet is always the same, in detail it is always different. Such life and energy is enhanced by sound and feel.

Water can be used in a great variety of ways, with the same source supplying different needs. It may lie in an isolated pool, in a canal, or perhaps define the boundary as a moat. It may give shape to a level in the bottom of a valley, imitating nature. It may rush down a rocky cascade, or fall in sheets over a high waterfall. It may soar up in the air in a thick column, or form a lacework of intersecting jets. Or it may be just a thin stream arching down into a lead tank. It can give breadth to a space, or draw the eye as a focus. It can dampen the air with a mist, and it can support waterside plants with rich foliage and textures that cannot be found elsewhere in the garden.

You must analyse what you want to do with the water and how the site helps or hinders this intention. A pool for swimming must be deeper than one that only has to support waterlilies. For reflections, you must consider the relative levels of the water surface, the height of the rim or the bank that contains the pool, and the height of your eye above the water surface. Water at ground level or slightly raised in a formal pool, with a low angle of reflection, appears more lively then one down in a pit, which can easily appear dull and stagnant.

Water must be considered as part of the structure of the garden, at the time of the initial planning. Its location and character will depend partly upon the levels of the site. A natural-looking pond must be sited in what appears to be a natural hollow, otherwise it will look wrong. A more formal body of water, however, may look perfectly satisfactory at a higher position. Consider the distance of the pool from the house: a natural pond is unlikely to look comfortable close to buildings unless you are skilfully playing on the contrast.

You must think of access and paths around or over the water, whether a bridge might be necessary and, if so, what are its visual implications. Perhaps stepping stones will suffice if they can be

Throughout history, water has been symbolic of life and fertility – a link powerfully confirmed by this fountain of the many-breasted Diana of Ephesus in the Renaissance garden of the Villa d'Este. Such an exuberant, joyful use of water might inspire us today.

A grand fountain *(left)*

Freestanding fountains that make use of sculpture have to balance the volume of water against the strength of sculptural form. Frequently, the volume of the jet is too small to stand up to the size and ebullience of the sculpture. The Pyramid at Versailles, shown here, cleverly solves the problem: when the fountain is turned on, the sculpture is masked by the cascade. This fountain is now available in reproduction.

made reasonalby safe and positioned at the correct intervals. Such access must be tied in with routes elsewhere. Pools will require cleaning, and a large pond or lake may need dredging from time to time, which implies access for heavy machinery.

Safety is a critical consideration, particularly for a family with babies or young children, who must be physically protected from the risk of drowning – perhaps by a temporary barrier. Even adults are at risk if they slip on ice or mud, so hard surfaces should have a slight fall to prevent water from accumulating. Another problem is the fall of leaves in autumn, which invariably end up in your pool. A net over the pool can prevent this, but unless discreetly detailed it can look unpleasant. You may find it more satisfactory to dispense with the net and dredge out the leaves every so often. If the leaves are allowed to silt up the pool, it will stagnate, become acid, and support little else but blanket weed. Ideally the water should be kept clear and sparkling, either by natural drainage and replenishment, or by recycling with a pump. It can also be kept clear by encouraging a balanced ecology, with oxygenating plants such as Canadian pondweed or water milfoil, together with snails and fish.

You must also think of the edge of the pool. If it is to look natural, the water should find its own level within the enclosing ground. If the ground has been shaped to impound the water, ensure that the embankment on the downhill side is really broad: otherwise it will resemble the rim of a container, giving the pool an artificial look. Waterside plants will help merge the pool into the surrounding land form. Trees also help the transition: alders, birches and willows would colonize naturally, or you can use more ornamental species such as the serviceberries *(Amelanchier)*, the tulip tree *(Liriodendron)* or the Caucasian wingnut *(Pterocarya fraxinifolia)* if space permits.

The shape of the more formal pools, in general, is better for being simple. Circles, ellipses, regular polygons and rectangles tend to make the most satisfactory shapes, but you must take into account the scale, shape and character of the surrounding space. A pool that is generous in scale, and tied into the enclosing patterns of paving and planting, will look inevitable and therefore pleasing.

Pool edges are often detailed to overhang the water, creating a shadow that obscures the true level (which may fall and rise with evaporation and refilling), and masking the scum line. But if you do this, reinforce the pool structure so that expanding ice in winter does not fracture the surround. Alternatively, you can make the surround without an overhang and with a smooth sloping wall so that the ice lifts upwards as it expands. Edges can be raised to lift the level of the water, but this will throw the edge into prominence. In the past, raised edges were made with beautiful mouldings, some of which are imitated today in artificial stone. Alternatively, the edge may be at ground level, where architectural elaboration is not necessary. Square stone slabs, perhaps with plants growing in the cracks, can look attractive; or, in a more precise setting, brickwork in various profiles may be suitable. If the pond is lower than ground level, a stepped edge can look pleasing, and perhaps be used as a shelf for large pots.

A shallow pool with a strongly figured or coloured lining will impinge on the eye as strongly as any reflection. This can produce some intriguing double images. If, however, you prefer your reflections to be unambiguous, make your pool deeper.

Fountains must be generous in scale, but related to their space. If the fountain is elaborate, make everything else subservient to it. If it is simple, tone the paving details and flower colour down to suit, making a quiet incident of it. Plan for the sound: catch and reflect it. At the same time, beware of the wind, which may blow the spray out of the pool; keep your fountain sheltered, or in a wide pool. Locate moving water where it can catch the sun, sparkling through the spray, making rainbows perhaps. Make a fountain that will thrill you.

Aquatic abundance

Waterside vegetation has a lushness not to be found elsewhere in the garden. Leaves tend to grow broader and longer, creating striking foliage textures. Perhaps the most dramatic are the vast leaves of *Gunnera manicata*, *Rheum* and *Peltiphyllum*. In contrast are the thin leaves of the rushes and sedges and waterside grasses. In this planting around a modest bridge, *Alchemilla mollis* and irises occupy the foreground, with ferns growing on the far side. In the pool itself is *Aponogeton distachyus*, the fragrant water hawthorn.

An oval pool

This oval pool at Dumbarton Oaks, Washington D.C., is quite shallow, so that the lining of precisely cut paving stone can be clearly seen through the water. At the same time, a silhouette of trees against a bright sky is visible in the still reflection, creating a curious double image. This part of the garden, known as the Lover's Lane Pool, is shaped like an open-air theatre, with terraces at one end (foreground) and a row of columns along one side, linked together by a looping chain to support plants.

A broad sweep of water *(above)*

There is no reason why a swimming pool should not make a positive contribution to the garden in the same way as any other ornamental pool. This particularly successful Californian example by Thomas Church is contained by the superbly shaped broad trees and a distant railing. The generous breadth of the pool and of its paving echo the estuarine landscape, where sky and water meet and merge. The central sculpture, by Adaline Kent, relieves the flatness of the pool and serves as an island on which swimmers can play or sunbathe.

Water geometry *(right)*

In this formal water garden at Longwood, Pennsylvania, the pools are laid out in a symmetrical plan, and are edged with ivy. Each quarter has a fence of narrow jets arching inwards, and in the central pool is a thicker, vertical jet echoing the form of the surrounding trees. The composition is reinforced with urns and stone baskets of fruit. Calmness prevails when the fountains are turned off, and lightness and sparkle when they are on.

SCULPTURAL FORMS

Sculpture has always exerted a compelling kind of magic, perhaps because it is a figment of the mind made solid. It elicits subconscious feelings that are hard to identify, let alone describe, ranging from strong emotions to peaceful contemplation.

In the past, at least in Western culture, sculpture has been created generally for a specific purpose, perhaps for religious reasons, perhaps to commemorate worthy people, or to tell stories. But it has seldom been the literal idea alone that has made a sculpture outstanding. The way the material has been fashioned, the relationship of voids to masses, the quality of the surface or the applied decoration, all combining to support and ennoble the literal theme, are what makes the sculpture arresting. It may even be a stretching or distortion of reality that holds the eye and stimulates the brain.

During the 20th century, artists and sculptors have explored abstract themes, and we are now perhaps attuned to look at sculpture in a more open-minded way – to enjoy pure form or texture or the flow of space. With a knowledge of non-Western traditions, we should now be able to enjoy sculpture or sculptural form in a wider range of manifestations than the merely representational – from the accident of a sea-tossed spar thrown up on the beach to a precisely engineered mobile in stainless steel.

Sculptural forms complement the garden. They are the projection of human personality into the realm of nature, an expression of the guiding hand that controls the garden, making it a place of pleasure. Sculpture can either make a focal emphasis that draws different parts of the garden together, or it can be an incidental accent that illuminates a corner. It can either dominate its space dramatically or offer a subtle hint of human presence.

The materials and workmanship of a painstakingly created sculpture stand in total contrast to plant forms and colours. So does the texture of a less self-conscious sculptural form, such as a pile of flat pebbles, a group of pots or an old staddle stone. The sculpture remains constant as the plants change and flower with the seasons. As leaves flutter in the wind, a sculpture remains still, untroubled and a reminder of peace. Yet its appearance is not entirely static: it quickly changes with the play of light and shade, and slowly weathers as it acquires the dignity of years.

When considering the use of sculptural elements in the garden, you should bear in mind the overall character of the garden, its spaces and views, planting textures and colours, and the nature of the light. In an intricate formal garden, a highly worked, finely carved sculpture in rich materials may fit in well. In a casual planting of large shrubs, something robust may be more appropriate. The whiteness of Italian marble, with its hard edges, may be both too bright and too delicate to stand under northern skies. Although the marble will weather to a degree, it will never acquire the subtle patina of a limestone, which carves more crudely but which will look rather more at home.

It is important to think of the background as part of the overall composition. The verticals of grass or bamboo may make it difficult to perceive a sculpture that relies on a particularly vertical emphasis. A background texture of *Fatsia* could all too easily swamp a small sculpture. Consider also its relationship to normal eye-level. Raised too high and seen against the sky, it may appear as an almost colourless silhouette; sited too low, it will escape attention. Think too of the scale: a small sculpture in a large space will be lost, and even a piece that looks large in a gallery will look a lot smaller once it is outside. But do not be concerned about the space being too small: if the sculpture is good enough, it may well benefit from appearing larger than it is.

Sculpture draws the eye, so use it to lead both body and mind around the garden. Place it statically at the end of a vista, or consider a more dynamic grouping where it counterbalances a strong planting. Use it as a pivot between two spaces or as a distant eyecatcher to point up a view. Or let the sculpture merely draw attention to itself, sited in an alcove or bower. Even a normally prosaic object acquires a significance with careful siting.

Sculpture must be used with discretion. If it is too fussy, it will compete with the plants, or the view. If there are too many pieces of similar size and character, they will fight each other for attention. One piece should dominate, or all the pieces should be treated as a single group. Sculpture should enhance the composition, supporting the overall theme – if it distracts, it is badly sited.

Traditionally in Western gardens, figurative sculpture has been widely used to conjure ideas. Today, antique statues may be prohibitively expensive, and there are few satisfactory reproductions in artificial stone, bronze or lead. Although some sculptors working in a figurative idiom indulge in the sentimental to appeal to an undiscerning market, others are producing some wonderfully vital works. Garden-owners with the means to employ such sculptors might consider embellishing their gardens with their own thematic programmes as patrons in the past sometimes did – surely a more exciting prospect than collecting whatever antiques happen to be available.

For the less well-endowed, perhaps an inventive use of an *objet trouvé* will give strength to the structure of the garden, or a lift to a sequestered corner. A rock, crude in form but mighty in presence, can make an awesome focus in a small space. A discarded stone door-frame and pediment can be an interesting illusion in a blank wall. There are also many artificial stone ornaments such as pineapples and urns, which, if adequately swathed in plants so that they are not examined too closely, can lend excitement. Functional artefacts such as seats, pyramids for climbing plants, even pots, also have a three-dimensional form that may be enjoyed as sculpture. So too has topiary, which has the singular advantage of

being inexpensive, even though it takes time to grow. Moreover, even in their natural form, many plants are highly sculptural, from the slim upright shape of *Libocedrus decurrens*, the incense cedar, to the horizontal line of *Viburnum plicatum tomentosum* (doublefile viburnum) or the spiky rosettes of yucca.

Perhaps the most exciting contrast in the garden is provided by modern abstract sculpture. Our unfamiliarity with such strange forms makes it hard to understand their purpose or message. But that, in a way, is their strength. They make us curious. Although they may seem outlandish indoors, when sited in a garden, framed by the familiar colour and texture of leaves, they somehow seem much more acceptable. In gardens it seems easier to take a dispassionate view, to accept abstract sculptures for their colour and texture, to take an interest in their peculiar forms. There is a certain irony that the garden, steeped in tradition and the past, should provide such a satisfactory setting for an art form so obviously groping for the future.

A frame for a staircase (left)

These columns topped by little statues at Iford Manor, Wiltshire, are supported on the backs of lions which look inward toward each other. Standing forward from the retaining walls, they create a space and suggest a pause before you ascend the steps.

A statue in winter (right)

An elegant Bacchus holding a bunch of grapes. Sited below the spreading canopy of a tree, the statue is treated as an incident in the garden, rather than a main focus.

A line of animals (below)

Hounds cast in bronze prowl across a lawn, adding a sense of movement.

An interplay of volumes (left)

A sculptural garden that wittily transforms classical themes, with timber features imitating stone. The central axis is focused on a timber arch designed to resemble rusticated frosted stonework. Behind is a rocky grotto.

A garden urn (page 101)

An urn with a beautifully modelled lid makes a punctuation mark in a garden composition. It is supported by a group of white peonies in front and a clematis which climbs around it.

Reflective surfaces

"Narcissus" by William Pye is made from polished stainless steel tube, which contrasts not only with the colour and texture of the foliage but also with its forms. The structure is precise, clearly defining its own implicit space. The craning wobble, as the top section looks down on the bottom section, introduces an element of uncertainty – perhaps humour. Glinting in the bright sun, the sculpture invites our curiosity and speculation.

STRUCTURE WITH PLANTS

For many gardeners, the growth and flowering of plants is the culmination of their work in the garden. Undoubtedly, flowers have an astonishing beauty that cannot be matched by any work of mankind. However, it is all too easy to forget that they also form part of a larger composition, and that their use merits the same kinds of design considerations as any other elements in the garden. The sensitive gardener will place flowers so that their beauty is enhanced by sympathetic surroundings. A background of confusing shapes and colours can make flowers difficult to see, whereas they will always stand out well against the green of a hedge.

The shape and proportions of the bed are also important. A narrow outline does not permit the flowers to be grouped in dense masses, and thus they appear straggly. A firm edge looks better than an untidy mingling of bed and gravel or bed and lawn, and the occasional plant flopping over the line is the foil that proves the point. A convoluted outline will only distract by its illogical form.

Equally important are the other species and varieties in the composition, particularly in terms of colour and flowering period. A herbaceous border whose flowers are coordinated for colour and timed for a climactic week in, say, August, can be sensational.

More durable than flowers are the plants with outstanding form or foliage, often evergreen, that make the permanent accents in a composition. Slim, upright conifers can be used as visual punctuation marks. Many types of evergreen can give shape and solidity, or anchor the corner of a bed. Such plants must be used with discretion, otherwise they will lose their point; but without them, planting compositions can look bland.

Plants can be used to make patterns on the ground. An interesting tradition is the "knot", in which geometric figures outlined in one kind of plant such as marjoram or rue are interlaced with figures outlined in another, such as germander or santolina. A more sophisticated development is the parterre, with box as the edging plant and the spaces filled in with coloured sands and gravels, or perhaps with flowers. Such designs give unity to spaces of almost any size and, provided that the area is relatively small, they do not present a maintenance problem; however, as soon as bedding plants are introduced, the labour required for maintenance becomes considerable.

Another form of ground pattern is the maze: an ancient idea which in its simplest form is cut in turf. Renaissance mazes appear to have been made most frequently with plants such as hyssop, santolina or thyme. These are low enough to permit the maze to be treated as a puzzle rather than just a confusion, and they smell delightfully as the maze-traveller passes by.

The turf maze is simple enough to make once you have worked out the routes on paper. You cut the paths in the turf and then fill them in with sand or gravel. Alternatively, you can line them in brick to make them more durable. For low-hedged mazes, box is perhaps the best plant to use for easy maintenance – most of the better-smelling edgings such as rosemary and lavender are apt to die off in the winter in cold, wet climates. For the taller-hedged mazes, any hedging plant that takes clipping will be appropriate, but it is important to plant the hedges far enough apart to permit proper growth.

Hedges are one of the most important structures of the garden, making solid, impenetrable divisions and giving privacy, freedom from wind and a better microclimate. They can give strength and unity to the garden, as well as a sense of style. The smooth, dark greens of yew or cypress are calm and restful and an excellent foil for subtle flower colours or for the free-arching forms of flowering shrubs. Hedges require regular maintenance, but for the slower-growing varieties this is not time-consuming in comparison with other gardening operations.

The tightest hedges are those made with plants that clip well and stay compact – for example, beech and hornbeam, or evergreens like box, privet, yew, cypress and holly. However, the species must be selected with care, with an eye to the conditions of the site. Yew can be badly burnt by the wind when young, and will not tolerate poorly drained ground. Some conifers such as cypress cannot regenerate from old wood, so they cannot be cut right back if they get too large. In areas of heavy snowfall, evergreen hedges are liable to be crushed if too much snow is allowed to pile up on top, although you could mitigate this effect by cutting the sides to a batter. The quicker-growing hedges, such as *Thuja* or *Lonicera*, may have the advantage of a rapid screening effect, but they also require increased maintenance.

Hedges can also be grown with plants that do not require regular clipping. Suitable shrubs, such as berberis, pyracantha or various roses, may be grown close together in a line and then, with judicious pruning, more or less left to find their own shape. They do not have the architectural strength of the clipped hedge, nor the height (unless they take up a great deal of space on the ground), but they are useful for making a softer line.

Hedges take time, and a quicker division can be made by training climbers over a high fence. The reviled chain-link fence makes an excellent frame for an evergreen covering of ivy. With a better-looking support such as a pergola or an arbour, you can use deciduous climbers flowering high off the ground and drawing the eye up. Alternatively, climbers can be used to decorate trees and shrubs, giving them an unexpected late flowering after their own flowers are over.

Another alternative to the hedge is the fruit tree trained onto a wire structure as a cordon or espalier. Fruit trees can also make three-dimensional shapes, such as pyramids or goblets. Pears are the most amenable plants, although apples and more tender fruits such as peaches and figs can also be trained.

On a larger scale, trees may be pleached to make a very tall hedge (sometimes known as a "pole" or "palisade" hedge), or perhaps they can be worked to form a tunnel. Pleaching is started on a frame of wire or bamboo. Each year, the branches are heavily pruned back to selected stumps at a predetermined level, each more or less pointing in the right direction. When mature, the hedge can be clipped or pruned more like a normal hedge. Often, the lower parts of the trunks are kept free of branches. Lime and

A chequerboard pattern *(right)*

A simple but striking ground pattern of red and yellow tulips, enclosed within a shaped yew hedge, shows that an ordered arrangement of plants growing in their natural form can be just as decorative as the more contrived forms of trained fruit or sculpted hedges.

Cones and squares *(page 105)*

Box trimmed into neat cones and surrounded by squares of low box hedging is repeated to give a unifying ground texture. Such repetition and clipping of plants open up many possibilities for interesting decoration – not only at ground level but, in the form of hedges and topiary, in the vertical dimension as well.

hornbeam are the most frequently used trees for this purpose, although for smaller structures, pears, apples and some sorbus are equally suitable.

Topiary uses the tree as living sculpture rather than as green architecture. Most topiary is carried out in yew or box, but you could also use thorns or Portugal laurels, which can be clipped to wide umbrellas. Ideally, the tree is shaped in a way that relates to its surroundings, and it is important to avoid too many highly elaborate specimens, or they will conflict with each other. You can make shapes that are not only beautiful but also give a sense of excitement and achievement.

Living geometry *(above)*

These smooth, shaven hemispheres of golden yew contrast with the pinks of *Phlox* and *Dimorphotheca*. The yew offers interesting colour variations, a fine texture, and above all a powerful sculptural presence.

A well-planned border *(below)*

This curved border is dominated by the blues of the delphiniums and *Thalictrum* rising in the rear. These are set off by the yellows of day lilies, purple geraniums and white daisies. Box cones give weight to the seat.

A tunnel of trees

This pleached avenue in a French
garden has become almost a tunnel as
each side leans in towards the other.
Grass grows satisfactorily only down
the centre of the avenue, where there
are no drips from overhanging
branches. The central grass strip is thus
flanked by gravel paths which
emphasize the linear thrust towards the
door of the house.

MOVABLES

The garden that is to fulfil all its owner's expectations, making the best use of the site, and coordinated for colour and flowering period, requires meticulous planning. But it would be a dry kind of perfection that made no allowance for some flexibility, for the possibility of local rearrangements within the overall structure – perhaps following the cycle of the seasons, or perhaps to accommodate changing preferences. Movable containers provide a means for such minor adjustments, giving the garden an additional distinction. Clay pots, timber planting cases and the like may be used to add a particular colour to a view or to change the shape of a space. Containers full of plants are remarkably versatile: they can bring greenery onto a balcony or a concrete-bound backyard, or they can embellish stately flights of steps or parterres&

Clay pots come in a variety of designs and sizes. Wherever possible they should be used in groups rather than singly, as they can look ridiculously small on their own when surrounded by open space. The clay colour can vary greatly – subtle pinks or creamy clays can be found – but all too often it is distressingly orange, although this becomes less aggressive with weathering. As a general rule, pots should have a relatively simple design that does not distract from the line and beauty of the plants that they contain. The big drawback of unglazed clayware, however, is its susceptibility to frost damage. Expensive pots should be taken in over winter, or protected with a covering, if severe frost is likely.

A vast range of cement-based artificial stone containers are also available. Many are handsomely modelled, although the cheaper versions may have surface inconsistencies and mould-marks. They do not have the subtle weathering characteristics of stone, but, given time, they can be improved by invading mosses and lichens. Cement-based stones tend to lack the finish of hand-worked stone, but casting techniques have improved dramatically over the last few years. Such containers are perfectly satisfactory for many situations, particularly when smothered with plants or located so that they are not subject to close scrutiny.

On a larger scale are the timber planting cases which can hold enough soil to support a small tree. Traditionally, these were planted out with tender trees such as citrus, and were hauled out of a conservatory for the summer to line the edges of paths and parterres. They come in a range of sizes and the better ones are lined with an impervious container to protect the wood. When used formally, such cases are large enough to have some architectural impact in the garden.

Plants grown in containers require much more attention than those grown in the ground. The container must have drainage holes in the bottom, otherwise the plants would become waterlogged. However, this does mean that drainage is very fast, and, particularly with unglazed clayware, there is water loss by evaporation through the container sides. Thus, in summer the plants need daily watering. They also need weekly feeding, as the nutrients tend to drain out with the water. But for the pleasure that plants in containers provide, and for an additional layer of form and colour that reinforces the design, the extra trouble is well worth taking.

Containers offer plenty of scope for improvising with discarded objects of various kinds. Old chimney pots or watertanks, disused sinks, barrels, even shoes, may be filled with plants. An old stone capital hollowed-out, or an ornate well-head, might be used as a raised pool or to support a small tree. Such adaptions introduce an element of the unexpected, a surprise that can highlight the beauty of an object hitherto unconsidered. They make useful accents, but should be used sparingly. Make sure that the salvaged item is a worthwhile piece and that it will fit beneficially into the place that you have in mind. There is no merit in using an object just because it is available: its contribution to the garden should always be a positive one.

A tulip pot *(page 109)*

This tall clay pot by Monica Young, as much a fine piece of sculpture as a useful container, resembles an unfolding tulip as the light catches the graceful lines and curling rim. The pot makes an excellent vertical accent for a small-scale space.

Subtle decoration *(above)*

The expensive swelling of this comfortably rotund pot contrasts with nearby foliage textures. A delicate pattern incised around the shoulders and waist gives the container added interest at close-quarters, but without distracting from its satisfying line.

While plant containers may be moved around for aesthetic effect, chairs and tables may be movable for functional reasons. The garden today is often conceived as an outdoor room which provides a place to relax, somewhere to sit and read, entertain, dine or sunbathe, and furniture for such activities must be practical, comfortable and portable. As the sun crosses the sky, casting ever-changing shadows, your chair must move too if you wish to remain cool in the shade or be warmed by the sun's rays. But furniture that is light enough to be moved around must be tidied away at the end of the day. It will not usually be robust enough to stay outside in all weathers: it will need to be taken indoors if it rains, and stored away over the winter. Thus, some ingenious lightweight folding chairs, beds and tables have been developed for the garden. Most of these are based on light metal or timber frames with canvas or similar materials stretched over. When choosing such furniture, you need to consider not only storage but also line, comfort and ease of operation. It is important to look closely at the materials in daylight: do not rely on the colours printed in a leaflet or catalogue.

There are, of course, other ways of providing for your ease. A hammock, for example, is the acme of summer leisure, as you doze in the dappled shade, intoxicated with the smell of lime or *Philadelphus*. The trees that give support are also an essential part of the image – without the leafy canopy overhead, the metal frames with which some hammocks are equipped can never give the same feeling.

Seats, and to a lesser degree tables, are the most obviously required garden furniture. Often, they will be fixed permanently in a favoured suntrap or at the end of a short vista. Permanent seating is always useful in the garden, as there is likely to be a limit to the storage space available for movable seating, and clearing up at the end of the day is always tedious.

There are interesting variations of the permanent seat that make it easier to use, particularly in relation to the weather. You could incorporate the seat in a little building, such as a mock temple, or under a rustic thatch. Some seats are given a simple pitched roof in canvas, erected on a frame attached to the seat itself. Stone seats may be detailed with a recessed area to take cushions, which you can easily take in at the end of the day. Another interesting semi-permanent seat is the kind with a wheel at one end and lifting handles at the other, in the manner of a wheelbarrow.

Movable seats and tables have been traditionally made not only in wicker or cane – hard to store but light and comfortable – but also in cast iron, which can be left outside at least during the summer. There is also a modern seat that uses steel mesh supported on a metal frame, combining comfort with an excellent texture.

If possible, movable furniture should be grouped where it will not impinge too much on the principal views around the garden. It is a good idea to site it in an area of partial enclosure, perhaps formed as a bay between flower beds, or gently closed in by small shrubs in pots. Ideally, the furniture should be placed against some kind of tall background: generally, we find it more comfortable to look out from a spot that is sheltered behind than from a site that is totally exposed. The same principle applies to the siting of permanent seating.

Movable structures may also be required for shade. Whereas tents may not be considered entirely practicable today, umbrellas make a useful alternative. Although many designs available look little better than makeshift, there are also large, off-white canvas umbrellas available, which are generous in scale and pleasant to look at.

Another useful portable item of equipment is the barbecue: there is an essential pleasure in the succulent smells of outdoor cooking. However, there seems little point in erecting a permanent cooking apparatus if its use is merely intermittent – especially if it leaves greasy brick and timberwork that needs frequent scrubbing. Good portable barbecues are available, and one that

White and grey (*above*)

This fine old lead tank has been converted to a new use, now serving as a handsome container for spring tulips. With its grey patina and simple raised pattern it makes its presence felt quietly but firmly, creating a modest point of interest behind a flower bed.

An antique chimney (*right*)

Old chimneypots have long been used as accents, sometimes planted up, sometimes on their own. This one has a strong sculptural quality and forms a pivot around which the path is turned. Rich foliage textures below create a firm visual base.

can be cleared away and cleaned in a sink seems eminently more practicable than a permanent structure.

Movable items for the garden have an aesthetic importance that should not be underestimated. Containers draw the eye by virtue of their use as temporary accents. Furniture is in the foreground because it is there to be used. After so much effort to make your garden a better place, it would be a pity to spoil it with ill-considered accessories.

A temporary display

A blue hyacinth in an old blue-and-white teapot is an utter delight. Here, the curves of the petals are on exactly the same scale as the daisies that embellish the pot. Matching plants to container in this way is one of the secrets behind a successful improvisation. When creating such effects, you must use your discretion: overdoing a clever idea will spoil the treat.

Victoriana

Cast iron was a popular material for garden furniture in the 19th century. Once the mould was made, it was relatively inexpensive to produce any number of castings. Now such items have considerable value as antiques, sadly putting them beyond the means of many garden-owners. If you manage to acquire an authentic cast-iron seat like this one, treat it with respect and give it the setting it deserves – here, a sea of *Anthemis* beneath a canopy of *Rosa* 'Nevada'. Beware of ill-considered reproductions, particularly if they are in aluminium.

Chippendale elegance

This seat made in a "Chinese Chippendale" design illustrates the best in garden ornament. It is generous, wide and comfortable, and, being painted in a subtle light blue-grey, it does not visually leap forward as white-painted furniture does, but rests with dignity, enfolded in a background of shrubs and roses. While such a seat may be relocated as the garden develops, it is more likely to become a permanent feature. It will need looking after, with periodic repainting. A well-drained stone base will prevent water from seeping up the legs and starting a rot.

CATALOGUE
OF
GARDEN
FEATURES

GARDEN STRUCTURE

The built structure of the garden is the framework that determines the spaces and proportions: an organization within which the plans may flourish in overflowing abundance. The choice of materials and construction can impose an overall character on the garden, which may blend or contrast with the surrroundings. A good structure lasts longer than most garden plants, providing a relatively constant form that supports the changing schemes of each generation. This form is just as important as the plants in helping to make the garden a memorable place.

EDGINGS

Edgings emphasize parts of the garden at ground level by a narrow band of contrasting texture, colour or shadow. A uniform edging treatment can bring neatness and unity to a design – a common denominator that makes separate beds part of the same family. More practically, edgings prevent earth from falling out of a bed and can make mowing easier by separating plants and grass. Their treatment should be in harmony with other structures, and consistent throughout each space.

In this edging, blue brick contrasts with the paler colour of reconstituted stone.

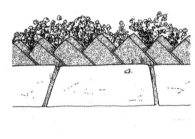
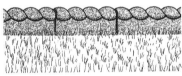

Two edging patterns: dogtooth brickwork (top) and "ropework" tiles (above).

Dwarf box makes a versatile edging requiring just one or two clips a year.

Stout timber edging to a raised bed makes a convenient seat. You must treat the timber with preservative.

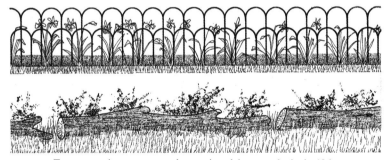

Two contrasting treatments: drawn wire edging, popular in the 19th century (top); and rough logs, for woodland gardens (above).

Parallel rows of bricks with an ivy infill at Dumbarton Oaks. You could also use box, or even bulbs or annuals.

Here, a low green hedge of yew fronts a retaining wall, emphasizing the path's geometry. Other evergreens would serve equally well.

PATHS AND PAVINGS

Paths connect places, or lead you on from scene to scene. Their details may encourage you to speed toward your destination or to take your time, admiring as you go a distant view or a nearby flower. Like edgings, paths can give unity to the design if they exploit a consistent material or pattern. Vary the material and the detail at the point where you want to change the mood. Paving is a versatile element that exerts a powerful influence on the way you see and enjoy your garden.

A delightful path formed by maintaining a close-mown strip among long grasses.

Reconstituted stone alternates with gravel, giving a stepping stone effect.

More stepping stones – of wood sections cut from a tree trunk.

Railway ties (sleepers) across a gravel path, in which thrift is colonizing.

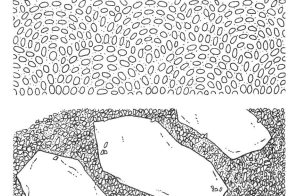

Cobbles and setts can be laid in fan shapes (top). Stepping stones (below) are a less formal treatment.

Rain as well as sun brings pleasure: here, stones of varying shapes and sizes glisten after a shower.

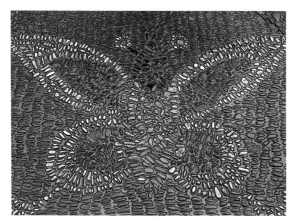

A butterfly depicted in carefully selected pebbles of various colours on a path in Peking.

Rectangular stones make a strong pattern, filled in by round pebbles.

Brickwork, fitting tighter than pebbles, gives a smoother texture. The pattern may be dynamic (top) or static (above).

Concrete setts in a circular pattern: you could use granite setts, bricks or cobbles for a similar effect.

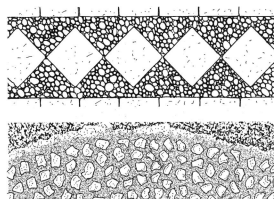

Stones turned through 45° and laid in a pebble matrix (top); and pebbles set roughly in mortar.

A chequerwork of flint and stone uses local materials. (Wiltshire, England)

A high-velocity path of bricks laid in "stretcher bond". Bricks laid across would slow the path down.

Rectangular stone slabs, laid uncoursed, make one of the best paved surfaces.

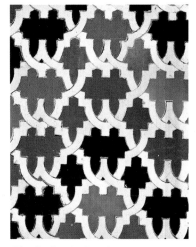

The rippling rhythm of a Moorish terrace, superbly crafted.

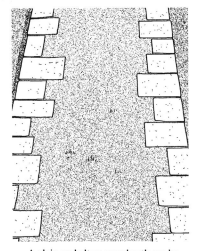

A plain asphalt or gravel path can be improved by a stone edging.

Cut stone flags make an elegant but relaxed path with a diamond pattern.

Stone surfaces can be enhanced by small plants: these steps are frilled with *Erigeron mucronatus*.

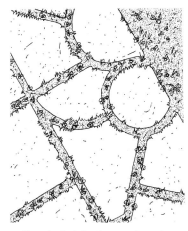

Grass in the joints between irregular stones can be mown for a netted effect.

Ancient thin bricks laid on edge have a warm and friendly, well-used texture.

Slabs treated with special paints make a colourful court. You may have to repaint as the surface wears.

A pattern of small concrete slabs relieved by irises. Not for walking on, but a pretty way to treat a bed.

Stepping stones slow you down: use them among plants to be admired closely.

Big flat polygonal stones make a combined path, bridge and edge in this Japanese garden.

STEPS AND STAIRS

Because they are designed specifically for human movement, steps have a consistent scale in all gardens. Their form may vary but the height of each riser is more or less the same all over the world. The bands of light and shade draw the eye up, underscoring each successive level. Ideally, steps are wide and generous: a steep, narrow stair may be suitable in a small area, but viewed from a distance it will look mean. Think of safety: slippery steps, long, unbroken flights or unprotected sides can lead to disaster.

An easy, safe, charming little stair of cobbles and stone risers. Stone balls give a hint of formality.

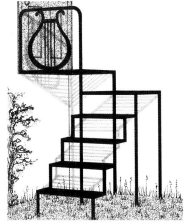

A light wrought-iron stair throws intriguing shadows on a wall.

Circular steps with a grass landing, designed by Lutyens (Great Dixter). The risers are decorated with *Erigeron mucronatus*.

Semi-circular steps present a simpler variation on the same theme. Here, the risers are colonized by a pretty *Campanula*.

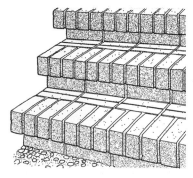

A brick stair with an overhanging nose that sharpens the definition.

A beautiful arrangement of stone risers and herringbone treads in thin bricks. (Campidoglio, Rome)

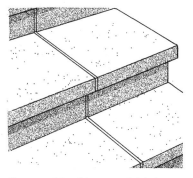

Cut stone slabs with stone or brick risers – a simple but elegant treatment.

Grass steps at Dumbarton Oaks continue the texture and colour of a lawn to the next level. Only suitable if there is little traffic.

At Hidcote, Gloucestershire, it is the risers that are green. The plant is *Cotoneaster congestus*, neatly trimmed.

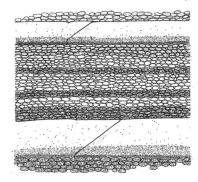

Ramp steps with stone risers, and a pattern of cobbles forming the treads.

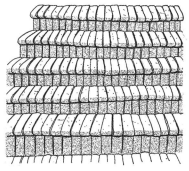

Thin tiles make pretty steps, but soggy leaves can make them slippery.

A change of colour in this path emphasizes the position of the steps – as do the tall pots.

A timber staircase with elegant thin balusters borrows support from a tree to climb a storey.

Steps of rough squared timber and gravel treads. If you wish, you can use textured concrete instead of wood.

Steps from tree trunks, bordered by fine-textured ground cover.

Logs again, set into gravel, with foliage providing important textural relief.

Logs on their sides are adequate in a woodland setting, but have a relatively short life.

An elegant ramp stair with water in a side channel to emphasize the rhythm.

Semi-circular cut stone steps. The shadow under the nosing improves their definition.

A fine stone flight with heathers and large shrubs which blur the edges.

Thick stone flags with a brick flanking wall set off by a beautiful red rose – a superb combination.

BALUSTRADES AND RAILINGS

The need to provide a safe edge for a high terrace has generated the balustrade. Whereas a parapet wall is satisfactory from a functional point of view, it may appear too heavy or too bland. The balustrade admits light between the balusters, so that it serves as a visual filter. It also introduces a rhythm that draws the eye along its length, unifying the composition of terraces and flights of steps. Railings serve the same end, but enclose more delicately, like a veil.

A Victorian pierced stone balustrade, with an urn accentuating the corner.

Each sweep of this rhythmically curved balustrade is dramatically reinforced by its shadow. (Peterhof, USSR)

Waisted stone balusters by Harold Peto for Iford Manor, Wiltshire.

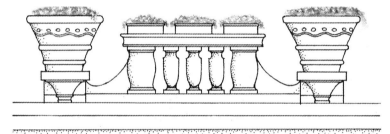

Short lengths of balustrade may alternate with large pots (top, Boboli Gardens, Florence). Above: a baluster with a fluted base.

A diagonally braced composition of steps and balustrades. (Italy)

A virtuoso pierced balustrade from India, reducing a slab of marble to a cobweb.

A pretty metal railing, its shadow as fascinating as the ironwork.

An 18th-century wrought-iron masterpiece by Robert Bakewell at Melbourne Hall, Derbyshire.

FENCES

Fences denote boundaries: a barrier to intruders. While they must clearly fulfil their functional role, they present opportunities to incorporate interesting textures into the design. The coarse textures of wattle or square trellis strengthen the sense of enclosure, although some fences can be so nearly transparent that space flows through. A repeated pattern of rustic poles can give unity to a space quite as well as the more sophisticated stone balustrade.

The texture of a simple garden trellis harmonizes with *Robinia pseudacacia*.

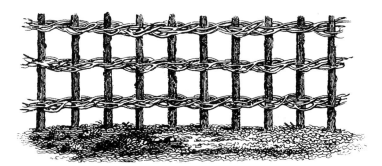

An unusual disembodied wattle fence from the 19th century, with hazel shoots woven around upright stakes.

Another Victorian curiosity: a hedge reduced to sprouting poles, with railings nailed across.

A cross-braced fence of large rustic poles is informal, simple and effective.

A covering of snow accentuates the form of a handsome timber fence, jointed and pegged.

A sturdy timber fence with a finial on the posts and rectangular windows offering a view beyond.

An iron fence, transparent, modest and stock-proof. This type of fence is typical of English parkland.

This timber fence, with a jagged rhythm of uprights, makes an attractive texture in the afternoon sun.

A simple picket fence, such as this one of larch, appears dramatic
when snow obliterates surrounding vegetation.

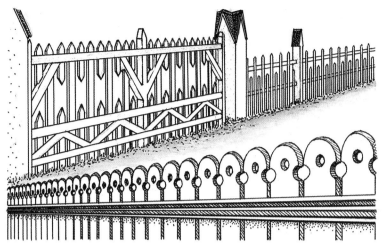

The picket fence can be developed into fanciful shapes and patterns,
and painted to suit an overall colour scheme.

A stout fence of vertically laid half-round posts.
Planting at the base softens the regularity.

Wattle fences, with their coarse texture,
give strong enclosure.

Split bamboo has a fine texture and subtle colour
variations that set off this simple composition ideally.

Diagonally laid stakes create an open texture that is enhanced by the
fine foliage and flowers of a briar rose.

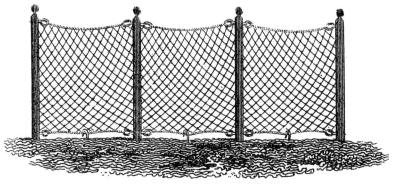

Black netting, to keep out sheep, disappears against a dark
background. It was an early alternative to the ha-ha.

GATES AND GATEWAYS

Gates are symbolic, and charged with associations – arrival, departure, a change of state. By their robustness they may discourage entry, or by their delicate transparency they may lead you on. They enhance the act of moving from one space to the next, making you pause and look around, or wait to read an inscription that prepares you for what lies ahead. Gateways should take account of the mood of the space that follows: wavy island beds, for example, may seem inappropriate after a triumphal arch.

A Chinese moon gate through a rippling dragon tail. To step over the threshold is a momentous event.

This Western moon gate divides spaces less decisively, but still concentrates the eye and mind.

A fantasy opening draws more attention to itself than to the view beyond. (Jenkyn Place, Hampshire)

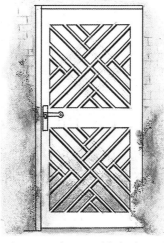

An openwork gate mainly for decoration, but with a view beyond if required.

A ceremonial-style gate at Nymans, Sussex, illogically designed with a low wall.

A simple picket gate framed by a majestic arch of yew presents a dramatic contrast of scale.

Stone obelisks over this gate do duty for a fanfare of trumpets.

An old arch on Tresco (Scilly) colonized by *Aeonium* – a variation on the theme of pleasing decay.

With care, materials can by mixed. This is a timber and wire gate by the author, split for separate pedestrian and vehicle access.

A handsome arched door in a brick wall. Doors prevent draughts better than gates.

A simple but decorative gate. White paint always draws the eye.

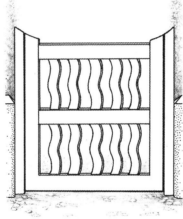

A square gate with a horizontal emphasis. Overhanging *Vitis coignetiae* provides a contrast of texture.

An individual little gate that gives the passing world a wave.

A beautiful timber gate, structurally logical, leading into a hydrangea walk.

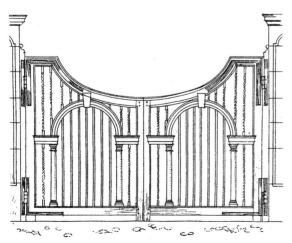

Magnificent vertically boarded gates with classical details (Canons Ashby, drawn by Inigo Triggs).

A studded oak door: note how the bolt heads are aligned on the diagonal.

A Japanese bamboo gate and fence. The bamboos of the gate are paired for strength and a change of texture.

More stout timberwork. Seemingly, it was easier to alter the piers than rebuild the gate to make it fit.

An arbour can act as a gateway. This one supports a climber, with light shining through the leaves.

This purposeful oak gate has delicate spindles giving a view through.

A Victorian metal fence and gateway. The pattern of the fence reflects the arch, unifying the design.

Set in a bamboo wall, this pair of doors in Japan (Shogaku-in) is emphasized by the roof above.

An ancient oak gate topped by a delicate iron-work arch.

A Victorian design for a rustic gateway in split stakes laid on a timber frame, setting a mood.

A "Post-Modern" door and canopy, designed by architect Charles Jencks for the garden of his London home.

A simple iron gate: the vertical bars are doubled in the lower half to keep out rabbits.

Wrought iron gates, delicate against the light beyond.

Cast iron, used for this gate, appears stronger and heavier than wrought iron.

A modern Italian gate, as valuable for silhouette and shadow as for safety.

Cast iron writhing in ecstasy: an elaborately scrolled design for a double gate.

A lighter metal gate painted a quiet blue-grey – visible but not shouting.

A pretty Victorian gate, enhanced by the rose growing over.

Here, strong vertical bars contrast with a riot of plants on the masonry.

The lightest filigree gate, revealing all beyond, secure but transparent.

TRELLISWORK

By this useful technique, light, open structures can be made which can support climbing plants. Being a constructed feature, trelliswork has instant impact in the garden – unlike a hedge or topiary. The regular texture can give a strong sense of enclosure, despite the transparency, and makes a good foil for plants. Modern preservation processes now give trellises an extended life. Treillage is the term given to complex latticework in architectural form.

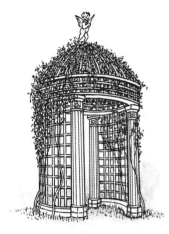

A circular arbour of square trellis and columns – expensive but delightful.

A trellis formed like a cloister. With overlapping trellises, be sure to avoid visual confusion.

A 17th-century French design of astonishing complexity – a masterpiece of treillage.

A pretty arched trellis laid on a mirror to increase the illusion of space.

A recent example by the author – an open timber entablature and roof on salvaged columns.

Although pretty, this example of treillage fails to work as an illusion: it appears more as a surface pattern than as a receding tunnel.

This little panel appears deeper, and is more inventive in its use of different trellis patterns and in the jaunty urns on top.

A *clairvoyée* with decorative metalwork is framed by a trellis built in a grid pattern. (Tryon Place, California)

An elaborate trellis pillar for a climbing rose from an early 20th-century catalogue.

A magnificent example of carpenter's work, in which mouldings give depth and solidity. (Old Westbury Gardens, Long Island, NY)

A timber obelisk by the author. Climbing plants are trained to run up inside.

The pattern of this light trellis is accentuated by training the *Ipomoea* closely to the timber diagonals.

An elaborate trelliswork arbour in an early 20th-century catalogue, adapted from a Dutch design and offered in oak, teak or painted oak.

PERGOLAS, TUNNELS AND COLONNADES

A path is transformed if it runs through a tunnel of plants. The sensation is best in strong sunlight, passing from bright glare to dappled shade, cool and heady with scent, with leaves and flowers lit from above in many shades of green. The idea derives from vine-growing practice, and tubular metal makes the modern equivalent of fine medieval carpenter's work. In summer the result is dreamy whatever the frame; but in winter the basic structure becomes more prominent, so let it be handsome.

This fine brick colonnade is so smothered in wisteria that it is beginning to lose its identity.

Vines trained over horizontal timber spars make a shady place for summer walks.

Stone columns supporting this pergola have a strong texture not entirely matched by the structure above – at least until it is covered by ramblers.

A plain-looking concrete pergola in Peking, with a wisteria giving its best under difficult conditions.

An elegant archway with an interesting curvilinear form.

An apple tunnel at Heale House, Wiltshire. There are big box balls at the end, waiting to pounce.

A metal tunnel sloping over steps, interesting with or without foliage.

A pergola of stripped chestnut poles over which roses luxuriate. The box hedges hide the bare stems.

A curved pergola with brick piers and a timber superstructure. The curved braces mark the entrance.

WALLS AND HA-HAS

A wall is the strongest possible division of space, and the feeling of strength can be increased by making it more highly modelled or by using coarsely textured blocks. Plinths and copings increase apparent mass, while buttresses, battlements or regularly spaced openings create rhythm. The colour may be grey, merging into the background, dominantly red, or white, so that it picks up shadows.

Walls are marvellous for applied or incorporated decoration. The ha-ha, however, is not for looking at – merely for looking over.

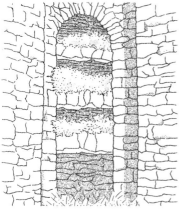

Troughs recessed into a stone wall provide a place for colourful annuals.

Fine sculptural buttresses model the rear of a wall at Longleat, Wiltshire.

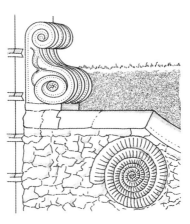

An ammonite built into a gate wall, with a robust console joining wall to pier.

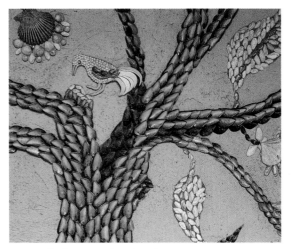

Shells from the beach, set in mortar, decorate this internal wall in a pavilion at Kerdalo, Brittany.

A plaque showing Geometry personified, set into a wall at Edzell, Scotland.

Disembodied stone hands make friends on a brick wall mottled with algae and lichens.

A crinkle-crankle wall at Heveningham Hall, Suffolk. The serpentine plan gives stability, as well as areas of light and shade.

The great sandstone wall at Edzell Castle, dressed in the Lindsay family colours of blue and white annuals in the niches.

Copings add character. Here, brick battlements create a lively rhythm.

Laying flat stones vertically, in the Cornish manner, gives good texture.

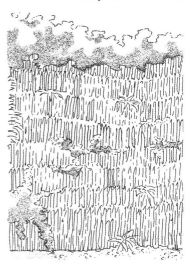

An extreme example of the same practice using slate.

A wall made from broken plates in mortar – a monument to domestic disaster.

A crisp modern concrete balustrade in the south of France contrasts with the robust texture of the stone wall below.

This brickwork balustrade can only be achieved with specially made bricks.

A humble cottage wall made distinctive by triangular battlements.

A brick ha-ha at Audley End, Essex, permits an uninterrupted view up the hill from the house, yet effectively keeps the cattle out.

At Lacock Abbey in Wiltshire, the stone ha-ha forms an edge to the formal area around the house.

BUILDINGS

By their form and their materials, buildings lend a characteristic feel to a garden – a calmness or busyness, a majesty or frivolity. Unless deliberately screened, they invariably make a focal point, often predominating. They look better for being generous in scale and well-built in sympathetic materials: meanness of construction is unbearably obvious. Buildings tend to be a major investment – make them worth it.

ARBOURS AND PAVILIONS

Not only useful for providing shelter from wind and rain, or from sun in favoured climates, arbours and pavilions are often visually important. Be sure to keep them in scale with the adjoining space, and pay as much attention to the roof as to the rest of the structure, giving it a sufficiently high pitch, or the building will appear insignificant. Wreathed in climbing plants, arbours offer an agreeable contrast between geometric structure and free-flowing foliage – a contrast that is agreeable in any well-designed garden.

The terminology of garden buildings is somewhat inexact. A pavilion may often be described as a gazebo – strictly defined as a small structure that overlooks the walls of an enclosed garden. The term kiosk is generally restricted to small pavilions with a Near Eastern flavour. An arbour is an open structure of metal or timber capable of supporting climbing plants; but when elongated into a tunnel, it is sometimes known as a tunnel arbour or pergola. However, a pergola may be one- or two-sided, and may or may not have a roof!

A Chinese pavilion with light bulbs that pick out its lines at night.

A tiny Indian pavilion sheltering pots emphasizes the corner of a pool.

A Western version of a Mughal pavilion, beautifully proportioned and set off by a dark cedar behind.

A tented arbour by the author. The tent is removed during the winter.

A wirework shelter, with a gauze-like texture that makes this a special, but public, place.

Roses wrestle with this wirework arbour, giving it an agreeable lean.

A simple metal arbour over a cast-iron urn and pedestal makes a telling focus.

A 19th-century design for a kiosk of Eastern inspiration, suitable for a garden or a railway station.

A classic stone corner pavilion, rusticated and pedimented.

A beautifully proportioned building at Wilton House, Wiltshire, with Ionic columns, and classical busts on the entablature.

Chinoiserie fantasies such as this are more common in design than on the ground.

A modern timber pavilion of simple design. Reflections in the glazed doors give it an attractive sparkle.

An orientally inspired pavilion raised on a platform. The timberwork is elegant and well-executed.

A 19th-century design for a half-timbered pavilion. A steep roof gives it weight.

A thatched summer house, with boarding that has weathered to a lovely silver-grey.

A curious pavilion of stout timber posts, and panels made up of bent elbows.

A pavilion at Heale House, Wiltshire, authentically built by Japanese labour.

An octagonal stone summer house, originally thatched, designed by Harold Peto for Iford Manor.

A modest little pavilion with an idiosyncratic roof makes a focus in a small urban garden.

A rock fantasy makes a powerful eyestopper in this 19th-century design.

A neat timber pavilion with a shingled roof, topped by a little dovecote.

A rustic arbour in larch, draped in roses and clematis, by the author.

A corner pavilion in Brittany. The battered base emphasizes its strength.

DOVECOTES AND AVIARIES

Pigeons were once an important source of winter food. Although pigeon consumption is no longer critical to the domestic economy, many dovecotes and pigeoncotes survive as important features in or near gardens, giving both visual and aural pleasure. The newer ones tend to be modest in size and constructed in timber. Aviaries are only for dedicated bird lovers.

A pretty converted barrel dovecote where the birds are the chief decoration.

A Gothick fantasy in stained timber, designed by the author.

A thatched dovecote with three arched entrances for the birds.

A late 19th-century dovecote from Cliveden, Buckinghamshire.

Dovecotes can be wall-hung; this one is from an early 20th-century catalogue.

A rectangular gabled dovecote with a handsome functional design.

The lantern provides access for the birds in this octagonal stone dovecote.

A finely constructed ironwork and metal-gauze aviary at the Villa Agnano in Tuscany.

The sumptuous aviary at Waddesdon Manor with finely detailed ironwork and a grotto in the middle.

CONSERVATORIES, GREENHOUSES AND ORANGERIES

The greenhouse was originally the house in which the greens (evergreens) were wintered. This developed into the orangery and, with the advent of industrial glass, the conservatory and the modern greenhouse. Such buildings warrant careful architectural treatment. Remember that glass, when reflecting the sun or sky, is a hard, shiny surface, but when not reflecting light, it appears black, throwing into relief the quality of the glazing bars.

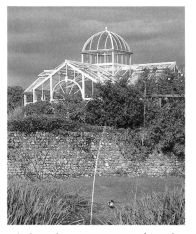

A modern Australian conservatory in timber and stone. The timber slatting provides the shade necessary in a hot climate.

An inventive conservatory can be made using standard greenhouse sections.

A delicate Victorian design in cast iron. The thin sections of iron permit maximum light to enter.

A lovely design at Osterley Park, near London, by Robert Adam. In the late 18th century, greenhouses still had solid roofs.

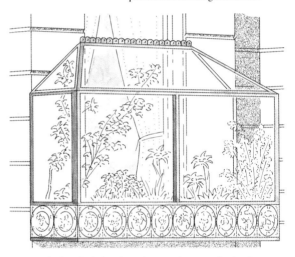

A glazed window box gives greater scope for tender plants, but be sure that they do not burn in sun.

An early iron conservatory, whose small panes give good texture. (Bicton, Devon)

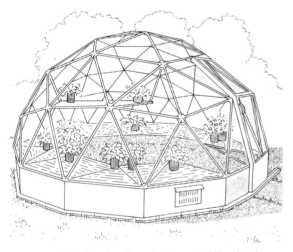

A well-designed modern glasshouse, both functional and economic.

The Camellia House at Culzean Castle in Scotland – a magnificent conservatory.

A distinctive modern glasshouse makes use of preformed ribs in an imaginative and efficient design.

FOLLIES AND TEMPLES

Such buildings were invariably sited and constructed as part of the stage scenery of a great garden, as distant eyecatchers or setting a mood. Many have disappeared, and those that survive today frequently need urgent restoration. Opportunities for such far-flung gestures, embracing a landscape, may be rare today, but the principle of siting objects to draw the eye remains the same. But remember to pay due regard to scale, and take care not to clutter the field of vision.

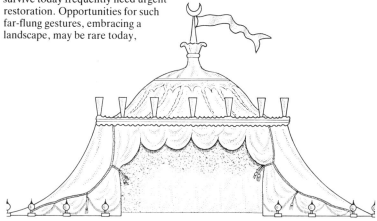

Although insubstantial, this 18th-century garden tent by Henry Keene introduces an element of fantasy as well as making an excellent eyecatcher.

The pinnacled outline of this mighty stone gateway makes an inspiring silhouette.

A ruin in the landscape, with its mood of antiquity and decay, is always an object of curiosity.

The pagoda fountain at Alton Towers, Staffordshire, with tinkling bells.

Sir William Chambers' pagoda at Kew Gardens – a landmark for West London.

The Bristol Cross at Stourhead: raised on a mound, it draws the eye across a lake.

A column at Stowe, Buckinghamshire: both commemoration and landmark.

A pair of columns supporting the she-wolf suckling Romulus and Remus.

The ruin at Uppark, Sussex. Light appearing through a silhouette is always particularly effective.

James Gibbs' Gothic Temple at Stowe: the outline makes a complex silhouette.

A beautiful temple by Sir John Vanbrugh, also at Stowe. It frames the long view from the house to the Triumphal Arch.

A Japanese-inspired Shinto temple, whose deeply eaved roof gives ample shade.

An agreeably eccentric structure with a clock and tower.

The Temple of the Four Winds at Castle Howard, Yorkshire, by Sir John Vanbrugh.

An elaborate neo-Grecian temple, attractive in a lakeside setting.

WATER

Water can evoke joyful well-being or seem sombre and brooding. With the advent of modern waterproofing materials and the small submersible electric pump, it is now perfectly feasible for any garden to have its pool and fountain. The wonderful size and shape of so many water-loving plants, such as gunnera and hostas, is a great asset, adding textures far bolder than those of the border or shrubbery. And the movement of water, tinkling in a thin jet or roaring in a cascade – changing yet the same – is endlessly fascinating.

BOATHOUSES

Although nothing more than the shelter for a boat, a boathouse makes that significant humanizing contrast with the trees and shrubs that colonize the shore. It is a merest mark of human control that makes the wild wood friendly.

A simple boathouse nestling under the trees at Shogaku-in, Japan.

A splendid white bargeboard shows up well against this dark entrance.

A brickwork boathouse. Again, note the bargeboard.

BRIDGES

Bridges offer opportunities for all kinds of fanciful design – from a simple timber plank to the great Palladian bridge that is also a building. Siting is critical, in that bridges are usually best viewed from the water, or from a path approaching from the side. When you are actually on the bridge, only the upper works can be enjoyed. Parapet walls and railings, normally needed for safety, give a chance for decorative construction, or for a frame for climbing plants.

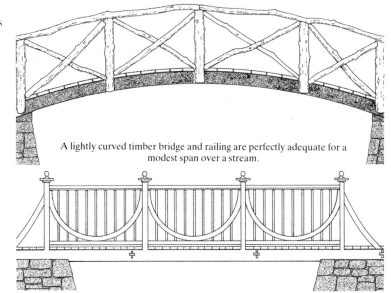

A lightly curved timber bridge and railing are perfectly adequate for a modest span over a stream.

A more elaborate and eye-catching design from an early 20th-century catalogue, functional but made pretty by its curved rails.

An elaborate mock bridge in a garden by Vernon Russell-Smith. (Chelsea Flower Show)

The awkward railing of this completely functional
timber bridge is used to support wisteria.

The stout railing of this Japanese bridge
emphasizes its gentle curve.

An interesting construction, partly arched, partly
suspended, at Middleton Place, South Carolina.

This oriental zigzag bridge is simply
constructed from posts and boards.

A Japanese-style painted bridge at Heale House, Wiltshire,
characterized by its grace and ease.

Two bridges, one brick, one timber, give
alternative views over a lake.

A minimal timber bridge, without rails, by
Alex Rota – unobtrusive and efficient.

An English thatched bridge, built over a
lane at Polesden Lacey in Surrey.

A white-painted bridge of simple construction is reflected attractively
in a lake. The open steps are an unusual feature.

A false bridge makes a grand feature and gives the impression that the lake goes on beyond.

A Japanese-inspired bridge at Wrest Park in Bedfordshire, built in 1876, has a graceful sweep.

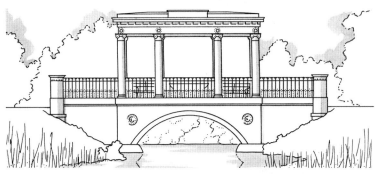

A simple Japanese bridge consisting of two stone slabs resting on a central prop. Functional but perilous.

A stout board can do similar service across a narrow span, but is liable to be slippery unless wrapped in wire netting.

This elegant stone composition inventively combines bridge and pavilion.

A substantial bridge constructed in stone, has a rugged yet graceful character. Urns mark the angles.

A simple stone bridge makes an excellent foil to the ferns and comfrey flowering in profusion.

The flints that face this bridge contrast in texture with the neat dressing of the arch and with the nearby plants.

A central shell and horses draw attention to this bridge, studded with ammonites.

Ironwork railings may have curious shapes – here, they imitate branches.

This bridge over a stream is destined to become a tunnel of roses supported on metal arches.

POOLS, CANALS AND LAKES

Still water puts the sky in unusual places: an area of brightness in the floor of a court or patio immediately draws the eye. The glassy texture of still water sets off lush waterside foliage to perfection. For reflections, little depth is required: all will depend on the angle from which the pool is observed. If the water is located in front of a dark background, with no possibility of reflections, it will appear deep and mysterious.

The strong foliage of waterside plants makes this stream a striking composition.

Serenity at Knightshayes, Devon. There are few elements in this composition, but they create a breathtaking space.

The sky's reflection in this pool echoes the view between the piers.

A pool in Kunming, China, where tiers of plants in pots form a changeable centrepiece.

A fountain and shallow basin in a Mughal garden, contrived to imitate spreading water.

A severe composition of arcade and pool makes a focus at Old Westbury Garden, Long Island, New York.

A sinuous rill by William Kent runs along a dark path at Rousham, Oxfordshire.

Water falling from a simple timber chute penetrates the stillness of snow.

Another view of Rousham (see above, centre): by eliminating all but the water, snow highlights the octagonal pool and rill.

An octagon, always an interesting shape, fits well in a rectilinear layout such as this one.

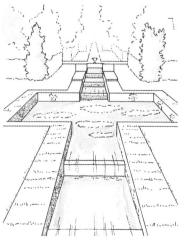

Water tumbling over steps gives life and sparkle to a canal.

This bird-shaped pool is a study in contrasting textures – water, pebbles and foliage.

Another textural contrast – a pattern of flat setts against the glassy water. (Pitmedden, Scotland)

A dark pool, of mysterious depth, is just as alluring as a pool with sparkling reflections.

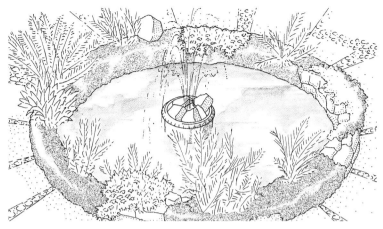

In this secluded pool the fountain and ferns complement each other with their upward thrust.

The regular shapes of stepping stones seen above reflected sky contrast well with foliage.

Steps contain this circular pool by Sir Edwin Lutyens at the Deanery, Sonning, Berkshire.

A textural composition of water, pebbles, rheum, hosta and ivy.

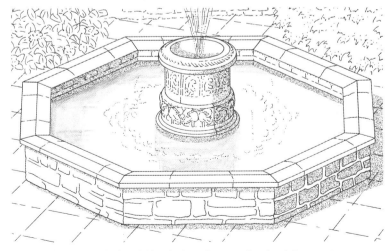

The octagonal edge of this raised pool is convenient for sitting on. The fountain is elaborately carved.

The gentle splash of water, a glint of darting fish, the texture of leaves and a comfortable seat are a delightful combination.

CASCADES AND FOUNTAINS

Water in movement animates the garden. Ideally, it catches the sun's rays and sparkles, but even in shadow it has an exhilarating effect. A light ripple on the surface can put a reflection into dancing motion, while a weighty head of water rushing down a cascade will foam and roar. Enjoy the sound of water – dripping, splashing, gurgling, hissing. Catch and reflect it. Water is a most potent element in the garden: exploit it to the full.

Fountains that catch the sun against a dark background sparkle joyously.

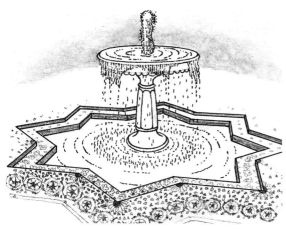

Islamic fountains contrast the fluidity of water against rich geometric patterns.

The Victorian fountain achieved a wonderful complexity of design.

The Mughal *chadar*, or water chute, makes water froth like a fine wool shawl.

A witty water chute into a swimming pool picks up the sculpted water flowing from the urn.

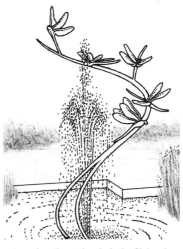

A modern fountain winds the flight of a dragonfly around a feathery jet.

Another modern fountain, in a New Zealand garden, arranged around a flight of birds alighting on a pool.

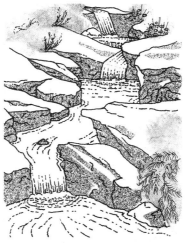

Water running over rocks is always a delightful effect.

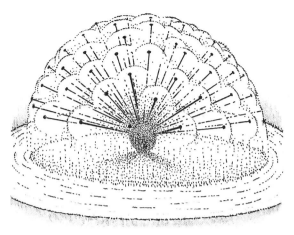

This cascade at Bowood, Wiltshire, is a superb artificial rockwork made on a grand scale in the late 18th century.

Frogs spurt water at Cotswold rams in this composition by Judith and Simon Verity.

A modern dandelion-head fountain, at the International Garden Festival, Liverpool, in 1984.

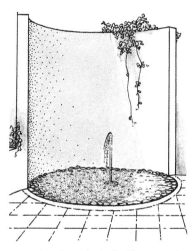

A modern fountain, backed by a curved wall that reflects the sound.

A pool arched with stone, with a thin jet falling from the carved keystone – by Lutyens at Hestercombe.

A triton and shell in reconstituted stone by the author. (Chelsea Flower Show, 1985)

A tiny satyr's head at the Villa d'Este, amazed by its own jet.

The curved forms of this fountain contrast with the directness of the jet.

A lusciously full cascade of water, perfectly balanced, streams out like an apron beneath arching jets at the Villa d'Este.

A tiny drinking fountain in a bronze surround, with fine brickwork.

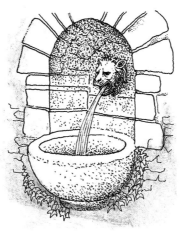

A more rugged stone fountain set in a wall. Water issues from the lion's mouth.

A wall basin supported by a kneeling girl, at La Mortola, Italy.

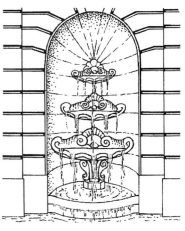

Tiers of stone shells in niches make a fine vertical display.

Sunlight catches a fine jet above a bowl on a pedestal in the sunken garden at Hatfield House, Hertfordshire.

An amusing little gilded lead fountain in a pool edged with lily pads. Water pours from the beak.

A dark hedge makes a good background for a fountain. This example is at Port Lympne, Kent.

An umbrella fountain, illuminated in sunlight. The stonework is attractively weathered.

PLANTS AND TREES

When considering the architectural and sculptural aspects of a garden, plants and trees must not be overlooked. Avenues are as architectural as topiary is sculptural; and in an age when constructed ornament is so expensive, green ornament comes into its own. The prospect of growing your own sculpture park from a few cuttings opens up all kinds of possibilities. And although the training of plants might have been ridiculed by Alexander Pope and William Robinson, do not underestimate the imaginative contribution it can make.

AVENUES

The regular spacing of trees in an avenue sets up a rhythm that leads on inexorably toward the end. Whatever it leads to must be worthy of such preparation. The choice of species, the width of the avenue and the interval between trees determines the overall character of the avenue and its harmony with its focus. The great forest trees such as oak, beech or lime are most commonly used for drives, while hornbeam or cherries or any of the smaller trees are useful for avenues closer to the house.

A fine avenue of cypresses, the shadows emphasizing the progression.

Small avenues can be made from plants in pots or planting cases, perhaps reinforcing an outer avenue of trees.

Yews or other conifers give a measured rhythm along an axis – but whatever lies at the other end must be worth the build-up.

Victorian topiary at Packwood, Warwickshire, leads to a fine gateway. The lack of uniformity creates an air of antiquity.

A double avenue of young lime trees give a rhythm to a broad lawn.
(Sandringham House, Norfolk)

A darker, more enclosed feeling is created by these old yew trees,
which meet to form a series of Gothic arches.

A curving avenue at Dumbarton Oaks,
where all the elements are in harmony.

Trunks of Spanish chestnuts flail away into the distance, their gnarled
textures contributing sculptural interest.

A paved avenue at Old Westbury, Long
Island, NY, makes a secret tunnel.

Closely grown limes, not old enough to
arch over, frame a rectangle of sky.

A widely spaced avenue of giant sequoia trees makes a stately approach
to a grand country house.

Regular rows of limes are broken
interestingly by the odd leaning trunk.

TRAINING

Tall divisions in the garden can be made effectively by pleaching: trees are planted at suitable intervals, their branches trained horizontally on wire or bamboo, and then treated as a hedge on stilts. Lower divisions can be made by fruiting hedges, most suitable in the kitchen garden, but equally usable elsewhere. Fruit trees are traditionally trained to make the crop better, but such techniques are also desirable for their decorative qualities.

Pleached trees can give additional height to a wall without obscuring its texture. Limes or hornbeams are commonly used.

In pleaching, side branches are trained outwards and pruned annually.

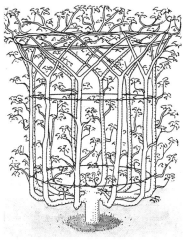

Pleached fruit trees in "goblet" form were popular in Victorian kitchen gardens.

This kitchen garden has apple trees in an early stage of training.

Pyrancantha neatly trained gives a house a pedimented door, a date and verdant rustication.

Another *Pyrancantha* wall cladding, this time in berry. A good way to attract birds.

A double espalier pear of considerable antiquity, probably around 100 years old. (Croxteth Hall, Liverpool)

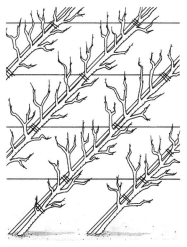

Cordons are grown diagonally, giving an interesting pattern to a fruit fence.

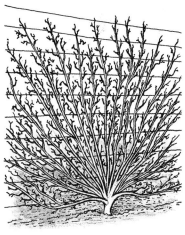

This apple is trained as a splendid symmetrical fan on an old stone wall.

Fans can also be formed on a fence of horizontal wires with bamboo canes.

Honeysuckle (*Lonicera*) trained as a basket to contain hydrangeas. (Nymans, Sussex)

MAZES

Mazes are an amusement that can easily be incorporated into a garden – space permitting. Not only are they fun, but their textural qualities can be exciting. The more difficult mazes are made with hedges above eye level, but so many miles of tall hedge become expensive to maintain. Turf mazes are altogether quicker to create and easier to navigate.

This maze (at Grey's Court, Henley, Oxfordshire) is of turf and brick and contains a central armillary sphere.

A young tree indicates the heart of this hillside maze.

This maze in box (Hatfield House, Hertfordshire) is in the process of being trimmed. Compare the texture of the untrimmed box beyond.

A maze like this should be visible from above, from a terrace or upper window, so that you can appreciate its texture and pattern.

A pattern for a turf maze, in which the path is long and winding but unambiguous.

Turf mazes rely on the play of light and shade for their strong texture. They look their best in bright sun.

Another turf maze pattern, again without blind turnings.

TOPIARY AND HEDGES

The architecture and sculpture of the garden can just as well be in living material as in brick or stone. Greenery costs less but takes up a lot more time. Topiary and hedges readily grow bigger if required, or into new shapes, but they need regular maintenance – although with yew and box you can just about get away with one clip a year.

Unconstrained by the mechanics of construction, you can use topiary to indulge the most fantastical whims.

In the Ladew Topiary Gardens, Maryland, neat pyramids frame steps and terraces in a formal composition.

Yew trimmed in diminishing tiers is a popular form, here offset by a seat.

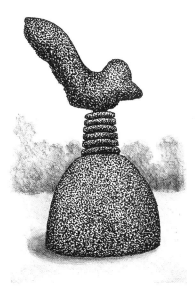

Birds are a frequent topiary subject, recognizable despite lack of detail.

Spiralled columns are often made, but need skilful setting out.

A topiary extravaganza: the Eiffel Tower straddling a tiny garden.

Cypress arches in this French garden have textural contrast at the base.

Golden yews form colourful buttresses to a dark yew hedge, creating a regular rhythm.

The great box balls at Heale House, Wiltshire, make a splendid centrepiece to the kitchen garden.

Topiary balls and battlements make a lively combination.

A cone of yew shelters a seat tucked inside, deep in the shade.

A 19th-century design for pleached hornbeams arching over standard trees in planting cases.

A fine avenue of arches with a venerable, slightly crumbling look.

More 19th-century designs: green architecture with piers, columns, arches and niches.

The scarlet *Tropaeolum* sparkles against dark yew. (Edzell, Scotland)

The inscription in box spells out the Lindsay family motto. (Edzell)

A hunt in full cry at the Ladew Topiary Gardens, Maryland. Tiresome for the mower but worth it for the fun.

An urban garden in which small-scale topiary provides an attractive low-maintenance solution.

A crumbly old box hedge, interestingly gnarled with years.

Ivy can be grown on a wire fence or timber frame to make a good evergreen hedge. But beware: it attracts flies when it flowers in the autumn.

The rose "Albertine" makes a secure hedge, thorny but fragrantly delightful.

A superb combination of urns and lavender.

Yew buttresses give a stately rhythm to the great retaining wall at Pitmedden, Scotland.

Bamboo as a hedge gives a totally different texture – interesting but difficult to maintain.

PARTERRES, KNOTS, BEDDING AND BORDERS

In the same way that paving can characterize a space, so too can planting patterns. The original simple geometric patterns of knots developed into complex arabesques of box and coloured gravels, and 19th-century patterns made full use of the newly available tender plants. Such patterns are best seen from a higher level, such as a terrace or the windows of a house. The border is a freer example of a planned arrangement. The best borders are orchestrated for a calculated colour effect and coordinated in their flowering times.

Three late 17th-century designs: box and gravel (left); flowers (centre); and a design for citrus trees in cases, brought out from the orangery.

The same ground surface inside and outside makes the hedge more prominent.

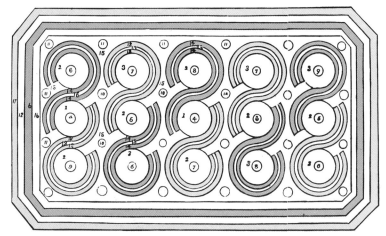

A complex pattern for a parterre from a 19th-century book: Nathan Cole's *Royal Parks and Gardens of London* (1877).

An elaborate parterre in the moat at Angers, France, still a little thin in April, but on the way to becoming a spectacular scheme.

A crisp design in green at Elvaston Castle, Derbyshire – a good idea but difficult to maintain.

A robust design for Albi in the south of France – unusual for the rounded tops to the hedges.

Hooped wire edgings give the impression of a basket containing flowers. Any tall flowers can be used.

A bedding scheme that takes advantage of raised beds to give it height.

Another illusion of a basket full of flowers, here using wallflowers planted in a tray.

A parterre of box, grass and gravel in a scheme at Little Moreton Hall, Cheshire, by the National Trust.

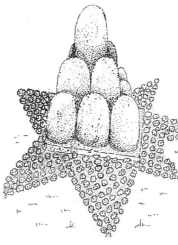

An unusual but imaginative bedding and topiary scheme. (Siena, Italy)

A cottage garden parterre of begonias, sweet alyssum and lobelia.

A parterre of box and sand mixed with plants – begonias in the centre, lobelia in the quarters.

A butterfly parterre with a concrete edging in a rose garden in China. Even the antennae contain planting.

This border concentrates on pink poppies and roses with white and red lupins, with an accent of grey near the gate.

This double border at Crathes, Scotland, terminated in a clipped tree, works round blues and pinks to make a stunning composition.

SCULPTURAL FORM

The worked surfaces of sculpture contrast with the apparently more chaotic forms and textures of foliage. Sculpture thus makes an excellent focal or terminal point, which draws the eye. Traditionally, sculpture in gardens has been figurative, although urns and other non-figurative embellishments have also been important. Modern sculpture, more diverse than ever in its concepts and materials, often seems more accessible in the garden than anywhere else. You can improvise your own sculptural forms from rocks, piles of stones or building fragments salvaged from demolition. Such features can make an accent as telling as a work of art, at a fraction of the price.

OBELISKS AND COLUMNS

To make a vertical emphasis is a useful ploy in garden design. The clean line of a man-made artefact such as a column or obelisk is far more arresting than, say, a tall upright tree whose outline is blurred. And if the column is placed in a cleft between the trees or on a skyline all on its own, the impact is all the greater. The space between observer and column, however wild, is brought under control by that single object. You need use only one such feature, as a focus for your entire plan.

A sculpture by Anne Christopher in aluminium and resin.

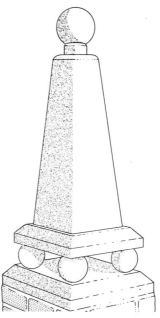

A small, homely obelisk in stone, mounted on stone balls.

Fluted columns surmounted by a sphinx draw the eye into a glade.

STATUES AND SCULPTURAL OBJECTS

In large gardens, statues have to be at least full-size or on plinths in order to register. Generally, they need framing or backing with trees. Only the very largest works, on the scale of the great Henry Moores, can compete with the sky unaided. Half- or three-quarter scale works should be reserved for more intimate spaces, where they can add a charm or create a mood that wonderfully reinforces the pleasure of the garden. Without sculpture, no garden is complete.

A huntress by Simon Verity in Rosemary Verey's Gloucestershire garden.

A lead statue in the white garden at Sissinghurst has a thoughtful air.

A beautiful bust on a pedestal makes a lively focus.

A stone Buddha well sited among rhododendrons.

A fine herm with a patina of algae against an ivy-filled panel.

A life-size gardener leaning contentedly on his spade.

A statue in Coade stone – an imitation stone popular in the early 19th century.

The Dying Gladiator by Peter Scheemakers at Rousham House, Oxfordshire, looking quite different in the snow.

This cloaked figure is in a corner, so that one comes upon it unexpectedly.

"Greeting the Day" by Polly Ionides (1985), carved in Ketton stone.

"The Green Man" by Simon Verity, with grass in his mouth, primroses in his hair.

A bust of John Milton enshrined in the Temple of British Worthies at Stowe.

A 3rd-century bust on a column rising above variegated pelargoniums.

A bust makes a useful terminal emphasis, here poised on a wall.

A flint sculpture by Peter Gough: the figure is curiously uncertain in form.

An improvised sculpture of flat stones on a rock base.

A boy with a goat (at Waddesdon Manor, Buckinghamshire) rise from a star-shaped bedding scheme of begonias.

"The Water Carriers" – a striking group in a Rock Garden, Chandigarh, in the Punjab.

A simple wooden sculptured head carved as a finial to crown a gatepost.

This "Barking Dog" constructed in elm (by Nick Deans) is a sculpture for play.

A magnificent lead peacock with finely detailed tail feathers.

A carved owl conjures up wisdom and vigilance.

A dragon makes a magnificent focus. This sumptuous example is in Peking's Forbidden City.

A life-size piglet in reconstituted stone adds a touch of humour.

A miniature sculpture of two little birds on a tufa rock makes a charming small-scale focus.

The lion is seen in many postures and expressions, often guarding entrances.

Salvaged griffins' heads (formerly supporting a stonework coat of arms) form an interesting group across a lawn.

A carved basket of fruit makes an apt terminal to a wall or pier.

The Weather Vane, a modern sculpture by Raef Baldwin, harmonizes well with bean rows.

A ceramic tree plaque with a Latin motto, by Ian Hamilton Finlay.

A pair of doves sculpted by Jacob Epstein at Holland House, London.

STONE SEATS

Stone seats are important in gardens not only for their convenience but also for their considerable visual impact. They tend to be large, with a strong horizontal line, and are often set back in the foliage of shrubs or hedges, with which they contrast well. Often they are elaborately carved, particularly on the arms and supports. Unfortunately, antique stone seats are costly, and reproductions of them are not a particularly commercial proposition for the companies that work in reconstituted stone. However, you can always try asking a sculptor to make one as a special commission, if your budget can stretch to it.

The long, cool, horizontal lines of this stone seat are set off by clumps of *Anthemis*.

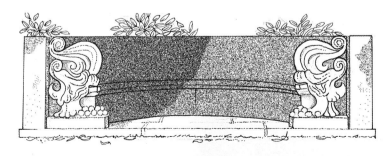

A curved seat with elaborately carved arms. The curved form gives a degree of enclosure and increases the intimacy.

Another curved seat, with griffins for arms and a lion's head surmounting the back.

This sumptuous seat at Jenkyn Place, Hampshire, with its massive arms, looks like a great sofa.

A more modestly sized seat, with finials, and supports in the form of sphinxes.

A medium-sized seat with arms of swirling foliage. Position such seats where the arms can be seen.

A simple stone slab supported by three square-section balusters. The algae add visual interest.

A gently curved seat with a shaped back, set in a frame of hedging. The steps give it prominence.

The seat on the outside of the Gothic Cottage at Stourhead, Wiltshire, has detailing to integrate it with the cottage itself.

Winged sphinxes form the arms of this elegant seat.

A terracotta chair, compact, decorative and functional.

SUNDIALS

Watches are now ubiquitous, yet sundials remain popular as a whimsically impractical way of telling the time – obscured by moss or cloud, and usually unadjusted for the time zone. Traditionally, they were supported on balusters or by figures such as "Father Time", the "Kneeling Blackamoor" or overfleshed cherubs. In Scotland magnificent faceted dials were made, full of astronomical complication. Sundials are apt to bear pithy messages such as *Ut Umbra Sic Vita* (As a Shadow, So Is Life). Hilaire Belloc's suggestion was: "I am a sundial turned the wrong way round and I cost my foolish mistress fifty pounds". Related to the sundial is the armillary sphere: a complex model made up of hoops to show the movement of heavenly bodies.

A sundial with an upright face mounted on an octagonal column.

A sundial supported on an elaborate wrought-iron pedestal.

A faceted sundial: each dial has its own gnomon. (Pitmedden, Scotland)

A faceted sundial supported on an obelisk. (Drummond Castle, Scotland)

An armillary sphere on a vigorously carved baluster.

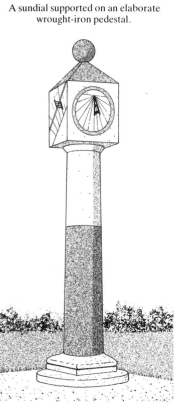

A handsome 17th-century pillar sundial topped by a stone ball.

A sundial on a graceful, spiral-fluted baluster, enhanced by a round base.

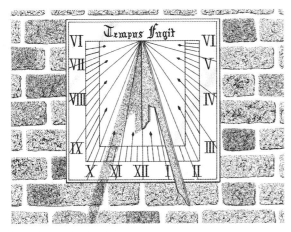

A wall sundial from an early 20th-century catalogue, complete with Latin motto stating the obvious.

A modest sundial with a pretty rope-waisted baluster support.

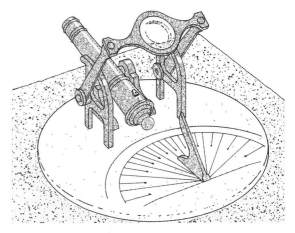

A marvel of solar technology: the sun focused through glass touches off the cannon at exactly midday.

URNS AND VASES

Urns and vases have long been important as sculptural garden ornaments. They may be terminal features on gate piers or mounted on pedestals, perhaps lining a path. Though mostly standing on their own, they sometimes contain plants. Antique examples are difficult to obtain and expensive. However, a number of reputable companies make reproductions in cement- or resin-based artificial stone or glass-reinforced plastic. So long as they are not liable to close scrutiny, modern reproductions may be quite adequate for use on a building. But where seen from close to, only the most sophisticated compounds can do duty for stone or lead.

A range of large terracotta amphorae are set off by the yew hedge at Hever Castle, Kent.

A stone vase, richly carved, with foliage on the lid and drapes around the middle.

A beautiful urn featuring Neptune in relief. The deep shadows create drama.

A fine fluted vase with a wreath of foliage around the neck.

A sarcophagus serves as an excellent planting box – here planted up with tender shrubs and annuals.

A historic vase with draped lion's heads and a key frieze.

A ram's-head vase and pedestal from an early 20th-century catalogue.

A marble urn with a subtle decoration of acanthus leaves. (Longleat, Wiltshire)

This urn on a rusticated pier forms a terminal to a wall.

A simple low-relief plinth contrasts with a scrolled plant-holder.

"Pope's Urn", designed by William Kent, is now available in artificial stone.

An elongated vase with a fluted neck springing from grotesque faces.

An almost spherical urn of terracotta sited on a stone pedestal.

A lead urn somewhat overdecorated with lion's heads, sphinxes and a spiral-fluted base.

This type of relatively simple urn is easily reproduced by moulding in artificial stone.

A terracotta draped urn with a key frieze. (La Mortola, Italy)

This urn makes a sinister-looking finial to a great stone seat.

This square urn in a cast terracotta flanks a short flight of steps at the end of a terrace.

A beautiful amphora-shaped urn, richly sculpted with lion's heads and garlands.

Like urns, simple rectangular planting troughs, with Adamesque ornament, are reproduced in cement-based artificial stone.

An old stone bath tub, set on a low stone platform, makes an excellent planting trough.

This stone fruit-basket celebrates autumn, with its grapes and ears of wheat.

An unusual vase carved with a vine curling round and a pair of rams' heads.

Although this sarcophagus could be used as a plant container, the plants would fight for attention with the carved panels.

GROTTOES AND ROCKWORK

Although the rock garden perhaps has a limited appeal today, mainly to enthusiasts for alpine plants, the use of rocks in the garden offers interesting possibilities. Rocks conjure a feeling of the primitive, of rugged nature, age and stability, and for these reasons are much admired in the East. They come in infinitely varied sculptural forms, subtle colourings and textures that always contrast well with foliage. They can be grouped together to form enclosures or used as a focal point in planting. They mix as well with shrubs as with alpines.

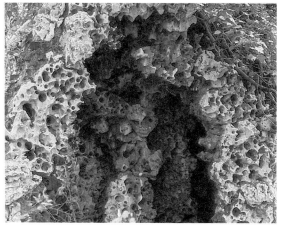

Limestone tufa surmounting a grotto has a wild, craggy aspect. (Painshill, Surrey)

An 18th-century grotto, in which water spills from a river god's urn towards an interior, toplit pool.

Tall rocks on end, like sentinels, make a dramatic enclosure in a Chinese garden.

This "frosted" rustication around a small fountain resembles dripping weeds.

A large flat rock raised on another makes a useful table, as well as a dramatic sculpture.

MOVABLE**S**

A garden requires movables – furniture in which to relax and pots to make temporary planting arrangements. The equipment required for these purposes should add to the visual pleasure of the garden rather than detract from it. This is especially true of items designed to remain outside throughout the summer. Good design exists, and does not always cost so much more than the mass-produced items that rely more on salesmanship than on quality. Make your garden better by hunting out well-crafted pieces, thoughtfully designed to satisfy their purpose.

GARDEN FURNITURE

Seats and tables together make a sizable group in the garden that all too often looks ungainly and untidy. They can benefit from being located on a special area of paving, to which their shapes, individually and as a group, happily relate; this helps to enforce a sense of tidiness. Consider their scale: they will generally look better for being partially enclosed, with their bulk partly obscured. A group of chairs and a table surrounded by an expanse of lawn disrupts the view and at the same time looks lost. If they must be in the open, try to anchor them visually to a tree or hedge.

A light decorative table with a cobweb design. (Chatsworth Carpenters)

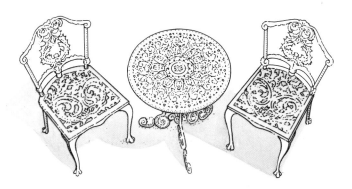

Cast-iron Victorian furniture. Beware of replicas in cast aluminium, which is much too light for cast-iron detailing.

A distinctive chair and double seat with a Turkish flavour, designed by John Stefanidis.

The simple, modest design of these stained timber chairs and table is enhanced by the circular base.

A set of three seats in Hornton stone and ash, together with a low table in Hornton stone. Designed by Bryant Fedden.

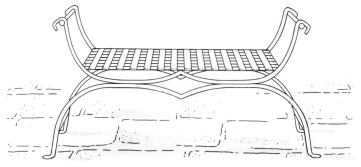

A graceful wrought-iron stool based on a Victorian design. It doubles as a table.

SEATS

Comfort and style are perfectly compatible. Think of the colour and pattern of your cushion material in terms of the leaves and flowers nearby. Look at the line of the seat you are thinking of buying and ask yourself whether you feel it is really beautiful, and whether it will remain so in your garden context. Is its colour justified by handsome looks? White, in particular, demands an elegant form. And, of course, you should also look at the seat in terms of durability: paint perhaps will chip, timber will rot, and steel will rust if there is water around.

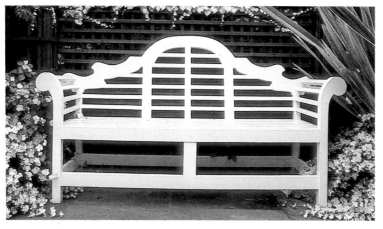

This fine timber seat by Lutyens has enough presence to make a focal point in any scheme. Modern reproductions are available.

A striking slatted timber seat with a fan-shaped back.

This sturdy, handsome chair by David Mlinaric is comfortable and capacious.

A beautifully designed and crafted timber seat by David Hicks.

A modern armless chair by Lucinda Leech, both sculptural and comfortable.

An elegant small folding timber seat, combining comfort and ease of storage.

This old, slightly curved timber seat has weathered to a quiet grey tone. It looks good enough to appear at the end of a view.

A wicker chair, well-used and friendly – but more suitable for a conservatory.

A massive timber seat designed by the author as a terminal feature in a garden. (Available from the Landscape Ornament Company)

This seat, designed to offer rest on a walk round the garden, gains by its modesty and directness.

A red-wheeled seat that can be moved along like a wheelbarrow, recently made to a 19th-century design.

A seat that is constructed from old cart wheels, with a simple board back and seat.

Tree seats are only worth making if there is a view all around. This handsome one has arms for comfort.

This cast-iron version of a tree seat, with a highly decorative back, draws the eye and thus requires careful siting.

A sculptural seat made from a curved treetrunk supported on short posts.

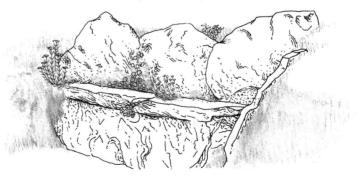

A seat made from unevenly sized stone slabs, colonized by various rockery plants.

A seat made of chestnut poles, painted brown. Simple to construct, but select the seat members with a thought for comfort.

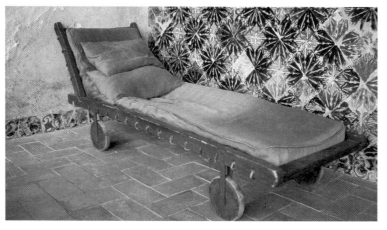

A movable day bed in a garden pavilion. The simple rope bottom is stretched over a timber frame.

This exotically curved wrought-iron chair looks good in silhouette.

A Regency wrought-iron conversation seat, ideal for harmless dalliance.

Wrought iron can be drawn into many patterns – here, a spiralling back and seat.

Elegant wrought-iron chairs with seats and backs made from iron mesh.

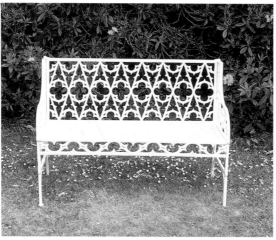

A Victorian "Gothick" seat in cast iron. The elegant white pattern stands out against a dark hedge.

A heavily decorated cast-iron seat overflowing with grapes and leaves.

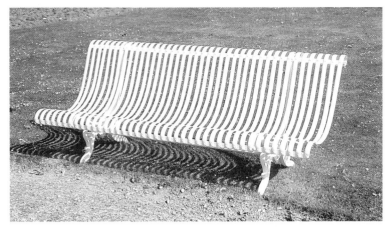

An elegant seat in wrought-iron strips is well-designed for its purpose, and comfortable.

A hammock is indispensable for an afternoon snooze. This one has a pretty valance.

PLANT CONTAINERS

Well-grouped plant containers, be they sturdy planting cases or terracotta pots, add a touch of luxury to the garden. Timber containers may be boxes or barrels. New boxes, in particular, should be lined, to prevent the water required by the plants from rotting the wood. Unlined boxes have only a limited life. Terracotta pots come in all shapes and sizes; not all are frostproof, so check carefully before you buy.

Triangular plant containers can be built up into a wall of trailing plants.

This old cast-iron fireplace makes an improvised container for *Impatiens* and ivy.

A fine Italian terracotta pot, boldly planted with *Canna*.

A cylindrical timber planting case, constructed on the barrel principle.

Stone troughs create special conditions for alpines and other small plants.

A simple timber case that looks good lining a path.

A Victorian stone water butt makes a fine plant container.

A small timber window box provides a place to grow a wealth of summer plants.

A stoneware pot with a bonsai bamboo trained and grafted back onto itself.

A tall pot with handles that are both practical and decorative.

A stone trough supported on slender brick pillars shows off a riot of *Osteospermum* to advantage.

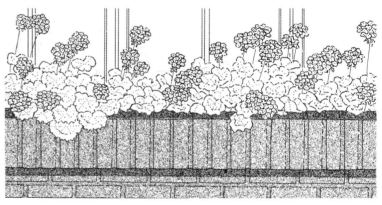

A window box made from bricks laid on end merges with the wall of the house, but is distinguished by the flowers.

These pots from New Zealand include some painted with geometric patterns, others dotted with painted shells.

These coiled and indented clay pots by Michael Hullis have a strong texture that looks good whether they are planted or empty.

Hanging baskets made of wire and lined with moss add high-level flower interest. Be sure to attend to the watering.

These beautiful pots have a strong texture. When pots like these are used for planting, make sure the foliage texture stands up to them.

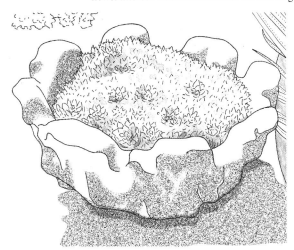

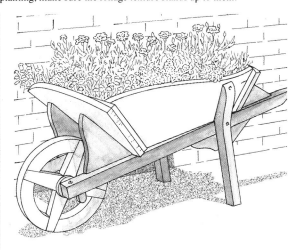

This stone container of carved acanthus leaves has a feeling of weight and solidity.

This old chimneypot makes an enchanting foil to the planting.

A superannuated wooden wheelbarrow can make a pretty planting box, but the wood must be treated.

A stoneware pot in the form of a compressed sphere, with incised decoration, in bronze and black.

A planting case by the author, with four steel straps that take carrying poles.

A simple clay pot by Jim Keeling. The horizontal banding is elegant and restrained.

Glossary

Cross references are given in CAPITAL LETTERS.

Allée A walk or ride cut through dense woodland, often with the trees on either side trimmed like hedges.

Aquatics Plants living in water, whether floating or submerged.

Arbour A construction with plants climbing over it. Generally consisting of a timber frame, arbours sometimes incorporate trellis walls and roof. Most often they are square, octagonal or round, but they might be extended to make a tunnel-arbour, or PERGOLA.

Armillary sphere A celestial globe that consists of metal rings to represent various divisions, such as the equator, the tropics, etc. These divisions revolve on an axis within another circle that represents the horizon.

Baluster A short pillar of circular or square section, in gardens normally made of stone, sometimes slender above and bulging below, sometimes waisted. The term comes from *balaustra*, the blossom of the wild pomegranate, which it resembles in shape.

Balustrade A series of BALUSTERS capped with a handrail or coping, normally sited at the edge of a terrace, or at the side of a flight of steps.

Bedding plants Plants used for temporary display in beds. They are planted, or "bedded out", in large quantities in their final position after they have been grown, almost to flowering stage, elsewhere – usually under glass. Bedding plants may be annuals, biennials or perennials, and either hardy or tender. They are arranged in schemes that make patterns of different flower and foliage colours.

Bosquet A plantation or thicket of trees in a park or garden. These might be trimmed to form large blocks of greenery as a background to stonework or statuary, as in the Italian garden, or they might contain a hidden garden, as at Versailles.

Caisse de Versailles A timber box or planting case. They originally contained small tender trees that were overwintered in the orangery and brought out into the open for the summer. Sometimes they were made with a removable side so that the root ball could be removed or pruned without too much disturbance. They were also provided with iron rings for lifting.

Carpenter's work The term used to describe elaborate timber structures, such as arbours, tunnel arbours and trellis fences, characteristic of late medieval and early Renaissance gardens.

Chadar A water chute with a profiled surface that breaks the flow of water, so that it foams like the white Kashmir shawl from which the *chadar* takes its name.

Chinoiserie A pseudo-Chinese style of ornament, particularly prevalent in the 18th and early 19th centuries. It was manifest mostly in pagodas and bridges, often with brightly coloured fretwork.

Clairvoyée An aperture in a wall or hedge enabling the surrounding countryside to be viewed from within the garden. Sometimes the opening is protected, particularly in Spain, by an elaborate iron grille. Such an opening is normally located at the end of a walk.

Coade stone An artificial stone, made of fired clay with additives. The compound, whose exact formula is now lost, was moulded and sculpted before firing. It was popular in England in the latter 18th century and early 19th century. There were various other similar techniques for making artificial stone.

Cordon A tree, normally a fruit tree, that is restricted to one or two stems by pruning. This allows several trees to be grown in a small space along a wall. They are often grown obliquely to allow a longer stem length within a convenient height.

Crinkle-crankle wall A wall that is serpentine on plan. Such walls have a regular series of sheltered bays, and are more stable than straight walls of similar thickness.

Espalier A system for training fruit trees on horizontal wires stretched on a wall or between posts. The tree is pruned to a central trunk, with branches stretching out horizontally, all in the same plane, at regular intervals above each other.

Eyecatcher A feature in the landscape or garden that acts as a focal point. This might be an arbour, garden house or statue, at the end of an alley or vista, or perhaps a ruin or folly on a hill.

Fan A form of fruit tree trained on a wall, or occasionally on horizontal wires, with branches radiating out from a short stem.

Folly A garden structure, usually an EYECATCHER, with no functional purpose. Follies are often quite unusual architecturally, taking the form of, for example, pyramids, towers or ruins.

Gazebo A structure commanding a view: either a turret or lantern on the roof of a house, or a separate garden building. The term also sometimes referred to a projecting window or balcony. It may have originated as a mock-Latin verb meaning "I will gaze".

Gnomon On a sundial, a pin or triangular plate whose shadow indicates, on the calibrated face, the time of day.

Goblet A form of fruit tree that is trained so that the branches reach outwards and then upwards from a very short trunk, somewhat in the shape of a goblet or vase.

Grotto Derived from the underground cave sacred to a local divinity, grottoes were made either in imitation of such caves, or as more architecturally finished structures above ground with inner rooms lined with shells, interesting geological stones, pebbles, glass, mirrors etc. Often filled with statuary and fountains, they were sometimes associated with theatres or used as a cool place for dining. See also NYMPHAEUM.

Ground cover The use of plants to cover the soil surface so completely that weeds are suppressed and the minimum of cultivation is required. Herbaceous perennials and shrubs may be used in this way.

Ha-ha A retaining wall or a fence sunk in a wide ditch below the level of the garden, separating the garden from the landscape beyond. A ha-ha does not appear in the view, yet keeps cattle or deer out of the garden. It became popular in the 18th century when landowners wanted their parkland to come right up to the walls of the house, apparently without a break.

Herbaceous border A bed or series of beds devoted to the cultivation of herbaceous perennials. It became popular in the latter part of the 19th century, particularly under the influence of Gertrude Jekyll. More popular today are mixed borders that include some shrubs as well as bulbs and annuals.

Herm A statue consisting of a square tapered pillar surmounted by a bust, often that of Hermes.

Hortus conclusus A medieval term signifying an enclosed garden, which was generally small in scale, possibly reminiscent of the monastic cloister. It was enclosed with a fence (sometimes of trellis), a hedge or a wall, and often had a central fountain.

Island bed A relatively large bed of mostly herbaceous perennials, often set in grass, that can be seen from all sides.

Jardin anglo-chinois A marriage of styles, derived from the *jardin anglais*, which was the European idea of the relaxed style of gardening practised in England, and CHINOISERIE. It was popular throughout Europe in the late 18th and early 19th centuries.

Knot A bed laid out in an intricate pattern made from low-growing or clipped plants such as box, santolina, thrift, germander etc. The spaces within the pattern were filled with coloured sands or gravels, or sometimes flowers. Knots were a popular Renaissance idea, perhaps of medieval origin, and were used throughout Europe in the 16th and 17th centuries.

Mount An artificial hill within a garden from which to view the surrounding countryside. Mounts appeared in many European gardens during the Renaissance. They were square or circular in plan and sometimes had spiral ramps running around them up to the top. They were open-topped or

surmounted by trees, or sometimes by a little banqueting house. They were located either in the middle of the garden or against an outside wall.

Nymphaeum A frequent feature of Renaissance and Baroque gardens. Derived from the GROTTO, the nymphaeum was a building dedicated to the nymphs who were believed to frequent sacred springs. It was often filled with statuary as well as with ornamental waterworks.

Parterre A level garden area containing ornamental beds of varying shapes and sizes. It is generally rectangular and surrounded by an enclosing element such as balustrading or a PERGOLA. Originally, the individual beds were often designed as KNOTS.

Parterre de broderie A PARTERRE made with an edging material (frequently box) laid out in a way that resembles embroidery. Originating in 17th-century France, this type of parterre was designed as an uninterrupted, unified pattern, specifically to be viewed from a terrace or from the principal rooms of the house. Variety was achieved by the introduction of curves and arabesques.

Pergola Originally a tunnel-arbour or covered walk, with plants grown over a timber structure; however, the term now often refers to a series of square or rounded arches at regular intervals along the length of a walk. A pergola may also be single-sided with the beams laid between upright columns on one side and a wall on the other. Confusingly, the word also sometimes denotes an open post and beam construction along just one side of a path, with no beams spanning across.

Pleaching Making a narrow, tall hedge by training the branches of suitable varieties of tree, such as lime or hornbeam, horizontally along wires or canes. Growth is controlled by regular pruning, and eventually the trees can be clipped like a hedge. The lower portions of the trunks are often left bare, making a "palisade" or "pole hedge".

Rustication A method of forming stonework with roughened surfaces and deeply recessed joints, in order to give it great visual strength.

Setts Small cubes of granite, varying between 4 and 8 inches in size, although sometimes rectangular. They are used for paving, bedded on sand, in a variety of patterns, including interlocking fans. Although expensive, they are very durable.

Staddle stone A mushroom-shaped construction in stone, about 2 feet high, originally supporting the corners of a grain store. The overhanging upper section prevented rats from climbing up. Staddle stone, are now frequently used as garden ornaments, flanking gates or serving as a local accent.

Stove An obsolete term for a hot-house. used in the 19th century.

Stumpery A 19th-century novelty, the stumpery was an area of tree stumps arranged in picturesque groupings, evoking rustic associations. The garden writer Shirley Hibberd recommended that a stumpery should be thickly planted with varieties of fern and trailing plants.

Tapis vert Strictly, an expanse of turf (literally, "green carpet"). Occasionally, the word denotes a PARTERRE with designs in dwarf box.

Term A statue or bust representing the god Terminus, the Roman divinity in charge of boundaries. The bust was normally mounted on a short pillar.

Topiary The art of clipping and training shrubs and trees into all kinds of shapes, from simple balls and cones to more complicated shapes, such as houses and peacocks. Topiary was practised by the Romans and was popular in the Renaissance and again in the 19th century. Many plants can be used, but yew and box are the favourites.

Treillage The French word for trellis, which is often used in English to denote garden structures such as ARBOURS, trellis tunnels or trellis houses.

Trompe l'oeil A visual deception or illusion. In the garden this can take many forms – the painting of a false view, trelliswork built to simulate a perspective, mirrors giving the illusion of another space. Another form of *trompe l'oeil* is the HA-HA, where a lawn appears to flow into the park beyond without a break.

Water parterre A shallow formal pool in which geometric patterns or arabesques are laid out in stonework, and the spaces between filled with water. See also PARTERRE.

BIBLIOGRAPHY

The books and articles in the following list may be of interest for further reading. Many of the older books, which are often well illustrated, give detailed accounts of historical precedents that might be usable in the garden today. Most of the sources listed have been consulted at first hand during the writing of *The Well-Furnished Garden*.

Abrioux, Yves, *Ian Hamilton Finlay*, Reaktion Books, Edinburgh, 1985
Acton, Harold, *The Villas of Tuscany*, Thames & Hudson, London, 1973
Adams, W.H., *Atget's Gardens*, Gordon Fraser, London, 1979
Amherst, Lady Alicia, *History of Gardening in England*, B. Quaritch, London, 1896
Arts Council of Great Britain, *The Arts of Islam*, London, 1976
Augustine, St, *De Civitate Dei* (tr. Henry Bettenson), Penguin, London, 1972

Bacon, Francis, *Of Gardens*, 1625
Balmori, D., D.K. McGuire & E.M. McPeck, *Beatrix Farrand's American Landscapes*, Sagapress, 1985
Bardi, P.M., *The Tropical Gardens of Burle Marx,* London, 1964
Batey, Mavis, "Regency Setting Restored", *Country Life*, London, April 26, 1984
Binney, Marcus, "Conserving Garden Sculpture", *Country Life*, January 28, 1982
Binney, Marcus & Anne Hills, *Elysian Gardens*, SAVE, London, 1979
Blomfield, R., & F.I. Thomas, *The Formal Garden in England*, MacMillan, London, 1892
Boccacio, *The Decameron* (tr. G.H. MacWilliam), Penguin, London, 1972
Boyceau, J., *Traité du Jardinage*, Paris, 1638
Brooke, E. Adveno, *Gardens of England*, c.1857
Brookes, John, *The Garden Book,* London (Dorling Kindersley) and New York, 1984
Brown, Jane, *Gardens of a Golden Afternoon*, Allen Lane, London, 1982
Brown, Roderick (ed.), *The Architectural Outsiders*, Waterstone, London, 1985

Chambers, Sir William, *Designs of Chinese Buildings etc.*, 1757
Gardens and Buildings at Kew, 1763
A Dissertation on Oriental Gardening, 1772
Church, Thomas D., *Gardens are for People*, McGraw-Hill, New York, 1983
Clifford, Derek, *A History of Garden Design*, 1966
Coats, Peter, *House and Garden Book of Garden Decoration*, Collins, London, 1972
Cole, Nathaniel, *Royal Parks and Gardens of London*, 1877
Colonna, Francesco, *Hypnerotomachia Poliphili*, Da Capo Press, 1969
Columella, *On Agriculture*, (tr. H.B.Ash), 1941
Comito, T., *The Idea of the Garden in the Renaissance*, Harvester Press, Brighton (Sussex), 1979
Confucius, *The Analects* (tr. D. C. Lau), Penguin, London, 1979.
Country Life, *Gardens Old and New*, London, 3rd edn
Cowell, F.R., *The Garden as a Fine Art*, Weidenfeld, London, 1978
Crisp, Sir Frank, *Mediaeval Gardens*, Hacker, 1966
Crowe, Dame Sylvia, *Garden Design*, 2nd edn, Packard, 1981
Crowe, S., & S. Haywood, *The Gardens of Mughal India*, Thames & Hudson, London, 1972

De Caus, Isaac, *Designs for Wilton*, c.1640
De Caus, Saloman, *Hortus Palatinus*, Frankfurt, 1620
De Crescentiis, Peter, *Opus ruralium . . . commodorum*
De Vries, Vredemann, *Hortorum viridariorumque formae*, 1583

Dodsley, R., *Description of the Leasowes*, 1764
Downing, Andrew J., *A Treatise on the Theory and Practice of Landscape Gardening Adapted to North America*, New York, 1841
Dresser, Christopher, *Principles of Decorative Design*, 1873
Du Cerceau, J. Androuet, *Les Plus Excellents Bastiments de France*, 1576-9

Edwards, Paul, *English Garden Ornament*, Bell & Hyman, 1965
Elliott, Brent, "We must have the noble cliff", *Country Life*, London, January 5, 1984

Farrelly, E.M., "The Triumph of Jellicoe", *Architectural Review*, London, September 1985
Foley, D.J., *Garden Ornaments, Complements and Accessories*, Crown, New York, 1972
Furttenbach, J., *Designs for Princely Palaces and Gardens*, 1628

Garden Club of America, *Gardens of Colony and State*, Scribner's, New York, 1931
Gardener, J.S., *English Ironwork of the 17th & 18th Centuries*, Batsford, London
Gibbs, James, *Book of Architecture*,
Girard, J., *Versailles Gardens: Sculpture and Mythology*, Sotheby's, London, 1985
Girouard, Mark, *Life in the English Country House*, Yale (New Haven) and London, 1978
The Return to Camelot, Yale (New Haven) and London, 1981
Gothein, M.L., *A History of Garden Art*, 1928

Hadfield, Miles, *A History of British Gardening*, Spring Books, Feltham (Middlesex), 1969
Harris, John, *The Artist and the Country House*, Sotheby's, London, 1985
A Garden Alphabet, Octopus, London, 1979
(ed.) *The Garden: A Celebration of One Thousand Years of British Gardening*, RHS, London, 1979
Harvey, John, *Mediaeval Gardens*, Batsford, London, 1981
Hellyer, Arthur, "Romantic Past, Bleak Future", *Country Life*, London, December 19, 1985
Hepper, F.N. (ed.), *Kew: Gardens for Science and Pleasure*, HMSO, Norwich (Norfolk), 1982
Hero of Alexandria, *Pneumatica* (tr. Bennett Woodcroft), 1971
Hibberd, Shirley, *Rustic Adornments for Homes of Taste*, 1856
Hicks, David, *Garden Design*, Routledge, London, 1982
Hill, Thomas, *Most Briefe and Pleasant Treatyse*, 1563
(Didymus Mountain) *The Gardner's Labyrinth*, 1578
Hobhouse, Penelope, *Colour in Your Garden*, Collins, London, 1985
Holme, C. (ed), *The Gardens of England*, The Studio, 1911
Homer, *The Odyssey* (tr. E.V.Rieu), Penguin, London, 1946
Hughes, J.A., *Garden Architecture*, Longmans, London, 1866
Hunt, J.D., & P. Willis, *The Genius of The Place*, Elek, London, 1975
Hunter, John M., *Land into Landscape*, George Godwin, London, 1985

Hussey, Christopher, *English Gardens and Landscapes, 1700-1750*, Country Life, London, 1967
Huxley, Anthony, *An Illustrated History of Gardening*, Paddington Press, London, 1978
Hyams, Edward, *A History of Gardens and Gardening*, Dent, London, 1971

Jacques, David, *Georgian Gardens*, Batsford, London, 1983
James, John, *Theory and Practice of Gardening*, 1714
Jashemski, W.F., *Gardens of Pompeii*, Caratzas Bros.
Jekyll, Gertrude, *Colour in the Flower Garden*, Country Life, London, 1908
Wall and Water Gardens, Country Life, London, 3rd edn
Jekyll, G., & C. Hussey, *Garden Ornament*, Country Life, London, 1927
Jekyll, G., & L. Weaver, *Gardens for Small Country Houses*, Country Life, London, 1913
Jellicoe, Sir Geoffrey, *The Guelph Lectures on Landscape Design*, Univ. Guelph, 1983
Garden Decoration and Ornament for Smaller Houses, Country Life, London, 1936
Jellicoe, Sir Geoffrey & Susan, *The Landscape of Man*, Thames & Hudson, London, 1975
Water: The Use of Water in Landscape Architecture, A. & C. Black, London, 1971
Johnson, Hugh, *The Principles of Gardening*, Mitchell Beazley (London) and Simon & Schuster (New York), 1979
Jones, Barbara, *Follies and Grottoes*, Constable, London, 1979
Jones, Owen, *Grammar of Ornament*, Van Nostrand Reinhold, New York, 1972
Juvenal, *The Sixteen Satires* (tr. P. Green), Penguin, London, 1985

Keswick, Maggie, *The Chinese Garden*, Academy Editions, London, 1978
Kip & Knyff, *Nouveau Théâtre de la Grande Bretagne*, London, 1708
Koran, The (tr. J. M. Rodwell), Dent, London, 1909

Langley, Batty, *New Principles of Gardening*, London, 1778
Lawson, William, *A New Orchard and Garden*, 1665
Lawrence, S., & G. Foy, *Music in Stone*, Frederick Müller, London, 1984
Lees-Milne, Alvilde, & Rosemary Verey, *The Englishman's Garden*, Allen Lane, London, 1982
The Englishwoman's Garden, Chatto & Windus, London, 1980
Lehrman, Jonas, *Earthly Paradise*, Thames & Hudson, London, 1980
Loudon, J.C., *Encyclopaedia of Gardening*, 1834
The Suburban Gardener and Villa Companion, 1838
The Landscape Gardening of Humphry Repton, 1840
Loudon, Mrs, *The Lady's Country Companion*, 1867

Markham, Gervase, *Countrey Farme*, 1616
Masson, Georgina, *Italian Gardens*, Thames & Hudson, London, 1961
Mawson, Thomas H., *The Art and Craft of Garden Making*, Batsford, London, 1901
McDougall, E.B. (ed.), *Fons Sapientiae*, Dumbarton Oaks, Washington DC, 1978
McLean, T., *Mediaeval English Gardens*, Collins, London, 1981
Miller, Naomi, *Heavenly Caves*, Allen & Unwin, London
Moore, S., "Hail Gods of our Forefathers", *Country Life*, London, January 31, 1985
Morgan, M.H., *Vitruvius: The Ten Books on Architecture*, Dover, 1960
Mowl, Tim & Brian Earnshaw, *Trumpet at a Distant Gate*, Waterstone, London, 1985
New Larousse Encyclopaedia of Mythology, Hamlyn, London, 1973

Page, Russell, *The Education of a Gardener*, Collins, London, 1983
Papworth, J.B., *Rural Residences*, 1818
Hints on Ornamental Gardening, 1823
Pereire, Anita & G. van Zuylen, *Private Gardens of France*, Weidenfeld, London, 1983

Physick, J., *Designs for English Sculpture 1680-1860*, HMSO, Norwich, 1969
Pliny the Elder, *Natural History* (tr. Packham and Jones), 1949
Pliny the Younger, *Letters* (trs. Betty Radice), Penguin, London, 1963
Plumptre, George, *Collins Book of British Gardens*, Collins, London, 1985
Pope, Alexander, "Epistle to the Earl of Burlington", 1731
Prest, John, *The Garden of Eden*, Yale, New Haven, 1981
Price, Uvedale, *Essays on the Picturesque*, London, 1794
Pückler-Muskau, Prince H.L.H., *Hints on Landscape Gardening*, Boston, 1917

Read, Benedict, *Victorian Sculpture*, Yale (New Haven), 1983
Repton, Humphry, *Sketches and Hints . . . Landscape Gardening*, 1795
Observations . . . Landscape Gardening, 1803
An Enquiry into . . . Landscape Gardening, 1806
Design for the Pavillion at Brighton, 1808
Robson, Eric, "Taking Gardens into Care", *Country Life*, London, December 13, 1984
Rowan, Alastair, *Garden Buildings*, Country Life, London, 1968
Rykwert, Joseph (ed.), *Leon Battista Alberti*, Architectural Design 5/6, London, 1979
(ed.) *Leon Battista Alberti: Ten Books on Architecture*, Tiranti, London, 1955

Shepherd, J.C. & G.A. Jellicoe, *Gardens and Design*, Ernest Benn, Tonbridge (Kent), 1927
Siren, O., *Gardens of China*, New York, 1949
China in the Gardens of Europe, New York, 1950
Strong, Sir Roy, *The Renaissance Garden in England*, Thames & Hudson, London, 1979
Stroud, Dorothy, *Capability Brown*, 1950
Switzer, Stephen, *Ichnographia Rustica*, 1718

Temple, Sir William, *Upon the Gardens of Epicurus*, London, 1680
Thacker, Christopher, *The History of Gardens*, Croom Helm, London, 1979
(tr.) "La Manière de Montrer les Jardins de Versailles", *Garden History*, September, 1972
Masters of the Grotto, Joseph and Josiah Lane, 1976
Thomas, Graham S., *Gardens of the National Trust*, Weidenfeld, London, 1979
Thouin, G., *Plans Raisonnés de Toutes Les Espèces de Jardins*, 1819
Tipping, H. Avery, *English Gardens*, Country Life, London, 1925
Triggs, H. Inigo, *The Formal Garden in England and Scotland*, Batsford, London, 1902
Garden Craft in Europe, 1913
Tunnard, Christopher, *Gardens in the Modern Landscape*, Architectural Press, London, 1938

Van der Groen, *Le Jardinier de Pays-Bas*, Bruxelles, 1681
Van der Horst, A.J., "A William and Mary Garden Reborn", *The Garden*, London, March, 1986
Varro, *On Agriculture* (tr. Hooper and Ash), 1954
Verey, Rosemary, *Classic Garden Design*, Viking, New York, 1984
Volkamer, J.C., *Nurnbergische Hesperides*, London, 1708-14

Walpole, Horace, *On Modern Gardening*, London, 1786
Weaver, Lawrence, *English Leadwork*, Batsford, London, 1909
Whateley, Thomas, *Observations on Modern Gardening*
Whinney, M., *English Sculpture 1720-1830*, HMSO, Norwich (Norfolk)
Wilkinson, E., & M. Henderson (ed.), *The House of Boughs*, Viking, New York, 1985
Willis, Peter (ed.), *Furor Hortensis*, Elysium Press, 1974
Worlidge, John, *Systema Horticultura*, 1677
Wright, Thomas (ed. E. Harris), *Arbours and Grottoes*

DIRECTORY OF ORNAMENT

The following lists of manufacturers, suppliers, craftworkers and sources of further information make no pretence of being comprehensive. All the individuals and companies mentioned either are known to the author or have been recommended to him. The author is aware that there are undoubtedly many more whose work, on the basis of quality, would warrant inclusion, particularly in areas outside his own field of activity. A mention here does not necessarily constitute unconditional approval of all the work produced or supplied by a particular source: taste and standards vary, and readers are advised wherever possible to inspect the products for themselves, in daylight, before making a purchase. It can be dangerous to rely only on catalogue illustrations. Many of the companies listed below export their products throughout Europe and the USA.

UNITED KINGDOM

MANUFACTURERS, SUPPLIERS AND CRAFTWORKERS

Acrise Pottery,
Ladwood, Acrise,
Folkestone, Kent
(030389) 3252
Clayware, traditional designs

Architectural Heritage,
Boddington Manor,
Boddington,
Nr Cheltenham,
Gloucestershire
(024268) 741
Antique ornament

Armstrong-Davis Gallery,
The Square,
Arundel,
Sussex BN18 9AB
(0903) 882752
Modern and antique ornament

Artisan,
Caxton Way,
Thetford,
Norfolk
(0842) 62321
Distributors of Swedish furniture, some good modern designs

Baldwin, Gordon,
Blue Giraffe Workshops,
1 Willowbrook,
Eton,
Windsor,
Berkshire SL4 6HL
(0753) 865064
Sculptor in stoneware and earthenware

Baldwin, Raef
Address as for Baldwin, Gordon
Sculptor

Barlow-Tyrie,
Springwood Industrial Estate,
Rayne Road,
Braintree,
Essex
(0376) 22505
Furniture

Barnsley House Garden Furniture,
Barnsley House,
Cirencester
(0285) 74561
Timber furniture

Bayer, Svend,
Duck Pool Cottage
Sheepwash,
Beaworthy,
Devon
EX21 5PW
(040 923) 282
Stoneware, large pots in good designs

Bell, Quentin,
81 Heghton Street,
Firle,
Lewes,
Sussex
(079 159) 201
Sculptor

Bulmer Brick and Tile Company,
Hole Farm,
Nr Bulmer,
Essex
(0787) 29232
Hand-made bricks

Chatsworth Carpenters,
Estate Offices,
Derbyshire Estates,
Edensor,
Bakewell,
Derbyshire DE4 1PJ
(024 688) 2242
Timber furniture. Good traditional designs

Chelsea Gardener, The
Sidney Street,
London SW3
(01) 352 5656
General ornament and furniture

Chilstone,
Sprivers Estate,
Horsmonden,
Kent
(089 272) 3553
Reconstituted stone

Christopher, Ann,
The Stable Block
Hay Street,
Marshfield,
Chippenham,
Wiltshire SN14 8PF
(0225) 891717
Sculptor

Churchill Sculptures
74 Lansdowne Road,
London W11 2LS
(01) 727 8891
Bird sculptures

Classic Garden Furniture Ltd,
Audley Avenue,
Newport,
Shropshire
(0952) 813311
Classic cast-iron furniture and general ornament

Clifton, Little Venice,
3 Warwick Place,
London W9
(01) 289 7894
Antique ornaments

Coombe House Antiques,
Malling Street,
Lewes,
Sussex
(0273) 473862
Reproduction wirework

Cooper, Paul,
Pendle College,
University of Lancaster,
Bailrigg,
Lancaster LA1 4YU
(0524) 65201
Sculptor

Crace Designs, Andrew,
Bourne Lane,
Much Hadham,
Hertfordshire
(027 984) 2685
Timber furniture

Crowther of Syon Lodge Ltd,
Syon Lodge,
Busch Corner,
London Road,
Isleworth,
Middlesex TW7 5BH
(01) 560 7978
Antique ornament

Crowther, T. and Son Ltd,
282 North End Road,
Fulham,
London SW6
(01) 385 1375
Antique ornament

Deans, Nick,
Loke Cottage,
Hall Road,
Aldborough, Norwich,
Norfolk NR11 7HH
(026 377) 423
Sculptor

Fedden, Bryant,
Castle Street,
Winchcombe,
Cheltenham,
Gloucestershire GL54 5JA
(0242) 602782
Sculptor

Garratt, Jonathan,
Coach House, Bartley Close,
Bartley,
Near Southampton,
Hampshire SO4 2LN
(0703) 812141
Clayware

Gibbs Ltd, Christopher,
118 New Bond Street,
London W1
(01) 629 2008
Antique ornament

Gough, Peter,
13 Southover High Street,
Lewes,
Sussex BN7 1HT
(0273) 472744
Sculptor in flints

Haddonstone Ltd,
The Forge House,
East Haddon,
Northampton NN6 8DB
(0604) 770711
Reconstituted stone ornament

Halliday's,
The Old College,
Dorchester-upon-Thames,
Oxfordshire
(0865) 340068
*Modern and antique statues and
    furniture*

Hawkes, Jonathan,
Professional Woodworkers,
1 Church Street,
Pewsey,
Wiltshire SN9 5DL
(0672) 62878
*Timber furniture, modern and
    traditional designs*

Hicks, David,
David Hicks International Designers,
1 Ponton Road,
London SW8
(01) 627 4400
Timber furniture

Hill, Stuart,
Claydon Forge,
Claydon,
Suffolk
(0473) 831000
Blacksmith: interesting modern designs

Hodgetts, Graham,
The Forge,
Newport, St Germans,
Cornwall PL12 5NS
(0503) 30411
*Blacksmith: modern and traditional
    designs*

Hullis, Michael,
7 Seven Gardens,
Burgh,
Suffolk IP13 6SU
(0473) 358107
Clayware, modern and traditional

Ionides, Polly,
5 Wickham Road,
Brockley,
London SE4
(01) 692 1939
Sculptor

Jobst, Paul,
19 Bow Street,
Alton,
Hampshire GU34 1NY
(0420) 87432
Blacksmith

Jones, Jenifer,
4 Tideswell Road,
London SW15 6LJ
(01) 789 4774
Clayware

Keeling, Jim,
Whichford Pottery,
Whichford,
Shipston-on-Stour,
Warwickshire CV36 5PG
(060) 884416
Clayware

Landscape Ornament Company,
Voysey House,
Barley Mow Passage,
Chiswick W4 4PN
(01) 995 9739
*Reconstituted stone, bronze, timber and
    clayware, statues, ornament and
    furniture*

Leech, Lucinda,
King Street, Jericho,
Oxford OX2 6DF
(0865) 56376
Timber furniture, good modern designs

Lister Green Bros.,
Freepost 95,
Hailsham,
Sussex BN27 1BR
(0323) 840771
Timber furniture

**London Architectural Salvage and
    Supply Co.,**
Mark Street,
London EC2A 4ER
(01) 739 0448
*Antique and modern furniture and
    statuary*

Machin Designs Ltd,
Ransome's Dock,
Parkgate Road,
London SW11 4NP
(01) 223 4340
Conservatories

Mallett at Bourdon House Ltd,
2 Davies Street,
London W1
(01) 629 2444
Antique garden ornament

Makepeace, John,
Parnham House,
Beaminster,
Dorset DT8 3NA
(0308) 862204
Timber furniture, good modern designs

Milner, Elizabeth,
40 Tarrant Street,
Arundel,
West Sussex BN18 9DN
(0903) 883445
Hammocks

Mlinaric, David,
61 Glebe Place,
London SW3
(01) 730 9072
Timber furniture

Naylor Conservation,
Unit H3, Hales Field 19,
Telford,
Shropshire
(0952) 583116
Restoration

Olive Tree Trading,
Twickenham Trading Estate,
Rugby Road, Twickenham,
Middlesex
(01) 995 5281
Imported clayware

Oxford Gallery, The,
23 High Street,
Oxford
(0865) 242731
Exhibitions of garden sculpture

Parkinson, Peter,
Heathfield House,
Shortheath Common,
Oakhangar, Bordon,
Hampshire
(042 03) 7191
Sculptor, modern sundials

Peschar, Hannah,
Black and White Cottage,
Standon Lane, Ockley,
Surrey RH5 5QR
(0306) 79677
Open-air gallery for garden sculpture

Pye, William,
43 Hambalt Road,
London SW4 9EQ
(01) 767 3588
Sculptor

Rattee and Kett Ltd,
Purbeck Road,
Cambridge CB2 2PG
(0223) 248061
*Sculptors, masons, conservation work,
    reconstituted stone*

Rooke's Pottery,
Hartington, Buxton,
Derbyshire SK17 0AN
(029884) 650
Clayware

Start, Peter,
Ashleigh House,
Ware Road,
Barby, Nr Rugby,
Warwickshire
(0788) 890971
Clayware

Stefanidis, John,
6 Burnsall Street,
London SW3
(01) 351 3436
Timber furniture

Taplin, Guy,
Anglesea Cottage,
Anglesea Road,
Wivenhoe,
Essex CO7 9JR
(020 622) 2160
Bird sculptor

Traditional Trellis Ltd,
24 Holland Park Avenue,
London W11 3QU
(01) 243 1090
Trelliswork

Van Dijk, Nenne,
6 Mount Adon Park,
London SE22 ODT
(01) 693 5366
Sculptor

Verity, Simon,
The Old Schoolhouse,
Rodbourne,
Wiltshire
(06662) 3837
Sculptor

Verey, Charles,
See **Barnsley House**

Young, Monica,
Reeth,
Richmond,
North Yorkshire DL11 6SP
(0748) 84487
Clayware, good modern designs

Winter, Faith,
Venzers Yard,
Puttenham,
Surrey
(0483) 810300
Sculptor

SOURCES OF INFORMATION

Brick Advisory Centre,
Building Centre,
26 Store Street,
London WC1 7BT
(01) 637 0047

Building Conservation Trust,
Apartment 39,
Hampton Court Palace,
East Molesey,
Surrey KT8 9BS
(01) 943 2277

Centre for the Conservation of Historic Parks and Gardens,
The Institute of Advance Architectural Studies,
University of York,
The King's Manor,
York YO1 2EP
(0904) 59861

Crafts Council,
12 Waterloo Place,
London SW1
(01) 930 4811

Garden History Society,
12 Charlbury Road,
Oxford
OX2 6UT

Historic Buildings and Monuments Commission,
25 Savile Row,
London W1X 2BT
(01) 734 6010

Landscape Institute
(information on landscape architects),
12 Carlton House Terrace,
London SW1Y 5AH
(01) 839 4044

National Trust,
36 Queen Anne's Gate,
London SW1H 9AS
(01) 222 9251

National Trust for Scotland,
5 Charlotte Square,
Edinburgh EH2 4DU
(031) 226 5922

National Trust Statuary Workshops,
The Tennis Courts,
Cliveden Estate,
Taplow,
Maidenhead
SL6 OJA

Royal Horticultural Society,
Vincent Square,
London SW1P 2PE
(01) 834 4333

Royal Incorporation of Architects in Scotland,
15 Rutland Square,
Edinburgh EH1 2BE
(031) 229 7205

Royal Institute of British Architects,
66 Portland Place,
London W1N 4AD
(01) 550 5533

Society for the Protection of Ancient Buildings,
37 Spital Square,
London E1
(01) 405 2646

Society of Landscape and Garden Designers,
23 Reigate Road,
Ewell,
Surrey
KT17 1PS

Stone Federation,
82 New Cavendish Street,
London W1M 8AD
(01) 580 5588

Timber Research and Development Association,
Stocking Lane,
Hughenden Valley,
High Wycombe,
Buckinghamshire HP14 4ND
(0240) 243091

FRANCE

MANUFACTURERS, SUPPLIERS AND CRAFTWORKERS

Blot-Galland,
36 rue Pascal,
77100 Meaux
(64) 33 00 39
Wood and metal garden furniture

Du Côté des Jardins,
14 rue des Jardins-St-Paul,
75004 Paris
(1) 48 87 21 41
Wooden garden seats, planters and trelliswork

Fonderie Saint Maur,
3 rue Chevreul,
75011 Paris
(1) 43 73 50 77
Bronze casting

Générale de Poteries d'Alsace,
B.P. 06,
67430 Diemeringen,
(88) 00 40 10
Some nice clayware

Jardinières,
40 rue de Maubauge,
75009 Paris
(1) 48 78 39 24
Good artificial stone castings

Lallemand,
Le Balmay,
F01430 Maillat
(74) 75 71 72
Garden furniture

Neyrat Peyronie,
B.P. 48,
71102 Chalon-sur-Saone,
(85) 48 35 23
Garden furniture in metal and wood; good umbrellas.

Poterie Clarous,
Mane,
31260 Salies-du-Salat,
(61) 90 54 54
Clayware

Ravel-Decroix et Fils,
Avenue des Goums,
13400 Aubagne
(42) 03 05 59
Clayware

Salin, S.A.,
Dannarie sur Saulx
F. 55500 Ligny en Barrois,
(29) 75 90 02
Cast-iron urns, statues and garden furniture; good reproductions

SOURCES OF INFORMATION

Fedération Françoise Du Paysage,
4 rue Hardy,
Versailles,
Cedex 78009
(1) 30 21 47 45

Ordre des Architects,
78 Avenue Raymond Poincaré,
75116 Paris

ITALY

MANUFACTURERS, SUPPLIERS AND CRAFTWORKERS

Angeli, Giorgio,
102 via Madonnina,
Querceta, Seravezza,
Liguria
Sculptor

Bernasconi, Enrica,
Via Montebello, 27,
20121 Milano
(2) 6551550
Ornament restoration

Cotto Ref SPA,
50023 Impruneta,
Firenze
(55) 2012180
Terracotta pots, floor tiles and general ornament.

De Vita, Alessandra,
Via Ponzio 78,
20123 Milano
(2) 235246
Ornament restoration

Fontanelle, Stradali,
Via S. Vicenzo 6,
20029 Turbigo,
Milano
(3) 31899318
Cast-iron drinking fountains

Gres Koppo Bitossi,
Via A. Gramsci 176,
50056 Montelupo Fiorentino,
Firenze
(55) 0571 51008
Glazed stoneware pots, traditional

Hartman, Veronica
Via Sarzanese 211,
55040 Capezzano Pianore,
Liguria
(584) 913327
Restoration

Italgarden,
Via Flaminia,
Km 37500,
00068 Rignano Flaminio,
Roma
(761) 509090
Reconstituted stone ornament

Via Aurelia,
Km 365.33, Pietrasanta,
Liguria
Sculpture

Mital,
50023 Impruneta,
Firenze,
Clayware

Morelli,
Via de Carracci 81,
40131 Bologna
(51) 634 4090
Cast-iron drinking fountains

Morselletto,
Via dell'Economia 97,
36100 Vicenza
(444) 5531355
Marble sculpture

Nenzi, Benocci & C.,
Via Madonnina 69,
I 53020 Petroio,
Siena
(577) 665012
Clayware, good traditional designs

Piolini, Daniela,
Via Airolo 23,
20159 Milano
(2) 686624
Restoration

Pizzinelli, Rossano,
Via Newton 34,
00100 Roma
Restoration

Poggi Ugo,
Via Impruneta 12,
50023 Impruneta,
Firenze
(55) 2011 077
Clayware, traditional

Prod. Gianni Pacchera,
Via Sant'Egidio 9B,
37121 Verona
(45) 32574
Wooden garden umbrellas

Regoli, Guido,
Via Giorgi Giovanni 35,
00149 Roma
(6) 5565431
Ornament restoration

San Marco Laterizi SPA,
Strada S. Dono 80,
30033 Noale,
Venezia
(41) 440124
Hand-made bricks

Sbigoli Terrecotte,
Via S. Egidio 4R,
50122 Firenze
(55) 2479713
Clayware

Simongavina Paradisoterrestre,
Bologna,
San Lazzaro
(51) 456001
Modern sculpture

Tagliolini, Alessandro,
Via Sarzanese 211,
55040 Capezzano Pianore,
Liguria
(584) 63327
Sculptor

Tongiani, Domenico, SPA,
Via Lottizzazione 10,
Massa
(585) 43206
Interesting marble pots

Vecoli, Mauro,
Via Umbria 2,
Pietrasanta,
Liguria
(584) 71120
Marble sculptor

SOURCES OF INFORMATION

Assoc. Italiano d'Architetti del Paesaggio,
2 Via Ricasoli,
20121 Milano
(2) 874073

Consiglio Nazionale degli Architetti Italiani,
Via Nazionale 69,
00184 Roma

THE NETHERLANDS

MANUFACTURERS AND SUPPLIERS

Haasnoot BV,
Lageweg 25,
Indstrieterrein 'T Heen,
2222 AG Katwijk ZH
(1718) 21744
Garden furniture and buildings, mostly large-scale

J.B.Huisman,
Buitendams 261,
3371 BE Hardinxveld-Giessendam,
(1846) 3084
Thatched timber garden buildings

Speelhout,
Postbus 59,
5300 AB Zaltbommel
(4180) 5150
Garden furniture, mostly for children

SOURCES OF INFORMATION

Vereeniging van Handelaren in Oude Kunst
(information on antique dealers who occasionally sell garden ornament),
Keizergracht 207,
1016 DS Amsterdam
(20) 238904

SOURCES OF INFORMATION

BNT
(institute of landscape architects),
Keizergracht 321,
Postbus 19610,
1000GP Amsterdam
(20) 254959

WEST GERMANY

MANUFACTURERS, SUPPLIERS AND CRAFTWORKERS

Erlau AG,
D-7080 Aalen/Württ.,
Erlau 16,
Postfach 1226
(7361) 595
Good wire-mesh furniture

Fuchs, Anton,
Bohnesmühlgasse 4,
8700 Würzburg
(931) 12051
Reproduction statues and ornament;
also restoration

Grünzig, Spielgeräte,
Postfach 1153,
2813 Eystrup
(425) 4651
Play equipment

Hiestand, Josef,
Postfach 129,
7200 Tuttlingen-Möhringen,
(746) 21322
Benches

Mesch, Erwin,
Grevenmarschstrasse 72,
Postfach 547,
D 4920 Lemgo 1
(5261) 12103
Furniture

Runge and Co.,
Grosser Fledderweg 89,
Postfach 36 46,
4500 Osnabrück
(541) 586184
Furniture

SOURCES OF INFORMATION

Bund Deutscher Architekten,
Ippendorfer Allee 14B,
5300 Bonn

Bund Deutscher Landschaftarchitekten,
Colmanstrasse 32,
5300 Bonn 1
(228) 655488

USA, CANADA AND MEXICO

MANUFACTURERS, SUPPLIERS AND CRAFTWORKERS

Cassidy Brothers Forge Inc,
US Route 1,
Rowley,
Massachusetts 01969-1796
(617) 948 7611
Ironwork, good traditional designs

Charleston Battery Bench Inc.,
191 King Street,
Charleston,
South Carolina 29401
(803) 722 3842
Cast-iron and timber benches

Chattahoochee Makers Company,
1098 Huff Road NW,
Atlanta,
Georgia 30318
(404) 351 7016
Hardwood furniture and planters

Clapper's,
1125 Washington Street,
West Newton,
Massachusetts 02165
(617) 244 7909
General suppliers, English teak
furniture

Dalton Gazebos,
7260-68 Oakley Street,
Philadelphia,
PA 19111
(215) 342 9804
Red cedarwood gazebos, good
trelliswork

Foster, Kevill,
5102 Weststate Street,
Westminster,
California 92683
(714) 894 2013
Timber planters, traditional

Garden Iron,
116 North Clifton Avenue,
Louisville,
Kentucky 40206
(000)
Garden ironwork, interesting frames for
climbers in pots

Gargoyles Ltd,
512 S. Third Street,
Philadelphia,
PA 19147
(215) 629 1700
Reproduction furniture

International Terra Cotta Inc.,
690 North Robertson Boulevard,
Los Angeles,
California 90069-5088
(213) 657 3752
General garden ornament

Iron Fence Co.,
PO Box 467,
Auburn,
Indiana 46706
(219) 925 4264
Iron fences

Lynch, Kenneth and Sons, Inc.,
PO Box 488,
Wilton,
Connecticut 06897-0488
(203) 762 8363
General ornament, restoration advice

Machin Designs (USA) Inc.,
652 Glenbrook Road,
Stamford,
Connecticut 06907
(203) 348 5319
Conservatories

Nampara Gardens,
2004 Golf Course Road,
Bayside,
California 95524
(707) 822 5744
Redwood garden furniture

Pem Fountain Company,
PO Box 426,
Richmond Hill,
Ontario L4C 4Y8
(416) 889 3201
Fountains

Ponzanelli, Gabriel,
San Miguel 18
Cayaacan,
0403 Mexico, D.F.
(689) 1605

Robinson Iron,
Robinson Road,
Alexander City,
Alabama 35010
(205) 329 8486
Cast-iron work, traditional

Smith and Hawken,
25 Corte Madera,
Mill Valley,
California 94941
(415) 383 4415
General suppliers, importing from the
UK

Washington University Technology Associates,
8200 Brentwood Industrial Drive,
St Louis,
Missouri 63144
(314) 645 5230

Wood Classics Inc.,
RD 1, Box 455E,
High Falls,
New York, 12440
(914) 687 7288
Timber furniture

SOURCES OF INFORMATION

American Society of Landscape Architects,
1733 Connecticut Avenue NW,
Washington DC 20009
(202) 466 7730

Canadian Society of Landscape Architects,
PO Box 3304,
Station C,
Ottawa,
Ontario K1J 4J5
(613) 564 0231

Horticultural Society of New York,
128 West 58th Street,
New York,
NY 10019
(212) 757 0915

Landmarks Preservation Commission, New York City
(general information on conservation)
20 Vesey Street,
New York

Marble of Institute of America Inc.,
(advice on restoration)
33505 State Street,
Farmington,
Michegan 48024
(313) 476 5558

National Sculpture Society,
15 East 26th Street,
New York,
NY 10010
(212) 889 6960

National Trust for Historic Preservation,
1785 Massachusetts Avenue NW,
Washington DC 20036
(202) 673 4000

INDEX

Page numbers in *italics* refer to picture captions.

Acanthus motif *177*
Acer *71*
Adam, Robert *139*
Adamesque style *169*
Addison, Joseph 36
Adel (W. Yorkshire) *62*
Aeneid *37, 38*
Aeolus, Temple of *92*
Aeonium *125*
Ailanthus altissima *61*
"Albertine" rose *157*
Albertus Magnus 23
Albi (south of France) 158
Alcazar (Seville) *18, 21*
Alchemilla mollis 99
Alders 98
Aldobrandini, Villa (Frascati) *25, 26*
Algae 70, *132, 165*
Alhambra (Grenada) *18, 18, 21*
Allegory *see* Symbolism
Allées *36, 180*
Allyssum *42, 159*
Alpines 77, *170, 175*
Alton Towers (Staffordshire) 44, *140*
Aluminium 91, *112,* 171
Amelanchier 98
Ammanati, Bartolommeo 27
Ammonite *132, 145*
Amphitheatres 77
Amphorae *167, 169*
André, Edouard 41
Angers 42, *158*
Annuals *167*
  in edgings *116*
  on walls *132*
Anthemis *112, 164*
Apertures, in walls 90
Apollo 30, *30,* 34, 37
Aponogeton distachyus 99
Appenines (sculpture by Ammanati) 27
Apple trees *153, 154*
Apple tunnels 91, *131*
Aquatic plants 97, 98, *99,* 145, *145, 146, 147*
Arbours 81-2, 90, *95, 96,* 106, 134, *134-5, 137*
  as gateways *127*
  medieval 23
  on mounds *80*
Arcades *146*
  Islamic 21
Architecture 91-3, *91, 94, 96,* 134, 137, 138, 140, *134-41*
  colour of 70
  in English landscape gardens 37, 38, *38*
  in Islamic gardens *18, 18,* 20, *20,* 21, *21*
  in oriental gardens *15,* 16
Ariadne *38*
Arley Hall (Cheshire) 42
Armillary spheres 166, *166,* 180
Arp, Jean 47, 48
Artemisia schmidtiana *69*
Arts and Crafts Movement 44
Ashridge (Hertfordshire) *41*
Audley End (Essex) *134*
Avenues 151, *151-2, 156*
  in French Baroque gardens 30
Aviaries 12, 137, *138*
Awnings (for shade) *19*
Azaleas *14, 71*

Babur, Emperor 20
Babylon 13
  Hanging Gardens of 12
Bacchus *103*
  Fountain of (Versailles) 31
Bakewell Robert 36, *122*
Baldwin, Raef *164*
Bali *78*
Balustrades *120,* 122, *122, 133,* 180
  brickwork *133*
  in Chinese gardens 17
  in Islamic gardens 21
  in Italian Renaissance gardens *25,* 27
  in "Italianate" gardens *43*
Bamboo 101, *153, 154*
  bonsai *176*
  for gates *126*
  hedges *157*
  fences 88
  split *124*
Banks 78, *78,* 81
Barbecues 47, 111
Bargeboard 91, *142*
Bark flakes 78
Barking Dog (Nick Deans) *163*
Baroque style 24, 25, *26,* 28-31, *28-31,* 35
Barrel containers 110, 175, *175*
Barry, Sir Charles 41, *43*
Baskets, hanging *177*
Bassin d'Appollon (Versailles) *30*
Bassins 30
Bateman, Richard 37
Bathtub *169*
Battersea Park (London) 43
Bay trees 27
Beaux Arts tradition 46
Bedding out *40,* 41, *42,* 47, 50, *105,* 158, 180
  criticism of 42
Bedding schemes 83, *158, 159, 162*
  raised beds 78
Beech 42, 151
  hedges 106
Begonias *159, 162*
Belloc, Hilaire *166*
Belvedere, Cortile del (Rome) 25
Benches *see* Seats
  in medieval gardens 23
Bengal Cottage, The 44
Berberis 76, 106
Berries 68, *153*
Berry, Duc de 23
Bethlehem (Kuskus) 32
Bicton (Devon) *139*
Biddulph Grange (Staffordshire) 41, 42, 44
Birches 98
Blenheim (Oxfordshire) 38
Blomfield 41
Blond, Le 32
Blue, as a receding colour 70
Boathouses 142, *142*
Boboli Gardens (Florence) *122*
Boccaccio 27
Bois de Moutiers 44
Bologna, Giovanni da *25*
Bolshoi Kapriz 32
Borders 105, *107, 158, 160,* 181
  colour schemes 70, *70, 71*
  Gertrude Jekyll and 42
  "Borrowing" the landscape 54
  in oriental gardens 16
Boschi 24
Bosquets 30, 31, 180
Bowood (Wiltshire) 38, *149*
Box

balls *131, 156*
  in bedding schemes 41
  dwarf *116*
  hedges 88, *106, 157*
  in Italian Renaissance gardens 27
  for mazes 105, *154*
  in parterres 31, *40, 43,* 71, 83, *86, 158, 159*
  topiary 107
Boyceau 31
Bramante, Donato 25
Brancusi, Constantin 47, 48
Brayton, Thomas 42
Brazil 46, 47
Brick
  colonnades *131*
  as an edging *116*
  for paths and paving 82, *86, 117, 118, 119*
  pergolas *132*
  for stairs *120, 121*
  walls 88, 90
  weathering of 70, *83, 119*
Bridgeman, Charles 36, *36*
Bridges 142, *142-5*
  Chinese 17
  false *144*
  Palladian *38, 39,* 142
Brighton, Royal Pavilion 50
Bristol Cross (Stourhead) *140*
British Worthies, Temple of (Stowe) 37, *39*
Brittany *132, 137*
Brooke, E. Adveno *43*
Brown, "Capability" 35, *35,* 36, 37, 38, *39,* 40
Buddhism 14
Buildings *see* Architecture
Bulbs, in edgings 116
Burlington, Lord 36, *36*
Burns, William 51
Bushell, Thomas 38

Caisses de Versailles 31, 180
Cafaggiolo (Italy) 24
California, gardens in 47, *100*
Campanula 120
Campidoglio (Rome) *120*
Canals 145, *146*
  in French Baroque gardens 30, *30*
  in Islamic gardens 20-21, *20*
Cane furniture 110
Canna *175*
Canon's Ashby (Northamptonshire) *126*
Canopus, Hadrian's Villa 13, *13*
Carpenter's work 23, 46, *130,* 131, 180
Cars 58
Cascades *26,* 97, 148, *148, 149*
  in Baroque gardens 30, 32
  in English gardens 38, 39
  in 18th-century gardens 32, *33*
  in Islamic gardens 21, *21*
Caserta (Naples) 32, *33,* 34
Cast iron
  edgings 41
  furniture 43, *44, 112, 171, 173*
  gates *128*
Castello (Florence) 27
Castello Sforzesco (Milan) 23
Castle Ashby (Northamptonshire) 41
Castle Howard (N. Yorkshire) 36, 38, *141*
Catherine the Great 32

Cavallo, Dr Joachim 49
Cedar 91, *135*
  western red 83, 88
Chadar 21, *21, 148,* 180
Chain-link fencing 88, 106
Chairs 110, 171, *171*
  folding 110
Chambers, Sir William 37, *92,* 140
Chamonix valley (Savoy) 43
Chantilly (France) 30
Charbonnier, Charles 32
Chard, ruby *69*
Charlecote (Warwickshire) 38
Charles II (of England) 35
Charles III (of Spain) 32, 34
Charleston (South Carolina) *84, 95*
Chatsworth (Derbyshire) 38-9, 40, 41
Chatsworth Carpenters *171*
Cheere, John *38,* 39
Chelsea Show *149*
Cherry trees 151
Chestnut 88
  poles *132, 174*
  Spanish *152*
Chevreul, Michel 67
Children 55, 56, *57,* 58, 87
Chimneypots, as plant containers 110, *111, 177*
China 14-17, *15, 17, 159*
"Chinese Chippendale" *113*
Chinese-style features 16, 41, 44, *125, 134, 135*
Chinoiserie 32, 34, *34,* 88, *135,* 180
Chiswick House (London) *36*
Christie, Miss 47
Christopher, Ann 160
Chromium 51
Church, Thomas 47, *48,* 100
Cibber, Gabriel 39
Clairvoyées *130,* 180
Claremont (Surrey) 38
Claude Lorraine 36, 38
Clay, Grady 51
Clay pots *109, 110*
Clematis 61
Climbers 63, 90-91, *127, 130*
  on arbours 134
  on trees or shrubs 106
Cliveden (Buckinghamshire) 138
Cloister gardens 22
Coade stone 43, *44, 161,* 180
Cobbles 71, *74,* 83, *83, 117,* 118
  for steps *119, 120*
Cole, Nathan 158
Collodi 27
Colonna 27
Colonnades 90, 131, *131*
Colour 67-71, *69, 70, 71, 72, 73, 76*
  of furniture 110, 172
  Gertrude Jekyll and 42, 67
  in 19th-century gardens 41
  in oriental gardens 14, *14*
  of swimming pools 57
Colour in the Flower Garden (Gertrude Jekyll) 67
Columns 65, *140, 141,* 160, *160*
Compartmented gardens 42, 45-6, *46*
Complementary colours 68
Compton Wynyates (Warwickshire) 42
Concrete
  balustrade *133*
  for paths and paving 82, 83, *118, 119*
  pergola *131*

for steps *121*
  textured *121*
Condé, Hôtel de 31
Confucius 14, 16
Conservation 49-51, *49-50*
Conservatories 58, *58,* 91, *96,* 138, *138*
Constructivist sculptors 47
Containers, plant *92,* 109-10, *110-12,* 171, 175, *175-7*
  in balustrades *122*
  to define space 59, 63
Copings 90, *132, 133*
Cordons 106, *153,* 180
Cornus alba 'Spaethii' *70*
Cotinus coggygria 'Foliis Purpureis' *69*
Cotoneaster congestus 120
Cottage gardens 55, *84*
Cottages in gardens 44
Cottam & Hallen 43
Cowden (Scotland) 47
Coysevox, Antoine *29,* 31, 34
Cranbourne (Dorset) 51
Crathes (Scotland) *160*
Crescentius, Peter de 23
Crinkle-crankle walls 90, *133,* 180
Crisp, Sir Frank 47
Croquet lawns 77
Croxteth Hall (Liverpool) *153*
Crystal Palace 40
Culzean Castle (Strathclyde) *139*
Cushions 172
Cypresses 20, 24, 27, *81,* 106, 151, *151, 155*
Cyrus, King 12

Daffodils *69*
Dartington Hall (Devon) *78*
Day lilies *107*
"De Agricultura" (Varro) 12
De Caus 38
De Médicis, Catherine 31
De Pigage, Nicolas 32
De Serres, Olivier 31
Deanery (Sonning) *147*
Deans, Nick *163*
Decks, timber 56
Delphiniums *107*
Desert gardens 44
Diana and Actaeon *33,* 34
Diana of Ephesus *24, 25,* 98
Dimorphotheca 107
Dining 56, 91
  in conservatories 58
Disabled gardeners 78, 81
Doors 90, *126*
Dovecotes 137, *137, 138*
Doves, The (Jacob Epstein) *164*
Downing, Andrew 41
Drainage 77, 78, 83
  fence posts 88
  paths 82
Drummond Castle (Tayside) *40, 166*
Dry gardens (*kare sansui*) 16, *16*
Drystone walls 89, 90
Du Cerceau 28, 31, 49
Du Pont, Pierre 46
Dubuffet, Jean 48
Dumbarton Oaks (nr Washington D.C.) 46, *47*
  avenue *152*
  edgings *116*
  pool 99
  steps *120*

Dying Gladiator (Rousham) *162*

Earth-moving 77-8
Eden, Garden of 13
Edgings 116, *116*
  in bedding schemes 41, 105
  to gravel 83
  pools 98
  wire *159*
Egypt, ancient 12, *12*, 13
Egyptian-style features 41, 42
Eiffel Tower, topiary *155*
Electricity 91
Elizabeth I 35
Elizabethan-style gardens 41
Elms 42
Elvaston Castle (Derbyshire) *158*
Elysian Fields (Stowe) 36, 37
Enclosure 59, *61*, 62, 87-93, *88-96*
Encyclopaedia (J.C. Loudon) 44
English landscape garden 35-9, *35-9*
Enstone 38
Epstein, Jacob *164*
Erdigg (Clwyd) 38, 50
Erigeron mucronatus 118, 120
Ermenonville 34
Ernst, Max 48
Espaliers 106, *153*, 180
Este, Villa d' (Tivoli) *24, 25, 27, 27, 149*
Estrades 23
Eyecatchers 180

Famille rose 17
Fans 154, 180
Farrand, Beatrix 46, *47*
Farrer, Reginald 47
Fatsia 102
Fedden, Bryant *171*
Fences 87-8, 123, *123-5*
  bamboo *124, 126*
  chain-link 88
  Chinese 17
  fruit *153*
  medieval *22, 23*
  metal 88, *127*
  picket 23, *124*
  trellis 22
  wattle 23, *123, 124*
Ferme ornée 36
Ferns *99, 147*
Fiesole 24
Filters, visual 63
Finance 54, 55
Finlay, Ian Hamilton 48, *164*
Firdausi 21
Fireplace, as plant container *175*
Flagstones 83, *84, 118*
Flemish gardens 22
Flint
  for bridges 83, *144*
  for paths *118*
  sculpture *162*
Floralia 13
Florence (Italy) 24, 27
Flower garden, in 19th century 42
Flowers 105
  planning colours 70, 105
Foliage, impact of 67, 68, *69*
Follies 140, *140-41*, 180
Folly Farm (Berkshire) 45
Football 56
Foreshortening effect 77
Fountains 98, 99, *100*, 147, *147*, 148, *148-50*
  in 18th-century gardens 32
  in French Baroque gardens 30, 31, *31*
  in Islamic gardens 18, 20-21
  in Italian Renaissance gardens 24, 25, *25*, 26, 27
Fouquet, Nicolas 28, *28*, 30
Four Winds, Temple of (Castle Howard) *141*
France
  Baroque gardens 28-31, *28-31, 32, 37*
  bedding schemes in 41
  paving patterns 83
Frederick the Great 32
Frost 77, 81
  and brickwork 83
  and pots 109
Fruit trees, training of 42, 106, 153, *153-4*
Function 55-8, *57-8*
Functionalism 47, *48*
Furniture, garden 171, *171-5*
  colours of 67, 70, 110
  movable 110-11, *112, 113*
  in Mughal gardens *19*
  19th-century 44
  stone seats 164, *164-5, 169*
Fuschia *61*

Gabo, Naum 47, 48
Gaillon 31
Galleries
  Italian-style 28
  oriental 16
Galvanization 88, 90
Gambara, Cardinal 25
Gamberaia, Villa (Italy) 27
Garages 91
Garden houses 94
Garden machinery 78, 81, 82, 91
"Gardenesque" style 41
Gateposts 90, *163*
Gates 90, 125, *125-8, 140*
  in China 16, *125*
  moon gates 16, *17, 125*
Gazeboes 134, 180
Generalife (Grenada) 18, *92*
George II (of England) 39
Geranium 107
Germander 105
Germany
  18th-century gardens 32, 34, *34*
  restoration in 49
Gibberd, Sir Frederick 65
Gibbs, James *141*
Girard, Dominique 32
Girardon, François *29*, 31, 34
Glass 138
Glasshouses *see* Conservatories
Glorietta 23
Gnomon 180
Goblets 106, *153*, 180
Gothick style 37, *37, 137, 174*
Gough, Peter *162*
Granite 83, *118*
Grass
  on avenues 108
  between paving stones *119*
  edgings for *116*
  paths *117*
  steps *120*
  for texture 75
Gravel 58, 82-3
  deterioration of 49
  for parterres 43, 83, *86, 158, 158*
  for paths *117, 118*
  raked 16, *16*, 82
  for steps *121*
Great Dixter (Sussex) *46, 120*
Great Exhibition (London, 1851) 40, 43
Greece, ancient 12, 13, 14
Green
  restfulness of 70
  shades of 67, 68
Green Animals (Rhode Island) 42
Green Man, The (Simon Verity) *162*

in medieval gardens 18, *22, 22, 23*
Greenhouses *66*, 91, 138, *138*
  origins of 40
Greeting the Day (Polly Ionides) *162*
Grey's Court (Henley) *154*
Grottoes 170, *170*, 180
  in ancient gardens 13, *13*
  in 18th-century gardens 32, 38, *38*
  in French Baroque gardens 30
  in Italian Renaissance gardens 25
  in modern gardens 51, *103*
Ground form 77-81, *78, 79, 80, 81, 82*
Gunnera manicata 99

Haddington, Lady 51
Hadrian's Villa (Tivoli) 13, *13*
Ha-ha 35, *132, 134*, 180
  alternatives to 124
Hakone Open-Air Museum 48
Ham House (Surrey) 50
Hamilton, Charles 36, 38
Hammocks 59, 110, *175*
Hampton Court Palace 35, 39
Hardwoods, treatment of 88
Harlow (Essex) 65
Harmonizing colours 67, 68
Hartwell House 51
Hatfield House (Hertfordshire) *150, 154*
Hawksmoor, Nicholas 35
Hazel 123
Heale House (Wiltshire) 47, *131, 136, 143, 156*
Hedges 30, 87, 105-106, *150*, 155, *156, 157*
  to define space 60
  Victorian *123*
Henley (Oxfordshire) 47, *154*
Henry VIII 35
Hepworth, Barbara 48
Herb gardens 22
Herbs 27
Hercules 13
  statues of 28, *29*, 32, 34
Herms 27, *161*, 180
Hero of Alexandria 13
Herrenhausen (Germany) 32, 49
Herringbone brickwork 71, *74*
Hesperides, Garden of the 13
Hesse, Landgrave of 32
Hestercombe (Somerset) 45, *149*
Het Loo 50
Heveningham Hall (Suffolk) *133*
Hever Castle (Kent) *167*
Hibberd, Shirley 41, *48*
Hicks, David *172*
Hidcote (Gloucestershire) 45, *120*
Hillside gardens
  Italian *24-5, 27, 25, 26*
  Mongol 20
  Renaissance 24, 27
Hoare, Henry 36
Holland House (London) *164*
Hollows 60, 77, *81*
Holly, for hedges 42, 106
Honeysuckle 63, 87, *154*
Hoole House 43
Hornbeam 42, 106, 151, *153*, 156
Hornton stone *171*
Horse and Lion (Peter Scheemakers) 37
Hortus conclusus 181
Hosta 70, *147*
Hounds *103*
Hullis, Michael *176*
Hunting parks, Chinese 15
Hyacinths *112*
Hydraulics
  in ancient Roman gardens 13
  in English 18th-century gardens 36
  in Islamic gardens 20-21
  in medieval gardens 23

Hyssop 105

Ilford Manor (Wiltshire) 45, *65, 103, 122, 136*
Impatiens 175
Improvising, containers 110, *111, 112*
India, Mughal 18, *19*, 20, *20*, 21, *21*
Ingleborough (Yorkshire) 47
Ionides, Polly *162*
Ipomoea 130
Irises *119*
Islamic gardens 18-21, *18-21*, 22
  fountains *148*
  paving patterns *118*
  inspiration for 12
Island beds *125*, 181
Isola Bella (Lago di Maggiore) 46
Italianate style 41, *42*, 42, 44, 46, *46*
Italy
  Ancient Rome 12, *12*, 13, *13*
  Renaissance 24-7, *24-7*
Ivy 106, *147, 161*
  in bedding schemes 41
  in edgings 116
  hedges *157*

Jahan, Shah 20
James, John 36
Japan 14, *14*, 15-17, *16*, 127, 142, *143*
Japanese-style features 47
  bridges *143, 144*
  gates *126*
  pavilions *136*
  stepping stones *119*
  temples *141*
Jardin anglais 32
Jardin anglo-chinois 34, 181
Jardin de Plaisir (André Mollet) 28
Jardin fleuriste 41
Jekyll, Gertrude 42, 45, 67
Jellicoe, Sir Geoffrey 48, 51
Jencks, Charles *127*
Jenkyn Place (Hampshire) *165*
Johnston, Lawrence 45
Julius II, Pope 25
Juniper 27
  Pfitzer's *76*, 77

Kabul 20
Kare sansui (dry gardens) 16, *16*
Kashmir 21
Kassel (Germany) 32
Katsura Palace 15
Keeling, Jim *177*
Keene, Henry *140*
Kennedy, Lewis *40*, 41
Kent, Adaline *100*
Kent, William 36, *36*, 37, *37*, 146, *168*
Kerdalo (Brittany) *132*
Kew Gardens (London)
  rock garden at 44
  Sir William Chambers at 37, *140*
Kinross, John *42*
Kiosks 134, *135*
Kitchen gardens 57, 153
  in Middle Ages 22
  in 19th-century 42
  siting of 77
Kneeling Blackamoor 39, *166*
Knightshayes (Devon) *145*
Knots 27, 28, 31, 105, 158, 180
Koran, The 18, 20
Kublai Khan 15

Kunming (China) *145*

La Granja (San Ildefonso) 32
La Mortola (Italy) *150, 169*
Laburnum 88
Lacock Abbey (Wiltshire) *134*
Ladew Topiary Gardens (Maryland) *155, 157*
Lakes 98, 145
  in oriental gardens 16
Landscape Ornament Company *173*
Lante, Villa (Bagnaia) 25, *25*
Larch *137*
Latona fountain (Versailles) 30
Laurel 71
Laurus, J. 12
Lawnmowers, origins of 41
Lawns, garden furniture on 171
Lazienki (Poland) 34
Le Brun, Charles *29*, 31, *31*
Le Gros, Pierre, *29*
Le Nôtre, André 28, *28*, 31, 32
Le Rouge, G.L. 34
Lead *38*, 39, *169*
  imitation 167
  tank *111*
Leasowes, The 36
Leaves
  colours of 67, 68, *69*
  in pools 98
  texture of 60
Leech, Lucinda *172*
Lenne, Peter 41
Libocedrus decurrens 103
Lichens 70, 72, *132*
  on pots 109
Lilium pyrenaicum 70
Lily, Turk's Cap *70*
Lime trees 42, *65*, 91, 106-107, *151, 152, 153*
Limestone 101
Lindsay family *133, 156*
Little Moreton Hall (Cheshire) *159*
Little Sparta (Stonypath) 48
Livre de Cuer d'Amours Espris 23
Lloyd, Christopher *46*
Lloyd, Nathaniel 45, *46*
Lobelia 42, *159*
Logs
  as an edging *116*
  for steps *121*
London and Wise 36
Longleat (Wiltshire) 36, *132*
Longwood (Pennsylvania) 46, *100*
Lonicera 106, *154*
Lotus, symbolism of 16
Loudon, J.C. 34, 40, 41, 44
Louis XIII (of France) 30
Louis XIV 28, *28*, 29, *29*, 32
Louis XV 32
Louis XVI 32
Lupins *160*
Lutyens, Sir Edwin 42, 45, *46*, 120, *147, 149, 172*
Lysicrates 44

Madresfield Court (Worcestershire) 43
Magnolia 78, *92*
Mahal, Mumtaz *20*
Manderston (Berwickshire) *42*
Mannerism 28
Marble 24, 31
  colour of 70, 101
  pierced balustrade 21, *122*
  urns 168
Marjoram 105
Marly (France) 30, 31
Marot, Daniel *50*

Marsy, B. and G. 31
Marx, Roberto Burle 46, *47*, 83
Mass production, 19th-century 43
Mausoleum (Castle Howard) 38
Mazes 27, 105, 154, *154-5*
Medici family 24, 27
Medieval gardens 22-3, *22-3*
  India 18, 20
  Spain 18, *18*
Melbourne Hall (Derbyshire) 36, 38, 39, *122*
Mesopotamia 13
Metamorphoses (Ovid) 25, *27*, 30
Microclimate 77, 78, 81, 87
Middleton Place (South Carolina) *143*
Middleton, Sir William *43*
Milfoil, water 98
Milton, John *162*
Mirrors 63, *129*
Mlinaric, David *172*
Moholy-Nagy, Lazslo 47
Molière *28*
Mollet, André 28, 31
Monasteries, medieval 22
Mongols 15
Montacute House (Somerset) 38
Montaigne 34
Montargis 31
Moore, Henry 48, 51, 161
Morris, Roger 39
Mosaics
  in Islamic gardens 18, 21, *21*
  on paths *17*, *17*
Moss houses 44
Mounds 60
Mounts (in medieval gardens) 23, 181
Movables 109-111, *110-13*, 171, *171-7*
  to define space 63
Mughal gardens *19*, 20, *20*, 21, *21*, 145, *148*
Mughal-style features *135*
Music in gardens
  Baroque France *28*
  Villa d'Este 24

Nadder, River 36
Narcissus 69
Narcissus (sculpture) *104*
Nash, Sir John *43*, 50
National Trust (Britain) 50, 51
Nebuchadnezzar 12
Nesfield, W.A. 41
Netherlands, The
  restored gardens *50*
  sculptors from *37*, 39
Netting
  for fences *124*
  over pools 98
Neuilly *34*
New Zealand 148
Nicholson, Ben 48
Nicholson, Harold 46
Nuneham Courtenay
  (Oxfordshire) 38
Nymans (W. Sussex) *125*, *154*
Nymphaea 13, *13*, 25, 181
Nymphenburg (Germany) 32

Oasis garden 18
Obelisks *125*, *130*, 160, *160*
Objets trouvés 102
Old Westbury Gardens, Long Island (NY) *94*, *130*, *146*, *152*
Old Windsor 37
Olmstead, F.L. 41
Orangeries 31, 138, *158*
Oriental gardens 14-17, *14-17*
Osteospermum *176*
Osterley Park (London) *139*

Outbuildings 91
Ovid 26, *27*

Pace, controlling
  with paths and pavings 62, 85
  with stepping stones 17
Packwood (Warwickshire) 42, *151*
Page, Russell 48
Pagodas 32, 44, *140*
Painshill (Surrey) 36, *37*, 38, 50, *170*
Paint
  colours of 70
  on furniture 172
  on paving 119
  for protection of timber 88
Palisade hedges 42
Palissy, Bernard 31
Palladian style 36, 38, *39*
Palladio, Andrea 36
Paris 28, 31
Parks, public 41, 44
Parterres 37, *40*, *50*, *86*, 105, 158, *158-9*, 181
  English 17th-century 36
  French Baroque 31
Parterres de broderie 32, 181
Parterres d'email 32
Paths 81-3, *83-6*, 117, *117-19*
  edgings for 116, *116*
  in Islamic gardens 21, *21*
  scale of 63
  around water 97-8
Patio de Los Leones (Alhambra) *18*, 21
Pavilions 134, *134-7*
  on bridges *144*
  in China *15*, 16
  colours of 70-71
  in Islamic gardens 20, *20*, 21
  in Japan *15*, 16
  in medieval Spain 23
  in 19th century 44
  origins of 23
  in 20th century 51
Paving 81-3, *83-5*, *86*, 117, *117-19*
  in Chinese gardens *17*, *17*
  crazy *84*
  planting of *118*
  scale of 63
Paxton, Sir Joseph 40, 41
Pear trees 91, 106, 107
Pebbles 82, *85*, 101
  mosaics *17*, *17*, 117
  in parterres 86
Pedro the Cruel (of Spain) 18
Peking 15, *117*, *131*, 163
  Summer Palace 17
Peltiphyllum 99
Pembroke, Fourth Earl of 36
Peonies 103
  symbolism of 16
Pepsico Sculpture Garden (NYC) 48
Pergolas 13, 87, 90-91, *90*, 106, 131, *131-2*, 134, 181
  medieval 23
  Renaissance 24
Persepolis 12
Persia 18
Perspective, laws of 62
Peter the Great 32
Peterhof (Russia) 32, 34, *122*
Peto, Sir Harold 41, 45, *122*, *136*
Petworth (W. Sussex) *35*
Pevsner, Antoine 47
Philadelphus 110
Philip V (of Spain) 32
Phlox 107
Picea pungens 76
Picket fences 23, *124*
Picturesque style 37, 41
Piers, gate 90
Pigeoncotes 137

Piglet *163*
Pincushion beds 41
Pineau, Nicholas 34
Pine trees 76, *78*
  symbolism of 16, *17*
Pinus mugo 76
Pitmedden (Scotland) *146*, *157*, *166*
Planting cases 63, 109, 151, 175, *175*
Plants 58, 151, *151-60*
  aquatic 97, 98, 99, 145, *145*, *146*, *147*
  for enclosure 87
  sculptural 103
  structural use of 105-107, *106-108*
  symbolism of 16, 20, 23
Plates, broken *133*
Pleaching 108, *153*, *156*, 180
Pliny, The Younger 12, 13, *25*
Pneumatica (Hero of Alexandria) 13
Pole hedges 42
Polesden Lacey (Surrey) *143*
Polished surfaces 71
Pomodoro, Arnoldo 48
Pompeii 13
Pondweed, Canadian 98
Pools 56, 97-9, *99*, 145, *145-7*
  dredging 98
  edgings 98
  in Italian Renaissance gardens 27
  octagonal *146*, *147*
  swimming 57, 77, *100*
Pope, Alexander 36, 38, *38*, 151
Pope's Urn *168*
Poppies 160
Porches, entrance *61*
Port Lympne (Kent) *150*
Portugal laurels 107
Post-Modernism *127*
Potemkin, Prince 32
Pots *92*, 109-10, *110*, *112*, 171, 175, *175-7*
  in balustrades *122*
  to define space 59, 63
Potsdam 32, 41
Poussin, Nicolas 36
Powis Castle (Powys) 51
Priapus 13
Prickly pear 45
Privacy, 87, 91, 106
Privet for hedges 42, 102
Pterocarya fraxinifolia 98
Pulhamite stone 43
Pumps, electric 142
Pye, William *104*
Pyracantha 42, 106, *153*
Pyramids 106

Quaracchi, Villa 27

Rabbits *128*
Railings 88, 122, *122*
Railway ties (sleepers) *117*
Ramps *78*, *120*
Recreation *see* Children
Red, as an advancing colour 70
Reflections 97, 99, *99*
  in perception of colour and texture 67
Regeneration 51
Renishaw (Derbyshire) 45
Repton, Humphry 37, 40, 41, *41*
Rheum 99, *147*
Rhododendrons 67, *161*
Ribbon gardening 41
Richelieu, Cardinal 28, 30
Robinia pseudacacia *123*
Robins, Thomas 37
Robinson, William 42, 45, 151

Rock gardens 170, *170*
  19th-century 43-44, *137*
  20th-century 47
Rocks 170, *170*
  around pools 57
  to canalize views 77
  in oriental gardens 16, *17*, 170
  in Renaissance grottoes 25
Rococo style 32, *34*
Rodin, Auguste 48
Roma Vetus et Nuova 12
Roman de la Rose 22, *23*
Rome
  ancient 12, *12*, 13, *13*, 24
  Renaissance 25, *27*, 120
Romulus and Remus *141*
Roof gardens 47, *163*
Roofs, pitched 62
"Rooms", gardens divided into 24
Root houses 44
Rope ladders *57*
Roses
  "Albertine" *157*
  against brick 121
  in borders 160
  on bridges *145*
  in hedges or fences 87, *124*
  in medieval gardens 23, *23*
  in 19th-century gardens 40, *41*, 42
  on pergolas and arbours *90*, *96*
Rota, Alex *143*
Rous Lench 42
Rousham House (Oxfordshire) 36, 37, 38, *146*
Royal Parks and Gardens of London (Nathan Cole) *158*
Royal Pavilion (Brighton) 50
Ruby chard 69
Rue 105
Ruel, Château de 30
Ruins *140*, *141*
Russell-Smith, Vernon *142*
Rustic Adornments 41
Rustic style 44, *94*
  gateway *127*
Rusticated stonework 27, *135*, *168*, 180
  frosted *170*
Ryoanji Temple (Kyoto) 15
Rysbrack, Michael 39
Rysbrack, Peter *36*

Sackville-West, Vita 46
Safety 81, 98
Sakuteiki 15
Salisbury, Lady 51
Samarkand 20
San Francisco *48*
San Ildefonso (Spain) 32
Sand, in parterres 31, *159*
Sandpits 56
Sandringham (Norfolk) *152*
Sans Souci 41
Santolina (cotton-lavender) 27, 105
Sarcophagus *170*
Sardis 12
Scale 60, *65*, 66
  garden furniture 171
  sculpture 65, 102
  steps and stairs 119
Scheemakers, Peter *37*, 39, *162*
Schleissheim 32
Schloss Bruhl 49
Scholar's retreats, oriental 15, 16
Schwetzingen 32
Screens 56, 87, 106
Sculptural forms 101-103, *103*, 104
Sculpture 65, *100*, 101-103, *103*, *104*, 160, 161, *160-70*, 164, 166, 167
  abstract 101, 103, *104*
  in Baroque gardens *29*
  colours of 67

in 18th-century gardens *33*, 34, *34*
  on fountains *98*
  in 19th century 43
  in polished materials 21, 101, *104*
  restoration of 51
  in Roman gardens 13, 27
  scale of 62
  in 20th century 47-8
Sculpture gardens 48
Seats *96*, 102, 110, *171*, 172, *172-5*
  in ancient gardens 13
  covered *94*
  to define space 63
  stone 110, 164, *164-5*, 169
Segal, George 48
Sequoia 152
Serapium (Hadrian's Villa) 13, *13*
Service areas 91
Serviceberry 98
Setcreasia 69
Setts 83, 85, *117*, *118*, 180
Seville (Spain) 18
Shade 111
Shahnama 21
Shells *132*, *176*
Shenstone, William 36
Shinto religion *141*
Shogaku-in *127*, *142*
Shrewsbury, Earl of 44
Shrubland Park (Suffolk) *43*
Siena 159
Siliceous stone 43
Sinks, as plant containers 110
Sissinghurst Castle (Kent) 46, *61*
Sitwell, Sir George 41, 45
Sizergh Castle (Cumbria) 47
Slate *133*
Slopes
  and drainage 78
  and pools 98
  and steps 81
  and views 77
Snow 106
Soane, Sir John 43
Softwoods, treatment of 88, 91
Soil mechanics 78
Sommer, Johann Jackob 34, *34*
Song of Songs 22
Sonning (Berkshire) *147*
Sorbus 107
Space 59-62, *61-6*
  attitudes to in oriental gardens 14-15, *15*
Spain
  18th-century gardens 32
  Islamic gardens 18, *18*, 21
  medieval gardens 23
Sperlonga 13
Spruce *76*
St Gallen 22
St Petersburg 32
Staddle stones 181
Statues 60, *65*, 101-103, *103*, 161, *161-4*
  to define space 63, *65*
  English neoclassical *37*, 38, 39
  French Baroque *29*, 30, 31, *31*
  Italian Renaissance 27
Steel, stainless *104*
Stefandis, John *171*
Stepping stones 16, 17, *117*, 119, *147*
Steps 78, *79*, 119, *119-21*
  dimensions of 78
  in Italian Renaissance gardens 77
  scale of 62
Stoa 13
Stone, E.D. 48
Stone
  paving 82, 83, *118*
  seats 164, *164-5*, 169
  substitutes for 43, *44*, 51, 83, 109, 164, 167, *169*
  urns 167, *167-70*
  weathering of 70
Stonypath (Scotland) 48

Stourhead (Wiltshire) 36, 37, *39, 140,* 165
Stowe (Buckinghamshire) 36, 37, 38, *39, 39, 140, 141, 162*
Stretcher bond *118*
Structure, garden 116, 117, 119, 122, 123, *116-29*
Studley Royal (N. Yorkshire) 37, 38
Stumpery 44, 181
Suburban Gardener and Villa Companion (J.C. Loudon) 40
Summer houses 91
Sundials 166, *166-7*
Surprise, element of 77
Surrealists 47
Sutton Place (Surrey) 48, *51*
Swimming pools 57, 77, *100*
Swings 56, *57*
Switzer, Stephen 36
Symbolism
  in ancient gardens 12
  in 18th-century gardens 34, 37
  in English landscape gardens 37
  in French Baroque gardens 28, *29,* 30, 31, *31*
  of gateways 124
  in Italian Renaissance gardens 25, *25,* 26, 27, 27
  in medieval gardens 22-3
  in oriental gardens 16, *16,* 17
  of plants 16, 23
  of water 13, 16, 23, 97

Tables 110, *170,* 171, *171*
Tafalla (Navarre) 23
Taj Mahal (Agra) 20, *20*
Taliesin West (Arizona) *44*
Tamerlane 20, 21
Taoism 14, 15
Tapis vert 181
Tarmac 58
Taurida (St Petersburg) 32
Tea-houses 181
  Japanese 15-16
  in the West 47
Teapot, as plant container *112*
Temples 44, *92,* 140, *140-41*
  neoclassical 37, *37,* 38
  at Stowe 37
Tennis courts 58, 77, 88
Tents *135, 140*
Terms 30, 181
Terraces 56, 77
  in Italian Renaissance gardens 25, *25,* 27
  in "Italianate" gardens *43*
  at Sans Souci (Potsdam) 32
Terracotta *165, 167, 168, 175, 175*

in 19th century 43
Texture
  of clipped evergreens 75
  of grasses 75
  of paving 74
  perception of 67
  of polished surfaces 71
  pools and *146*
  and shadows 71
  of shrubs 76
  of trelliswork 76
Thalictrum 107
Theâtre d'Agriculture (Olivier de Serres) 31
Thetis 30
Thorn 42
  topiary 107
Threave (Dumfries and Galloway) 69
Thrift *117*
Thuya 106
  plicata 88
Thyme 56, 83, 105
Tiberius 13
Tietz, Ferdinand 34
Tifurnum 13
Tiles
  for paving *85*
  roof *17*
  "ropework" *116*
  for steps *120*
Tiltyard *78*
Timber
  bridges *142, 143*
  as an edging *116*
  for conservatories 91
  decking 56, 83
  fences 88
  for gates *126*
  planting cases 109
  staircases *121*
  weathering of 70
T'ing 17, 37
Tints 68
Tivoli
  Hadrian's Villa 13, *13,* 27
  Villa d'Este *24, 25,* 27, *27*
Tokufuji Temple, Kyoto 16
Topiary 107, 151, 155, *155-7, 159,* 181
  in ancient Roman gardens 13
  in Italian Renaissance gardens 24, 27
  in medieval gardens 23
  in 19th-century gardens 42, *151*
  as sculpture *102-103*
Tradition, importance of 44, 51
Training of plants 42, 153, *153-4*
  in medieval gardens 23
Tree of heaven 61

Tree seats *173*
Tree trunks *173*
Trees
  artificial 21
  in Italian gardens 27
  as vertical accents *81,* 105, 160
Treillage 31, 63, *129,* 181
Trelliswork 63, *63,* 76, *95,* 129, *129-30*
  ancient Roman 23
  to define space 59
  fences 123, *123*
  French Baroque 31
  medieval 22, 23
  texture of 71
Trentham (Staffordshire) 41
Très Riches Heures (Duc de Berry) 23
Tresco (Scilly) *125*
Triads, colour 68
Trianon gardens (Versailles) 31, 32
Triggs, Inigo *126*
Trompe l'œil 63, 129, 181
Tropaelum 156
Tryon Place (California) *130*
Tsarskoe Selo (Russia) 32
Tubi *29*
Tudor gardens 23, 35
Tuileries (Paris) 31
Tulip tree 98
Tulips *106, 111*
Tunnels 62, *90,* 108, 131, *131, 132, 134, 152*
  laburnum 88
  in medieval gardens 23
Turf mazes 56, 105, 154, *154,* 155
Turf seats 23, *23,* 56
Twickenham (London) 38
Tyninghame (Lothian) 51
Tyrconnell (Maryland) 88

Uppark (Sussex) *141*
Urns 30, *64,* 102, *157, 167, 167-70*
  on balustrades *122*
  on bridges *144*
  to define space 63
  in fountains *148*
USA 46, *46,* 47, *47,* 48, *48,* 88, 99, *100,* 116, *120, 152, 155, 157*
  19th-century 41
  restorations 50, *50*

Van Nost, John 39
Vanbrugh, Sir John 34, 36, *38, 141*
Varro's aviary *12,* 13

Vases 167, *167-70*
Vaux-le-Vicomte 28, *28*
Vegetable gardens *see* Kitchen gardens
Vegetables 57
Veitschochsheim 34
Verey, Rosemary *161*
Verity, Judith *149*
Verity, Simon *149, 161, 162*
Versailles 28, *28, 29,* 30, *30,* 31, *31*
  influence of 32
  Pyramid fountain 98
Viburnum 58, 103
Views
  framing 62
  pergolas and 91
  slopes and 77
Villandry 49, *49*
Villas, Italian
  Aldobrandini (Frascati) 25, *26*
  d'Este (Tivoli) *24, 25,* 98, *149*
  Gamberaia 27
  Garzoni (Collodi) 27
  Hadrian's (Tivoli) 13, *13*
  Lante (Bagnaia) 25, *25*
  Quaracchi 27
  Rotonda (Vicenza) 36
  Taranto *81*
Vine-growing 131
Virgil 37
Visione Amorosa (Boccaccio) 27
Vitis coignetiae 126
Vizcaya (Florida) 46, *46*
Von Sporck, Graf 32

Waddesdon Manor (Buckinghamshire) 43, *138, 162*
Walls 88, *89-90,* 132, *132-4*
  in Chinese gardens 16
  in medieval gardens 23
  retaining *81, 83, 116*
  serpentine 90
Water 97, *99-100,* 142, 145, 148, *142-50*
  in ancient gardens 13
  colours of 67
  in 18th-century gardens 32, 38, 38, *39, 39*
  in English landscape gardens 38, 38, *39, 39*
  in French Baroque gardens 30, *30*
  in Islamic gardens 20
  in Italian Renaissance gardens 25, *25,* 26, 27
  in medieval gardens 23
  in oriental gardens 16
  personified (by Pierre Le Gros) *29*

symbolism of 13, 16, 20, 23, 25, 97, *98*
Water parterres 46, *47,* 181
  Italian Renaissance 25
  French Baroque 30
Water staircases *26,* 30, 32, *33,* 120
Waterfalls 21, *21,* 97 *see also* Cascades
Wattle 71, 123, *123, 124*
Weather Vane (Raef Baldwin) *164*
Weikersheim (Würzburg) 34, *34*
Westbury Court (Gloucestershire) 38
Wheelbarrow
  as plant container *177*
  seat 110, *173*
Wicker furniture 110, *172*
Wilhelmshohe 32, 34
William of Orange, Prince 50
Williamsburg (Virginia) 50, *50*
Wilton House (Salisbury) 35, 38, *39,* 41, *135*
Window boxes *139, 176*
Wingnut, Caucasian 98
Wirework
  as an edging *116*
  19th-century 43, *96*
  shelters *96, 135*
Wisteria 78, *131, 143*
Woodland gardens
  edgings for 116
  steps for *121*
Wren, Sir Christopher 35
Wrest Park (Bedfordshire) 38, *144*
Wright, Frank Lloyd *45,* 47
Wright, Thomas *37*
Wrought iron 44
  furniture *171, 174, 175*
  gates *128*
Wurzburg 34, 49

Xenophon 12

Yew
  avenues *151, 152*
  in bedding out *40*
  golden *107*
  for hedges 42, *62,* 106, *106, 116, 125, 156, 157*
  topiary 106, 107, *155*
Young, Monica *110*
Yucca *45,* 103

Zwinger (Dresden) 49

PICTURE CREDITS

Abbreviations
B: bottom   **C**: centre
L: left   **T**: top

1 Jean-Loup Charmet
2 Tania Midgley
6T Jerry Harpur (Barnsley House, Gloucestershire)

6B Paul Miles. Designer: Thomas Church
7 Heather Angel (Tyninghame, Dunbar, East Lothian)
8T Roger Pennington (Sheffield Park, E. Sussex)
8B Tania Midgley (Tresco, Scilly)
9 Jerry Harpur (Haughton Hall)
10 Archiv für Kunst und Geschichte, Berlin (Hans Bol, *Parklandschaft mit Schloss, Gemaelde, 1589*)

12L British Museum
12R Mary Evans Picture Library
13 C. M. Dixon
14 Japanese Tourist Office
15T Robin Laurance
15B Heather Angel (Yuantong temple, Kunming, China)
16 Heather Angel (Tofukuji temple, Kyoto, Japan)
17TL Christie's Colour Library

17TR Heather Angel (Summer Palace, Beijing, China)
17B Heather Angel (Forbidden City, Beijing, China)
18 John Sims
19 Claus und Liselotte Hansmann
20 Jane Taylor/Sonia Halliday Photographs (Taj Mahal, Agra, India)
21T MacQuitty International Collection (Shalimar, India)

Architecture and Landscape Gardening
135BC Michael Balston
135BR Mansell Collection
136TL Rob Herwig (Harlow Car, Yorkshire)
136TR Derek Fell (Swiss Pines Gardens, USA)
136CL John Arthur Hughes, *Garden Architecture and Landscape Gardening*
136C Heather Angel (Brodick Castle, Arran)
136BL Michael Balston
136BC H. Inigo Triggs, *Formal Gardens in England and Scotland* (Iford Manor)
136BR Pamla Toler/Impact Photos
137TL Mansell Collection
137TCL Derek Fell
137TCR Michael Balston
137TR (Kerdalo, Brittany)
137BL The Iris Hardwick Library (Longleat, Wiltshire)
137BR Michael Balston (Heale House, Wiltshire)
138TL F. H. C. Birch/Sonia Halliday Photographs
138TCR Derek Fell
138TR (Nymans, W. Sussex)
138CL Hazel le Rougetel/Biofotos (Villa Agnano, Tuscany)
138CR Tania Midgley
138BL Pamla Toler/Impact Photos. (Ballarat, Victoria)
138BR Tania Midgley
139TL *MacFarlane's Castings*, volume II, Trickett & Webb Limited
139TR Michael Balston
139C S. & O. Mathews
139BL The Harry Smith Horticultural Photographic Collection
139BR John Glover (Blagdon House)
140TC The Harry Smith Horticultural Photographic Collection
140TR Jean-Loup Charmet
140CL George Wright
140BL Blanche Cirker (ed.), *1800 Woodcuts by Thomas Bewick and his School*, Dover Pictorial Archive Series
140BC Michael Balston
140BR The Harry Smith Horticultural Photographic Collection
141TL George Wright
141TC National Trust Photographic Library
141CL Michael Balston
141CR Tania Midgley (Tatton Park, Cheshire)
141BL (Brympton d'Evercy, Somerset)
141BC The Harry Smith Horticultural Photographic Collection
142TL MacQuitty International Collection
142TC Robert Saxton (Scotney, Kent)
142TR Michael Balston (Audley End, Essex)
142BR The Harry Smith Horticultural Photographic Collection
143TL The Harry Smith Horticultural Photographic Collection
143TC MacQuitty International Collection
143C Michael Balston
143CR The Harry Smith Horticultural Photographic Collection (Chyverton, Cornwall)
143BL Jerry Harpur. Designer: Alex Rota
143BR Michael Balston (Stowe, Buckinghamshire)
144TL Michael Balston (Kenwood, London)
144TR Tania Midgley
144 2nd row L Japanese Tourist Office
144 3rd row L (Audley End, Essex)
144 3rd row R Michael Balston
144BL Derek Gould (Hidcote, Gloucestershire)
145TL Tania Midgley (Hinton Ampner House, Hampshire)
145TR Michael Balston (Audley End, Essex)
145CL Derek Gould
145CR The Harry Smith Horticultural Photographic Collection
145BL (Hestercombe, Somerset)

145BC Heather Angel
146TL Jerry Harpur
146TC Michael Balston
146TR Nigel O'Gorman
146CL Heather Angel
146CR MacQuitty International Collection
146BC MacQuitty International Collection (Kirstenbosch, S. Africa)
147TL Nadia Mackenzie
147CL The Harry Smith Horticultural Photographic Collection
147C Lucinda Lambton/ARCAID
147CR The Harry Smith Horticultural Photographic Collection
147BR Nadia Mackenzie
148TL MacQuitty International Collection (Taranto)
148CL J. C. Loudon, *The Suburban Gardener and Villa Companion*
148C MacQuitty International Collection
148CR John Glover
148BC Hazel le Rougtel/Biofotos
149TL Michael Balston
149TR Manufacturer: Ustigate Ltd
149TC (Barnsley House, Gloucestershire) Tania Midgley
149C Tania Midgley
149CR Heather Angel. Designer: Michael Balston (*Vogue* Scented Garden, Chelsea Show 1985)
149BL Michael Balston
149BR Michael Balston
150TL Tania Midgley (Hampton Court)
150TCR Tania Midgley (La Mortola)
150CL Michael Balston
150CR Tania Midgley (Hever Castle, Kent)
150BL Derek Gould (Port Lympne, Kent)
150BR Tania Midgley (Sezincote, Gloucestershire)
151TL Hazel le Rougetel/Biofotos (Villa Continale, Tuscany)
151BL The Harry Smith Horticultural Photographic Collection (Stanton Harcourt, Oxfordshire)
151BR The Harry Smith Horticultural Photographic Collection
152TL Jerry Harpur
152TR The Harry Smith Horticultural Photographic Collection
152CL Jerry Harpur
152C Visual Arts Library (Croft Castle, Hereford and Worcester)
152CR Jerry Harpur
152BL Jerry Harpur (Sir Frederick Gibberd's garden, Harlow, Essex)
152BC Heather Angel (Kimbolton, Cambridgeshire)
152BR Michael Balston (Erdigg, Clwyd)
153CTL Michal Balston
153C Heather Angel
152CR Linda Burgess
153BL Pat Brindley
153BC Michael Balston
154TL The Harry Smith Horticultural Photographic Collection
154TR Tania Midgley
154CL Mark Cator/The Illustrated London News Picture Library
154BL Derek Fell
154BR Derek Fell (Deerfield)
155TL Mansell Collection (Ripon Common)
155TC John Glover (Troy Town Maze, Somerton, Oxfordshire)
155TR Mansell Collection (Shernton, Nottinghamshire)
155CL Derek Fell (Ladew Gardens, Monkton, Maryland)
155BCL F. H. C. Birch/Sonia Halliday Photographs
155BCR The Harry Smith Horticultural Photographic Collection
155BR Tania Midgley
156TL (Rotherfield Park, Hampshire) Heather Angel
156TC Michael Balston
156CL (Anthony House, Cornwall) The

Harry Smith Horticultural Photographic Collection
156C Jean-Loup Charmet
156CR (Alton Towers, Staffordshire) The Harry Smith Horticultural Photographic Collection
156BL Jean-Loup Charmet
156BC Michael Balston
156BR Michael Balston
157TL Derek Fell (Ladew Gardens, Monkton, Maryland)
157TR Pamla Toler/Impact Photos
157CL (Audley End, Essex) Michael Balston
157CR Tania Midgley
157BL (Wakehurst Place, West Sussex) Jerry Harpur
157BC Michael Balston
157BR The Harry Smith Horticultural Photographic Collection
158TL Jean-Loup Charmet
158TR The Harry Smith Horticultural Photographic Collection
158CL Nathan Cole, *Royal Parks and Gardens of London*, Design Z, photographed at the Lindley Library, RHS, by A. C. Cooper Ltd.
158CR Michael Balston
158BL Heather Angel
158BR Tania Midgley
159TC Derek Fell
159CL Michael Balston
159CR John Glover
159BL Linda Burgess
159BR Heather Angel
160TL (Heslington Manor, York) Jerry Harpur
160TR Michael Balston
160BL Ann Christopher
160BR (Lacock, Wiltshire) Michael Balston
161TL (Barnsley House, Gloucestershire) Michael Balston
161TC (Sissinghurst, Kent) The Harry Smith Horticultural Photographic Collection
161TR (Waddesdon Manor, Buckinghamshire)
161BL (Compton Acres, Dorset) The Harry Smith Photographic Collection
161BCL Robert O'Dea (Blickling Hall, Norfolk)
161BCR (Burton Agnes, Humberside)
161BR Michael Balston
162TL Heather Angel
162TC Nigel O'Gorman
162TR Elizabeth-Ann Colville. Designer: Polly Ionides
162CL George Wright
162CCR Heather Angel (Hever Castle, Kent)
162BL Michael Balston
162BC Cynthia Woodyard
162BR Michael Balston
163TL Hazel le Rougetel/Biofotos (Chandigarh, Punjab)
163TC (Gaulden Manor)
163TR Michael Balston. Exhibited: Oxford Gallery at High Walls, Oxford
163CL Michael Balston (Powis Castle, Powys)
163CR Archiv für Kunst und Geschichte, Berlin
163BL Michael Balston. Sculptor: John Bradbury
163BC Cynthia Woodyard
164TL Heather Angel (Wallington Gardens, Northumbria)
164CL Michael Balston
164C Michael Balston. Designer: Ian Hamilton Finlay with David Ballantyne
164CR "Doves" by Jacob Epstein. The Harry Smith Horticultural Photographic Collection
164BC Linda Burgess
164BR Michael Balston (Knightshayes, Devon)
165TL Michael Balston

165TC Michael Balston (Jenkyn Place, Hampshire)
165TR Michael Balston
165CL Heather Angel (Falkland Palace, Fife)
165CR Michael Balston (Knightshayes, Devon)
165BC Robert O'Dea (Parham, Dorset)
166TL Heather Angel (Penshurst Place, Kent)
166TR Hazel le Rougetel/Biofotos
166BCL Heather Angel (Jenkyn Place, Hampshire)
166BR Michael Balston (Hatfield House, Hampshire)
167TC Michael Balston (Lacock Abbey)
167C Heather Angel
167BL Archiv für Kunst und Geschichte, Berlin (Schloss Nymphenburg, Munich)
167BC The Iris Hardwick Library (Corsham Court, Wiltshire)
167BR Michael Balston (Blenheim)
168TL F. H. C. Birch/Sonia Halliday Photographs (Cliveden, Buckinghamshire)
168TR Michael Balston
168TR Michael Balston (Fonthill, Wiltshire)
168BCL Heather Angel
168BR Robert O'Dea (Cliveden)
169TL Tania Midgley (Sissinghurst, Kent)
169TR Tania Midgley
169CL Michael Balston (Wilton House)
169C Michael Balston (Knightshayes, Devon)
169BL Manufacturer: Haddonstone
169BR The Harry Smith Horticultural Photographic Collection
170TL Pat Brindley (Hidcote, Glos.)
170TC (Orchardleigh, Somerset)
170TR Michael Balston (Iford Manor)
170CL Michael Balston
170CR Heather Angel (Goldney, Bristol)
170BL Hazel le Rougetel/Biofotos (Wuxi)
170BC Michael Balston (Drummond Castle)
170BR Cynthia Woodyard
171TL Design: Chatsworth Carpenters
171CR Jerry Harpur
171BL Michael Balston. Designer: Bryant Fedden (exhibited at Oxford Gallery at High Walls, 1985)
172TL Nadia Mackenzie
172CL Michael Balston
172CR Lucinda Leech
172BC Michael Balston
173TL Michael Balston
173TR Nigel O'Gorman
173 2nd row L Michael Balston (Stoneleigh Abbey, Warwickshire)
173 2nd row R Nigel O'Gorman
173 3rd row R Tania Midgley
173BL Heather Angel (Elvaston Castle, Derbyshire)
174TL Heather Angel (Alton Towers)
174TR Cynthia Woodyard
174C The Harry Smith Horticultural Photographic Collection
174BL Heather Angel
174BC Paul Miles (Arlington Court, Devon)
175TL Paul Miles (Clandon Park, Surrey)
175TR Linda Burgess
175CL The Harry Smith Horticultural Photographic Collection
175CR Linda Burgess
175BL Michael Balston (Blenheim)
175BCR Jerry Harpur
176TCL Nigel O'Gorman
176TR Michael Balston. Designer: Monica Young (exhibited at Oxford Gallery at High Walls, Oxford)
176CL Linda Burgess
176BL Pamla Toler/Impact Photos
176BR Michael Hullis
177TL Judith Patrick/EWA
177TR Cynthia Woodyard
177C Michael Balston
177BL Jenifer Jones
177BR Landscape Ornament Company